Ruth
thanks for
all the help.
Roger Storkamp

Pvt. Richard Lee Leslie

ROGER STORKAMP

Pvt. Richard Lee Leslie

Copyright 2017 by Roger Storkamp

All rights reserved

No part of this book may be reproduced, stored in a retrieval system, or transmitted by any means electronic, mechanical, photocopying or otherwise without written permission of the author.

Books and Birch, Publisher
www.RogerStorkamp.com
3016 Haddon Drive
Las Vegas, NV 89135

ISBN 978-0-9893585-2-1

Dedicated to the 503rd
Airborne Combat Regiment
"General Douglas McArthur's secret weapon"

Last Men Standing

Friendships of the 503rd Airborne Combat Regiment billowed and blossomed like the parachutes that landed them on Japanese-held islands in the Pacific sixty five years ago. A few men short of a platoon gathered in Arizona, where they, as did the mythical bird of Phoenix, rose from near ashes to restore their comrades' achievements lost to the dusty pages of history.

While my father-in-law, Richard Leslie, registered us at Grace Inn, Laurie and I gazed at the wall-to-ceiling poster proclaiming that General Jones and his 3000 thieves had landed. Her father's stories about the antics of the 503rd regiment had been confirmed, and I eagerly awaited meeting his octogenarian buddies.

Although war stories were available on demand, most conversations dealt with the bonding of the men, their wives, and families, and, of course, honoring fellow members who have mustered out since last year's meeting.

The five day conference mostly centered around hospitality and sight-seeing in the Phoenix area, culminating with business meetings and banquets. In addition to tweaking the nuts-and-bolts of the organization, the members endorsed an official web site, www. Corregidor.org. Their web master, Paul Whitman organized eyewitness accounts and pictures, official from government photographers and candid like those Chester Nycum confiscated from Japanese cameras. They give a face to the heroism as well as the human toll on the rock remembered as Corregidor.

Like the call of the Alamo, the theme of the meeting was *Remember us who took Corregidor.* The 503rd, cobbled together from remnants of the 502nd and ultimately sandwiched into the 101st, suffers from the middle child syndrome. The association sadly endorsed a last-man-standing bases for termination of the 503rd as an active Association, relegated to the history books and web sites.

In the course of five short days, Laurie and I gained insights into the horror of war, its affect on the men who fought and the human bonding that resulted. We have a deeper understanding and respect for torment that plagued her father most of his life. Our greatest generation must not be forgotten.

"Sir, I present you Fortress Corregidor."

Col. Jones to General McArthur, March 2, 1945

A Message from the Author

My father-in-law, Richard Leslie, served in the Army Airborne under General Douglas MacArthur throughout the Philippine Islands Campaign during WWII. He made three combat jumps, most notably to retake the island of Corregidor from the Japanese. Enlisting at age seventeen, Richard's education had been interrupted until age 59 when he earned his GED, an achievement he considered only second to his military honors.

His story offers an honest view of courage, fear, and self preservation strategies. Atrocities committed on both sides created an emotional toll that plagued him throughout his eighteen months of combat and continued to haunt him throughout his life.

He asked that publication of PVT. RICHARD LEE LESLIE be withheld until his ashes "dusted the breeze."

He passed away on Good Friday, 2013.

Chapter One

"Let's talk about Australia." A voice oiled with chicken fat, it seemed to Richard, attempted another prime-the-pump strategy to break loose his patient's painful and locked-in combat experiences. Richard glanced at the wall clock and counted—actually mouthed—the tic tocks. *Gotta be here, don't have to talk.*

"Surely those memories shouldn't be that difficult to discuss." Lieutenant Colonel Renford, uniform void of any combat ribbons, brushed an imaginary speck of dust off each epaulet.

Richard ignored the psychiatrist's wide-eyed gaze and fought back recurring images: *Geronimo—Kilroy—Jenkins—Heidt—Reed—Jennings.*

***

The Japanese soldier writhing a few yards from the still smoking fifty-caliber machine gun possibly experienced flashes from his boy-hood days back in Tokyo, but his buddy missing half a head instantly sacrificed his life to Japan's emperor, *bonzai* his final testament.

Innocence of childhood masked the devastation his weapon had caused.

An arm around his midsection, butt planted firmly against the hip of his nine-year-old sister, bounding across railroad tracks near their home, down the well-worn path to town's center; Pvt. Richard Leslie's earliest memory. Fourth of July parade down Main Street, Melrose,

Minnesota, 1929, details beyond a four-year-old boy's comprehension, except from Margaret's retelling their story many times at family gatherings. Cherished details: plopped down curbside, cheering and waving as vintage automobiles chugged and belched fumes with an occasional blast from a Model T Ford's Klaxon.

"Cigarette?"

The single Lucky protruded from its pack like a pistol barrel, but Pvt. Richard Leslie, hands locked on the rifle's grips, eyes glued to his fresh kill, responded, "Margaret."

Geronimo's glance shifted from his gunner to the white package in his grip, its red eyeball glaring back—*Lucky Strike Green had gone to war*—and raised it to his lips. He shook the last five from the pack and passed them around; Kilroy, Jenkins, Heidt, Reed, and Jennings. *Guts-to-go Kilroy* shielded a flame, touched it to his cigarette, and ditched the match; no predawn target for a sniper to zero in on.

Geronimo crushed and tossed the empty pack, its cellophane wrinkling and smoldering atop a pile of spent cartridges, and reached for Kilroy's lighted cigarette passed between the squad. "Margaret?" A cloud billowed through flared nostrils.

Richard shrugged, his stare unbroken.

Geronimo peeled the seal from a fresh pack with his teeth, stamped out a clump of cigarettes, and shoved it in Richard's face. "Have one. Get the taste of cordite out of your mouth."

Richard considered cigarette smoke no less harsh than that from spent ammo, but pinched one from the cluster and pressed it to a smoldering butt passed forward.

"Margaret?" Geronimo repeated his question. "Doesn't matter." Its tip a glowing cherry, he snuffed the cigarette, wrapped a field jacket around the barrel of the Fifty Caliber, and, muscles bulging, hoisted the weapon with tripod still attached.

"Better get our asses out of here." He dipped his head toward Richard and remarked to the guys shouldering carbines and lugging ammunition. "Gotta take care of the little guy."

Richard knew who would carry his lifeless body to field headquarters if a sniper got lucky and scored a gunner.

He shook off the image of his bullet riddled body and reconstructed—piece-by-piece—the picture of his father sloshing water across the kitchen floor. Giggling on top the kitchen table with his legs dangling, Daddy lifted the mop as if to scrub the table clean of his youngest child. Done in jest, at least then. Beyond a few such incidents, Richard would never get to know the father who abandoned him and his family prior to the birth of his younger sister, Rita.

With her five children decked out in store-bought clothes, Richard's mother, six-months pregnant, boarded the same train whose company dispatch had frequently denied her husband their bed, requiring layovers at distant hotels—and shady ladies.

The last straw, one of these strumpets at her doorstep, baby in arms. "I would like to present another of your husband's handiwork. I'll just leave it here with his home-made bunch, one more won't make a difference."

"Morgan Leslie doesn't live here," and she slammed the door. She should have said, "Morgan's *family* no longer lives here."

Leaving an empty house and a huge debt at the local mercantile, she resettled her family in St. Paul, Minnesota, sharing an apartment with her married daughter, Edna. Margaret remained Richard's beacon until she eloped and hitchhiked to California about the same time he graduated from juvenile court to the adult system and was forced to make a choice, prison or Army.

***

Lt. Col. Renford glanced up from his clipboard. "You and your buddies caught a ride to Sidney. Perhaps you got tickets to an opera at the Town Hall. I know you listen to classical music."

"Yeah I do. No I didn't go." Richard's gaze dropped and his head began to sway.

"Don't leave me."

"I ain't going no place. We've got another half an hour together."

"You know what I mean when I call you to attention, Private Leslie."

"I'm not a private. Haven't been since the war with the Japs ended and mine began. Maybe you meant *private* citizen."

"Sorry, I misspoke."

Richard braced himself for the colonel's silent treatment, no more questions, no sound but the clock; their entire previous session a wall of quiet between them, his head loaded with World War Two unchecked.

Today's session, he had allowed his psychiatrist to resurrect the carnage buried beneath weeks of drinking, carousing, screwing, and fast cars. He can't allow that to happen again.

Australia seemed a safe place to dwell, but not to share.

***

"A beer please."

"Sorry, Mate. Don't know what that is." The barmaid swiped a damp cloth and rearranged the dust into a swirl in front of Pvt. Leslie.

"Yeah, beer. That foamy stuff you got pictured out front, comes in those round kegs and piped to that spigot." Richard anticipated the butt-end joke about his youthful appearance, a beardless one-hundred-thirty-five-pound nineteen-year-old rascal, and his tone intended to aggravate the surly barmaid. He assessed his situation: one grungy looking fellow a few stools to his left downing what appeared to be beer, Geronimo and the rest of his squad out buying trinkets to send stateside.

"Ain't no beer for you makes its way through them pipes." A curl of a sneer as the barmaid gestured with her head toward the mysterious figure, beckoning him forward.

The surge of anger pulsating through Richard's temples erased the metallic taste of fear in his saliva, a rage not felt since he challenged his drill instructor to a no-holds-barred fight under the rules of combat. When the sergeant smirked and turned away, Richard threatened to hunt him down off base and kill him.

The sergeant's response, "That ain't gonna happen, Soldier, 'cause you're shipping out tomorrow. Besides, the day will come when you will thank me."

Had that day arrived even before actual combat? He clustered the fingers of his right hand for the deadly plunge into the throat as the man approached, Akruba slouch hat, brim sides curled and tacked, eyes shaded.

"I think this young pup wants more than just beer." He forced his left arm around Richard's neck and, with his right hand, tapped the tripod of fingers poised to attack. "No need for this, Mate." Richard's hand surrendered to the Aussie's firm grip. "Give us a couple o' pints of ale. That's what Yank here craves." One last shake and a firm hand squeeze, eyes penetrating, "Mate?"

"Mate!" Richard's enthusiastic response transcended three years and resounded in a psychiatrist's office at Ft. Snelling, Minnesota.

***

"Aha! Something interesting occurred in Australia." The psychiatrist shifted his bulky bottom that filled the space between arm rests. "Remember what I told you. That shit can swirl around in your head, but like a bowel movement, it has to come out."

A nail hit squarely on the head. The colonel's smug expression brought a curl to Richard's lips. *Two wrong hits*—his determination *not* to cooperate, and *misjudging this soldier's use of slang.* Richard never succumbed to the vernacular that many people associate with combat veterans. A part of him still clung to an English heritage through his mother's side, but he harbored a reserve of his Scotch father's intensity when threatened.

Richard struggled to retrieve his interrupted memory, R & R in Australia that he had yet to earn through combat.

***

"What's your unit, Yank? Trousers tucked inside your boots tells me something I might want to know about."

"We're not allowed to divulge that information."

"Your secret is safe here. We're on your side."

Richard eyed his companion and succumbed. "The 503rd Parachute Regiment."

"That explains the missing insignia." He rubbed his chin stubble. "General MacArthur's secret weapon." He tipped his hat revealing a deeply etched face, testimony to years in the Outback. "What Company? A, B, C, D?"

"None. We're Battery. We drop alongside whichever company requires artillery."

"Just what I wanted to hear." He grabbed both pints from the bar handing one to Richard. "We gotta clang glasses and chug-a-lug over that good bit of information." Mugs crashed and ale splashed. The Aussie gulped. "I don't cotton to jumping out of perfectly good airplanes."

Richard took a long sip but drank little. "You a paratrooper?"

"Was 'til now that you guys got here. Your crazy colonel commandeered our artillery unit, jammed us into C47's, and shoved us out the door over Markham Valley. Not many of us ever even been up in a plane."

Richard shook his head. "Crazy." He understood how tough a jump would be without proper training.

"Yep, crazy 'cause that colonel shot himself after a victory celebration with his officers."

Richard acknowledged that fact with a nod. The news of the 503rd commanding officer's suicide had reached his squad even before they disembarked. He respected the regiment's replacement, Lt. Colonel Jones.

Banging his empty glass on the bar, the Aussie flashed two fingers toward the barmaid. "A couple of our guys got busted up on the jump, but the action on the ground was hardly worth our while."

Not the account Richard's tent mates back at base had described, but that had been their first taste of combat.

"You guys come in on the USS Young America?" Richard nodded. "Supposed to be the fastest ship afloat. What took you so long?"

Twenty eight days aboard ship, forced to sleep below deck even crossing the equator, and confined aboard ship during repair work at Pearl Harbor, none of which he wanted dwell on, especially the tangle of half sunken ships still blocking much of the harbor.

***

"A lot of sheep in Australia." Lt. Col. Renford's musing edged out the image of the Aussie soldier.

The scene at the pub interrupted, Richard grimaced and tried to refocus. *Just a few minutes left on the clock, and he wants to talk about* sheep!

He released a calculated amount of anger. "I didn't attend an opera, and I didn't encounter any sheep the few weeks my outfit spent in Australia." A flash of memory broke through his rant at the colonel. "Montana's where I learned to herd sheep."

Richard checked himself. *Whoever breaks the silence loses.* He had mastered that sales strategy as a preteen selling magazines door-to-door. At the critical moment, stop the pitch, look the customer in the eye, and hand him the pen and order form.

Richard locked eyes with the colonel, a dangerous maneuver if still in uniform.

Lt. Col. Renford returned the glare, consuming minutes that had suddenly become precious.

Richard blurted, "I was fifteen, didn't turn sixteen until September of that year." The urge to talk about his Montana experience overwhelmed his desire to be coy. "Summer of 1940 and again in '41."

He had broken silence but didn't care. "Me and my brother Edward, he's…was…two years older." He shook off a painful memory. "Me and Edward hitched rides west with no destination in mind. Just an adventure with my older brother. We joined a bunch of bums riding an empty boxcar out of Williston, North Dakota, and got kicked off by the railroad bulls. Just to be mean, they waited 'til we were ten miles out of town and had to walk back.

That's where we split up. Edward was fond of this girl back in St. Paul. Got lonesome, horny I teased, and headed home. I kept going. Had to prove I could make it on my own. Bumming food was easier than peddling magazines. I'd offer to chop wood, but no mother would make a starving boy work for food, and sometimes they would offer a little cash on the side."

Richard anticipated a reaction, but the psychiatrist remained stone faced.

"I never took money unless offered." He glanced at the clock. "Got as far as Billings. Stopped at a ranch where two big dogs met me at the gate. I always loved animals, and they seemed to take a shining to me. I impressed the owner, a guy with a ruddy face and a hearty laugh."

"'Them's sheep dogs. Do you understand sheep?'"

"I told him I'd worked with sheep and cows and hogs. And that I rode horses to tend my trap line. I didn't tell him I was a city kid ordered by juvenile court to a Wisconsin farm for attitude adjustment, and that I was still in grade school at the time."

"He said, 'Come with me while you're resting,' as if hitchhiking was hard work. We piled into an old International pickup, two dogs and a bunch of supplies in the back. I expected a short drive, but we rode that rattling old truck most of the afternoon.

Up in the mountains on a sloping grassy plateau, the field off in the distance appeared white."

"'Six thousand sheep,' his voice bursting with pride. 'Just one man and half a dozen dogs.' His eyes locked onto mine. 'Think you can handle it? I try to deliver supplies every week, but the cabin's stock could last twice that long.'"

"I told him all he needed was to show me what to do."

"'My herder walked off the job yesterday. Couldn't stand the isolation. I was planning to do the job myself, 'til you come along. I can stay with you a few days 'til you get the hang of it, and for the dogs to accept you as their master. I saw you work with the two sheep herders we brought with us—they'll join the others until we bring the flock back this fall. Pay ain't too good, but no place to spend money up here anyhow.'"

***

"I'm afraid I have to call *time*."

Richard's story had been interrupted, and he resented the slight, until he glanced at the clock. He had talked half way through the next patient's appointment time.

Chapter Two

Flat on his stomach, hands covering his head, Richard quivered and then began to sob.

"Are you okay?" Rita's voice accompanied a wedge of daylight that shot across the floor of his darkened bedroom.

"Don't come in!" one hand swiped tears from his eyes, the other grabbed the sheet off the bed to cover himself.

Rita ignored her brother's command, as he should have expected from a teenaged sister who reported everything to Ma.

"What happened? All I did was knock, and then the ruckus. Did you fall out of bed?"

Richard clamped his forehead as if it were a pimple about to burst. "Nah, I slept this way last night," he lied. "Cooler than in bed." Mind cleared of haze but not the pain, he had yet to control or even understand his violent reaction to unexpected loud noises.

She seldom gave much attention to her brother's strange behavior, an issue his family tiptoed around, literally, something guys at the bar found funny when they'd sneak up and clap their hands behind his back. He'd get over it, no thanks to the psychiatrist he'd been forced to see every week, or lose his disability pay. After a few beers, loud noise didn't bother, and the guys would lose interest in trying to startle him. His bigger concern, the nightmares, screams that brought his mother running to his room. He denied his single overwhelming fear, even to himself.

"What do you want?"

"There are two soldiers at the door waiting to talk to you."

Richard jumped to his feet, sheet dropping to the floor. Rita turned away as he covered the slit in his boxer shorts with his saluting hand; eyes fixed on his sister's back as he stepped into his pants. "What do they want?" An unnecessary question since he skipped yesterday's appointment. He'd only stopped at Frankie and Johnnies for a quick beer, and one thing led to another.

"Are they MP's?"

"How should I know? They just said I should get you up."

"You told them I was still in bed?" He glanced around for the clock, but last week he'd smashed it against the wall because the ticking annoyed him. "What time is it?"

"Two o'clock." She slowly turned to face him. "I was going to get you up anyway, because you promised we could go to Sears & Roebuck to order Ma her new washing machine."

"That might have to wait." He tossed the sheet back onto the bed. "Tell them I'm sick."

Rita stepped out into the hall.

"No, wait. I'll go, but give me a minute."

She stuck her head back into the room. "I'll tell them you're on your way, but hurry. They're scary."

***

"You're lucky I had an opening this late in the day. I wouldn't want to report you AWOL." Lt. Col. Renford gestured for Richard to sit in the usual client's chair across the desk from him.

"I told you, I'm not a soldier anymore."

"Yes, but under care of the US Army, and drawing compensation."

"A small token for eighteen continuous months of combat, and the explosion during mop-up that earned me a ticket home aboard a hospital ship. What I do now is my business."

"Your business is to let go of what happened in the South Pacific, and my job is to help you. Both our paychecks depend on the effort we put toward this goal."

"What do I have to do to show what combat did to my head? Go out in the street and kill someone?"

"What I want is for you to stop killing yourself a little bit at a time. But for now, I want to hear about your life before the war."

"Hasn't the government got access to my court record? It kept me from going to jail, which I'm sure I'd be out of by now without this dark cloud over my head."

"Dark cloud. A good analogy. Why don't you release thunder and lightning and let loose the downpour locked up in there."

Richard repeated the only statement that usually got a rise out of the Colonel. "Would it please you if I went out onto the street and shot someone?" He half stood and plopped back onto the chair. "That's what they trained me to do."

"Just the enemy, and right now we have no enemies."

"You haven't been in my shoes, lately."

"No, but I would like you to step out of them, take a chance and go barefoot for a while. Let down your guard." He glanced at the closed folder on his desk. "Last week we talked about Montana. I gather that was a bright time in your young life."

"Sheep don't mess with your head."

"Touché Soldier."

Fists clinched, "Stop calling me soldier."

Gazes locked, "Then stop acting like one, just itching for a fight."

Richard blinked, refocused his stare into empty space, and, biding time, willed his anger to recede. A rustle of papers from the menacing manila folder perched strategically at the middle of the desk,

Renford, no doubt, searching for an incident that would break into his safe place. It didn't take long.

"Would you really have killed that farmer with a pitchfork? You were only what, twelve years old at the time?"

The puppeteer had jerked the correct string, and Richard relinquished his defense. "He slugged me first, and not with an open hand like Ma had to do sometimes."

"You gave your mother cause to resort to corporal punishment?"

Safe for the moment, but the pitchfork incident would come up again and bite his backsides. "She had to because Pa wasn't there to punish us. He left us when I was only five years old. Rita wasn't even born, yet."

"What did you do that made her mad?"

"Skip school mostly. One time in the fifth grade the principal called her to a meeting in his office."

"Why did you hate school?"

"I liked school, but I had other responsibilities. If I left my shoeshine spot for more than a few hours, I'd have to fight to get it back. Ma needed that money for food."

"So, you were the man in the house?"

"Edward was older, but he was sent away." Talking felt okay, almost good. "He got me started shining shoes." Richard glanced at his boots, still military as were his dominant characteristics. Damned if he'd go barefoot just to make a point.

"I had the best spot between 3M and the pub where the higher-ups went for lunch. I'd get them shined so they could flirt with the waitresses or when they decided to shape up and return after an extended lunch. Late afternoon I'd get a few, but if I wanted to score big, I'd have to hide from the curfew cops until some half drunk guy would leave the bar after dark. They were my biggest tippers."

"What happened when you got caught?"

"I was forced to join the Army."

"When still in grade school?"

"No, but that's what it finally came to? Cops dragged me home. My mother…"

A trap! A quick glance at the clock and back to the pair of eyes penetrating his…soul?

"Your mother…?"

Richard's vision blurred. He mumbled, "Crossed the line."

"Who?" Stare intensified.

"I…she said…" Cotton filled his mouth. A flash of light and a presence in the doorway.

"Bring Richard a glass of water."

Eyes glued to the door, Richard conjured the St. Paul cop bursting open the door to his mother's apartment, her vagrant nine-year-old son in tow. Grip on Richard's collar relaxed, and a fatherly hand settled on the misguided kid's shoulder. "Your boy should not be out roaming the streets after dark." A not too gentle shove into the kitchen. "Your son was accosting business men outside the St. Paul Hotel. If you recall, last week it was outside the Landmark Post Office."

"I got a business to take care of and that's where I find my best customers," Policeman number two held the shoe shine kit with both hands. "You better give that back. Ma needs all the money I can earn."

"Is there a Mr. Leslie?" Cop number one overstepped, crossed the line.

"He's dead! I will take care of this matter."

Cops gone, door slammed. "My dad is not dead,"

"He is to us. Next time, don't stay out on the street so late."

Richard glared at the Renford's secretary too eager to make him drink. "I couldn't abandon my hard fought-for spot unattended before cocktail hour ended at the hotel." He grabbed the glass, gulped a single swallow and set it down. Pleading eyes sought Renford's attention and then affixed to the door until the secretary left the room.

"I'd drop to my knees in front of a guy waiting for the valet to bring his car around and snap the polishing cloth across the toe of his shoe. If he didn't jerked his foot back or push me away, I'd won, probably cheated the valet out of his tip."

A nine-year-old Richard demonstrated his shoeshine story to a rapt audience of one. "I'd grab a tin of brown or black polish and say, 'These scuff marks will need a little extra work.' When the guys car arrived, I'd hold out my hand and say, "Thank you, Sir" even if the loose change had been intended for the valet.

Occasionally, a hand would pull out an empty pocket lining, but that didn't deter me. Disappointment etched on my face, I'd keep an extended hand until he either got into his car or pulled out his wallet for paper money."

Embarrassed by his nostalgic outburst, Richard focused on the water in front of him but didn't drink.

"Are you saying your mother condoned your violating curfew?"

"She knew the score. 'Fight your own battles,' she'd tell me." Her voice resonated in his. "'Run away from a fight with a bloody nose, don't come home crying for sympathy. I'll just bloody it some more.'"

"How did that make you feel?"

Richard sat up. "Like a man, in front of my sisters. In that small town where we used to live—when my dad was still around—kids down the street from our house used to beat me up. I was only four or five. My sisters told me to go to their house, throw rocks at them playing in the back yard, and then run like hell. They chased me, and the girls ambushed them. They didn't bother me after that. By the time we moved to St. Paul, my sisters got too old for such shenanigans, and I had to fend for myself."

"What was it like, living in a house with all those women?"

"Isabel and Hazel got married and moved, Margaret eloped and ran off to California, and Edna died in a car accident. Only me and Rita lived with Ma. Edward too, but he wasn't home much."

"Were you assigned household chores?"

"I did some cooking and baking. Ma said I'd make a good chef some day. I did most of the shopping. The butcher down the street had eyes on Ma, so she avoided going to his shop. She'd send me there to buy a dime's worth of hamburger, partly to show how poor we were. Then, I'd ask for bones about to be thrown to the dogs. He'd pull a hock out from the cooler and trim off maybe half the meat. 'Tell your Ma to make some soup.'"

"It galled me to have him think Ma only made soup, like Tiny Tim's family in Dicken's Christmas story." Richard noticed the pen in Renford's hand scratch a few words onto his note pad.

"Ma was a good cook and so were the older girls. That's how they got their husbands interested, to my way of thinking."

He avoided eye contact. "Ma is a proud English woman—parents immigrated just before the *Great War*; that's what they called the World War One. She set a fine table, even when food supply ran short near the end of the month. Table cloth and place mats, all washed by hand."

He remembered his promise to Rita. "I'm supposed to be buying a washing machine instead of rattling away here." Out of the corner of his eye, he checked for the Colonel's attention. "See, I do some good with the Government's money. Don't just piss it all away."

His mind returned to his mother's table; knives, forks, and spoons all in their proper positions alongside the plates, water glass, and tea cup on either side.

He leaned forward and peered into the officer's cup on the desk, its milky residue puke yellow. "Ma taught us to drink tea, but the army insists on coffee, makes fun of the Limeys with their tea time. I remember once on Negros Island, I was battling the head-high and razor-sharp Kunai grass, but you wouldn't know about that."

He took in a satisfying breath. "I heard voices, not Japs, I could smell them a mile away. A squad of Limey's had trampled an area to take their tea. I took a break from my hunt—I used to track down Japs like game back in Wisconsin—and we had a spot of tea together."

A quick glance to check if his slip of the tongue about a war-related incident might have found its way to the note pad only to reappear in the form of a question later. The pitchfork incident would be easier to discuss.

"You made reference to Dickens." The pen scratched out words. "Did you read a lot when you were young?"

"Not until after Juvenile Court sent me to Wisconsin. It cost me my shoeshine operation, but I did learn to read in the process."

"Yet you wanted to harm the farmer who took you in."

That guy didn't *take me in*. He negotiated with the court for a slave to work on his farm for free." Richard shifted his weight. "Mr. Munson...." His frown relaxed. "Mr. Munson and his wife, Bertha, *took me in* after the court declared my former placement too dangerous."

Richard checked for Renford's silent *go ahead* expression. "They didn't treat me like a hired hand, and I worked hard; got up for chores at five, back in the house for a hot breakfast at seven, and then off on my horse to the country school in time for the bell at nine. After school I'd jump back on my horse and tend my trap line."

Renford's expression resembled that of a cat about to pounce on a field mouse, but Richard continued. "Got five dollars for skunk fur, but skinning one was a bit of a problem. Bertha made me undress outside before letting me into the house."

Renford's mouse seems to have escaped the cat. "At night after chores, Bertha would help me with my home work. She taught me to read for comprehension, not just sounding out the words. By the time I returned to St. Paul, I had read Dickens, knew my geography, and tested high enough in math to skip the ninth grade. Country school ended at the eighth grade."

"Why did you leave the Munson's?"

"To dodge the draft."

"At age twelve?"

"Not me but his twenty-year-old son. If I had stayed on, Munson couldn't claim hardship to operate the farm. My mother didn't have that option when I got drafted."

"It says here ..." he pointed to the file folder, "you enlisted. Had to make an exception because you were still a minor."

"Read further. The Army wasn't the only institution on my case."

"Your mother didn't try to intercede?"

"With only one teenager left at home, she had no grounds to claim hardship." Muscles in his face tightened. "When Edward got killed in Italy, she requested her only son be returned to civilian life, but the government claimed they had too much invested in my training." He glanced at his hands. "I must have signed off on that right when I joined the paratroopers after basic training." His spirits brightened. "Got an extra fifty bucks a month on top of combat pay. More money than any foot soldier of my rank, and even a few officers."

"Yes, of course." A shuffling of papers, a pause followed by a glare. "You mustered out of the Army less than a year ago with thousands of dollars back pay, and God only knows for what else. What did you do with all that money?"

He had penetrated the colonel's shield. "Raw whiskey, wild women, and fast cars. I don't know, the rest just sort of got pissed away."

Face blotchy. "But your mother will get her washing machine."

"Yeah, and a Frigidaire, too." He will have to borrow some of Rita's babysitting money. "Let's get on with what you called me in here for. I gotta see a man about a horse." *Sixty of them, all crammed under the hood of a Thirty nine Ford.*

"That's it. We've used up the time. Next week be here pronto." He placed the folder into his brief case. "You're dismissed..." A grin slid across his face. "Soldier."

Chapter Three

Richard drew in a deep breath; cathedral time, his favorite part of the day. The hospital's shadow sliced through the mauve tinged sunlight, crept across the sidewalk onto the freshly mowed boulevard fronting the streetcar tracks, and wrapped itself around anything in its path. The session had gone better than expected, considering the circumstances.

The MP's, so eager to deliver him earlier, were nowhere in sight; apparently their door-to-door escort service operated only one way. Rather than wait for the last streetcar, he'd called his friend, Virgil, who owned Trumel's Automotive Repair with his father. A customer's car might need to be road tested, burn out the carbon on the stretch of road out to Fort Snelling and back.

A few more months until the third anniversary of his induction into the Army, physical taken in the medical building he just exited. Virgil never got drafted; forming a partnership with his father kept that from happening. Now he's a pain in the old man's ass, or, as Virgil thinks, the other way around. Richard pondered a relationship with his father, probably not possible after the way he abandoned his mother and sisters. Margaret, who returned from California with two kids and no husband, talked to their dad who'd been reassigned to the railroad out west. She refused to give Ma his address, but mentioned that he fathered two more daughters.

Girls. With Edward gone, women—mother, sister, and girl friends—complicated his life. How did Milton Morgan Leslie deal with mother, wife, and daughters?

Having step sisters made him uneasy, the grandmother they shared made him angry.

The streetcar pulled to a stop, and the other riders who'd been waiting filed on board. Richard couldn't break free of the stare he'd locked into.

"Hey, you." The driver yelled from inside the streetcar. "The last chance to catch a ride. No more units out this far until tomorrow." He stepped out of the car, his grizzled face directly in line with Richard's stare. "I know you guys got problems, but it's my ass if I leave one of you crazies stranded at the funny farm." He peered into Richard's eyes and turned back toward the car repeating, "Last chance." Hand on the lever, "I got a schedule to meet."

Freed from his stare, Richard's gaze locked onto the retreating conductor, but his body remained rigid. If he released one tensed muscle, he'd lose control and the consequences frightened him. He didn't relax until the streetcar screeched and disappeared down the track. He had overcome an impulse, what psychiatrists told him couldn't be done by will power alone. They understood his problem, but only he had the solution. He was engaged in a different kind of war where concentration, not action, was the main strategy. His deepest fear, it might not always work.

He'd keep calm. Virgil agreed to come to get him if he missed the last streetcar. Buddies got him through the war, and buddies like Virgil will help him adjust to the peace. He'd allow himself to doze.

Tell him I don't have a grandson. A crone's voice crackled from inside the house. *Only two granddaughters.*

Uniform cleaned and pressed with leggings tucked into polished boots, Richard stood at the door facing the maid who offered a sympathetic smile; no need to repeat the response from a grandmother he will never get to see.

Only two granddaughters, echoed on the train ride all the way back to the infirmary at Fort Ord, California, and again stranded at the Veteran's hospital at Fort Snelling, Minnesota.

***

Awakening from a deep sleep, Richard fought back the urge to flail his arms, only to realize they'd been restrained. Through the din of falsetto voices fussing about, he recognized Virgil's harsh but hearty tone.

"What the hell happened to you?"

His head had cleared, but his situation remained confused. "I don't know. I was sitting on a bench when things seemed to go crazy. I'm not sure but I think four or five guys jumped me. At least something happened to land me here. This is a hospital bed, isn't it?"

"Yes, you are in the emergency room, and so are a couple of MP's who tried to restrain you." The guy in the white gown hooked the clipboard at the foot of the bed. "You're under sedation, but we will remove the restraints if you assure us your outbursts are under control." He glared at Richard. "Do we have your word?"

Virgil said, "He's good."

"I need to hear Richard say it."

"Yeah, I'm okay. But I want to know what happened."

"That'll be explained tomorrow at nine hundred hours. It's all in the report we sent to Colonel Renford at his home." He cast Richard a doubtful glance. "Are you back in control? Yes or no."

"Yes! Now can Virgil take me home?"

"Nine hundred hours. Do we need to send the M.P.'s? Again?"

Virgil said, "I'll bring him." His gaze followed the aides as they loosened the straps. "Hell, he can take one of Pa's cars and drive himself. He's a war hero. No need for a baby sitter."

Richard thanked him with his eyes, rubbed his wrists, and sat up. "We better get going. Ma will be worried."

"I'll check your vital signs one more time, and then you'll be free to leave with your buddy." He shook his head. "I don't think getting discharged at this time is a good idea, but the decision was made above my pay grade."

***

Virgil tossed the keys to Richard as they approached the Ford. "You drive."

"Are you sure you want to trust me behind the wheel? Especially this car? I just had some kind of relapse."

"Gotta start sometime." Virgil slid onto the passenger seat and remained quiet until they reached an open stretch on Minnehaha Boulevard. "Gun it!"

Using the passing lane, Richard breezed by a couple of slower cars and cut back in to shoot ahead of the traffic in the cruising lane.

After swerving in and out, and the needle hovering around eighty miles an hour, Virgil yelled, "Hey, enough." The Ford's speed dissipated. "When you get back from your session tomorrow—driving one of Dad's street vehicles—we can open this one up on Stillwater Road."

Richard double clutched to gear down, shot back up to cruising speed, and dropped into high gear. "Not bad for a sixty horsepower flathead."

Virgil said, "Shaved those heads within a witch's breath of blowing the bottom half the engine. It'll be ready for the State Fair next week." He chuckled. "If you can stay out of trouble that long."

A rush traveled up and down Richard's spine, assured he wouldn't disappoint his pit-stop mechanic.

Virgil cracked the window an inch, shook loose a cigarette from its pack, and lit it. "Never guess who stopped by the shop today asking about you."

Richard, who seldom smoked, held out an open hand. "Who?"

Virgil passed him the smoldering Chesterfield and lit another. "Frank Kelly."

"Yeah?"

"Sounds like he's been keeping an eye on you. I didn't know you were buddy-buddy with the mob."

"He and his associates pretty much controlled East Side back when I had my shoe shine location. I did his shoes once. Didn't really need a shine. Probably every kid in a thirty block area earned his dime that afternoon."

"He mentioned that episode. Said he'd like to talk to you."

"When?"

"Didn't say, but I'd seek him out real soon. You know he hangs out at the Rusty Scupper, probably owns the place, or, for sure, gets his cut."

Richard crushed his cigarette into the ashtray and accelerated to a careless speed considering that section being heavily patrolled.

Chapter Four

Minutes, hours it seemed, ticked off as Richard fidgeted across from Lt. Col. Renford whose attention locked onto the report supposedly delivered to his home the previous evening. Why hadn't he already read it?

"Excuse me for a minute." Renford tucked the report into the file folder on his desk and left the room.

Richard eyed the ever expanding packet within arm's reach. Was he being tested? He had no desire to read a collection of infractions he'd nearly erased from memory. However, waking last night restrained to a bed with no memory of how or why he got there felt very similar to his hospital ship experience shortly after the war had ended. Amount of time lost was the only difference, a few hours yesterday compared to two months under sedation after the explosion in a booby-trapped Japanese bunker.

He called upon last night's conversation with Frank Kelley to blot out the emerging images of buddies who led him into that bunker but didn't survive the blast. And to block out the temptation peek into his file.

***

"I noticed you and Virgil got a pretty hot car ready for the races at the Minnesota State Fair." Frank Kelley sunk his teeth into the stub of a cigar gone cold, and, with his feet atop half an acre of mahogany, indicated the leather arm chair where Richard assumed he should sit.

"Yes, Sir. We done that." The leather creaking might have been mistaken for an inappropriate release of gas, something Richard avoided even when drinking beer with the guys.

"You come a long way since your shoe-shine stand on East Seventh."

Richard followed Kelley's gaze to the shoes adorning the desk top, their 4-bit shine obvious.

"A few nickels and dimes to take back to Ma. Just a couple sisters left at home when you stopped for a shine."

"Did I leave a good sized tip?"

"Yes, Sir. Silver dollar and a few pennies. Said that was all the change you had at the time."

"Are you sure it wasn't just the dollar? I seldom carried pennies."

"Maybe I got it mixed in with my pocket change. Pennies back then could still buy a handful of candy."

"That's what I want to talk to you about."

"Candy?"

Frank dropped his feet to the floor. "And pretzels and beer. I need someone to make delivers through the back doors in some pretty tough neighborhoods, not always during daylight hours." He paused, as if assessing a piece of property he might want to buy. "I'm sure you can handle those problems, but how about kegs half your weight?"

"I used to deliver ice before the war, eighty pound cakes up to second and third story apartments."

"Some time after your shoe shine operation, no doubt. I often wondered what happened to you until I heard you enlisted."

"Had a few problems with school and the cops. I survived."

"I'd ask if you can handle a truck, but I saw what you and Virgil did with automobiles. Any questions?"

"Just, when do I start?"

"Next week. I'll have Tommy ride shotgun until you get the route established in your head." He glanced down at the dead plug between his lips and tossed it into the waste basket.

"And point out the dangerous places." His glaze remained fixed on the no longer visible cigar butt, as if it were an old friend. "I got just one more question."

Richard squirmed as the mobster's eyes penetrated.

"Do you play cards?"

Richard nodded, relieved.

"Me and some of the boys get together off-and-on for some cribbage and maybe a little poker. I'll keep you in mind."

***

Renford returned with another report that he placed on the desk. "Sorry for the wait." He sat and held eye contact a few moments, as if Richard should initiate conversation. "What happened yesterday when you left our afternoon session?"

"You tell me. I didn't get copies of the reports."

"I want to know what caused the incident that generated those reports." He tapped the folder as if seeking answers to every one of Richard's mysteries. "Two MP's and a security guard required medical attention, Mr. Hermendez released just minutes ago. What the hell got you so riled?"

Hermendez. Mexican Hermendez. Richard just stared.

"The streetcar driver from the afternoon run said you waved him away after the other guys got on board. Said he considered driving back with his personal car to check if you were still stranded. He's the kind of guy who cares about his usual riders."

Crazies at the funny farm. Richard tucked the insult into his private list of triggers that could cause loss of control. "I was waiting for my ride, not the streetcar."

"That was confirmed by Trumel's presence at the emergency room. We need to establish what caused you to attack the security guard who was concerned about your safety."

"I fell asleep. That much I remember. Hermendez, if you can understand his accent, will have to fill in the details."

"I believe he has." Renford read from the report. *"Security guard Hermendez noticed Mr. Leslie didn't get on the streetcar, the last one for the day. Approximately forty-five minutes later—the end of Mr. Hermendez's shift—Mr. Leslie appeared to be sleeping. Mr. Hermendez approached to offer a ride home since he, too, commuted from downtown St. Paul, but Mr. Leslie appeared to have died with his eyes open. Mr. Hermendez made the sign of the cross and attempted to close Mr. Leslie's eyes. If two MPs hadn't happened by, Mr. Hermendez felt sure Mr. Leslie would have choked him to death."*

Renford tucked the sheet of paper into the packet on his desk. I don't think you need to hear the MP's accounts of the struggle. Cracked ribs and a broken nose can add a negative tone if not an actual bias to any report.

Silence, an obvious strategy shift from *your turn to speak* to *just think about it for a moment*, and Richard resented the manipulation. He redirected the discussion. "I was offered a job last night after I got home from the hospital."

"What kind of interview happens that late in the day? Bar tending? Or, considering your facial cuts and bruises, maybe a bouncer?"

"I got beat up *here* on government property last night, remember?"

A quick glance at the colonel's deadpan reaction. "A business man called me to his downtown office. He never asked personal questions about my face." Richard resisted touching his swollen eye that began to throb. "If anything, a few battle scars enhance rather than deter in this line of work. Next week I begin driving a delivery truck."

"How do you see this job as a means of curbing your anger?"

"I won't have to beg any more money from Ma." Richard locked onto the psychiatrist's glare. "I won't be coming here anymore."

"I won't recommend disability pay."

"I won't need it." Sarcasm topped.

***

The State Fair cancellation that year due to the polio outbreak disappointed Richard, but the delivery job pleased him and others; mother, sister, psychiatrist. Until an incident in the alley behind Fitz's Tavern.

"He'll never be able to talk again," the court appointed attorney's plea for leniency, his client at his side shrinking into his oversized suit jacket.

"On the bright side, he'll never rat on his buddies," whispered Frank Kelley into the ear of his employee he'd been summoned to vouch for. No need for an attorney, because Richard hadn't been charged, although attempted manslaughter could have been a possibility.

Up Near Frog Town during a pre dawn delivery, Richard returned to his truck and found three guys rummaging through the van assessing whatever they could run off with. He yelled and all but one disappeared down the alley and jumped a fence, creating the slight annoyance Richard had come to expect. The remaining assailant, courage backed up with a knife, slashed a gash in Richard's jacket, a costly miss.

"I don't wan' no trouble, jus' hand over the keys." Richard had exaggerated the black man's dialect at the police station, the culprit no longer able to speak for himself.

That unfortunate phrase raised the charge from *robbery* to *hijacking*, but Richard cared little about such details; three fingers to the throat and the knife dropped to the street, followed by the hijacker onto his knees gagging blood. "I only wanted him to drop his weapon. If I wanted him dead, he wouldn't be on trial today."

Richard whispered back to Kelley, "What are the MP's doing here? This is a civilian matter."

Frank Kelly, Richard's play-acting attorney, said, "I'll deal with it." He faced the judge. "Your Honor, I can only assume the uniformed men at the door are here to show respect for a former soldier—war hero—performing his civic duty."

"The court will deal with that matter when the docket is cleared. The defendant has pled guilty and expressed remorse. Bail denied, until sentence is pronounced at a later date. Case dismissed."

Bailiffs escorted the prisoner down the aisle and out the door still flanked by two military police officers, his attorney trailing.

The judge continued. "The Army has no jurisdiction in this court, but *have* been granted permission to speak in defense of their former soldier." He acknowledged Frank Kelley with a nod almost as a boss to an employee.

"Mr. Kelley." Frank stiffened as if some ordinary roles had suddenly reversed. "You placed your employee in a dangerous situation without any kind of support, relying on his special skills that could render him vulnerable in a court such as this."

Frank gnawed at an absent cigar as the judge continued. "This did show bad judgment on your part, but certainly within the law, and I can only assume you will carry on as usual now that this issue is settled. You are excused, but Mr. Leslie, if it please the court, remain at your seat."

"Hey, I did nothing wrong. You can't charge me with anything."

"This is true. However another jurisdiction holds sway over your behavior, and has been invited to assist this court with what it deems necessary."

"Your Honor." Frank, two fingers readied to remove the non existent cigar, returned his hand to his pocket. "I'm staying. I'm not an attorney, but you can't leave this man with no representation."

"Suit yourself." The Judge continued, "The St Paul Police Department, in conjunction with outlying law enforcement departments, has has made a request of this court, and The Department of Veteran Affairs has concurred. We just witnessed what this man is capable of in hand-to-hand street fighting, and have been informed of various other lethal hand maneuvers he may be able to perform."

"You can't cut off a man's hands for what he might do with them," Frank Kelley, who probably doled out such punishment, stated defiantly. "As a matter of fact..."

"Yes, yes. We are not some primitive desert society where such an act could be condoned. Quite the contrary. Our actions are to preempt possible harm to an officer should he find cause to approach Mr. Leslie unaware of the weapons he possesses."

Kelley smirked. "If *Mr. Leslie* promises to use his hands solely for gainful employment and to wipe his ass, will the court be satisfied?"

"Mr. Kelley, that would cost you a *contempt* if court were in session." The judge stepped down from the bench, and the MP's moved forward. "What we are asking of Mr. Leslie is to register his hands with the St. Paul Police as lethal weapons. These officers are prepared to present the military's rational for such an act as spelled out by one Lieutenant Colonel Renford."

Chapter Five

"Ma, sit down." Richard pulled the chair back from the table. "Rita, make Ma sit. The colonel might walk through that door any minute."

"Can't wait to get home and tack this etching up on the wall." Richard's mother unwound the scroll, a gravestone-sized sheet of white paper she had bummed from the butcher on East Seventh Street." She glanced at her teenage daughter. "Which room do you think?"

Richard shoved the chair back against the table, not wanting the colonel to make any assumptions about his relationship with his mother to bring up at a future session. Meeting at least once a month for a year pretty well used up all topics he agreed to discuss. "Keep it out of my bedroom. I got enough stuff bugging me without opening my eyes every morning to a sketch of my brother's grave stone."

"Come, help me keep this from rolling back up so I can read his epitaph"

Richard caught Rita's attention and motioned for her to hold the paper open for Ma. He sat across from where his psychiatrist would probably sit. He wished they could meet in his office, but his secretary thought it would be crowded.

With her finger, his mother traced the shaded etchings, the scrapings of charcoal from pens she purchased at Woolworths where she insisted Richard stop on their way to Fort Snelling. She read in a soft voice, "Edward A. Leslie, Minnesota, Private, 363 Infantry, World War Two, born May fifteenth, nineteen hundred and twenty one."

35

She brushed back a tear and whispered, "Died October thirteenth, nineteen hundred and forty four."

Richard grimaced. The darn fool went in as a medic but volunteered, actually argued his way into the infantry. Caught a bullet the first day at Monte Casino, his wife from one week's leave claimed the ten thousand dollar Army insurance policy that his Ma would have been entitled to.

"Oh, my Edward! I knew he was dead the moment it happened." She gave Richard a teary-eyed glance, but he pretended not to notice. "Got the telegram a week later, but I felt his dying in my sleep—his crying out to a mother who couldn't comfort him. When I awoke, he was gone."

Yeah, and tracking her remaining son in the Philippines, letter demanding revenge. No matter that a German shot Edward. Enemy is enemy. As if the number of dead Japs hadn't already evened the score. A hundred more she demanded and wanted proof. What? Ears? Noses? penises? From my mother? I chalked it off as grief, yet I couldn't help myself. I began hunting and counting and…

His mother dropped her edge of the paper and shook her finger at Richard. "I fought for you." She paused until he made eye contact. "Wrote I don't remember how many letters. Came out here at Snelling to state my case, no sole surviving son should remain in harm's way. I got the attention of the base commander, General Something or Another. He couldn't protect you because you volunteered—were warned but no, you wanted adventure, glory."

Rita stood guardian to her brother's headstone.

Richard mumbled, "And fifty dollars a month jump pay, and fifty more combat pay."

"And what good does that money do now. I got a Maytag and a Frigidaire and a son who has to borrow money from his widowed mother to carouse the streets every night."

"Pa ain't dead, Ma." Richard returned his gaze to the table.

"To me he is. To his children he is."

The door swung open and, on impulse, Richard stood. "Colonel, this is my mother and my sister, Rita." Embarrassed and defeated, he sat, locked into an empty stare.

Lt. Col. Renford stood at attention acknowledging the older woman and then her daughter, each with a nod. "Mrs. Leslie. Rita." He stepped closer and extended his hand toward the sketch. "I see you've visited Richard's brother's grave." He shook his head. "A terrible sacrifice for any mother to have to make for her country. You have my deepest sympathy."

From the corner of his eye, Richard caught the familiar quiver of his mother's chin, forewarning a beating when he was a child, but just frustration since he moved back home. Recently, being slapped would have felt better.

Rita rolled the paper, took her mother's arm, and seated her at the table, placing the scroll on her lap.

"One year ago this week Richard mustered out of the army, returning to your home a war hero. As in most cases, this comes with a price. Time to adjust to civilian life varies depending on the amount of time a soldier had been involved in combat. The 503rd, Richard's regiment, experienced continuous combat for eighteen consecutive months."

Richard's mother interrupted. "How many men?" She had yet to extend eye contact to the colonel since they sat down.

"Pardon?" Renford's startled response.

"How many were in Richard's regiment?"

"Richard, I believe you could give your mother a better estimate than I could."

Richard resented being drawn into a conversation that smelled like a trap. "About three thousand, Ma. You knew the size of my outfit."

Mrs. Leslie shot her son a grimace and then glared at the colonel. "Are all of them meeting with psychiatrists since the war ended?"

37

"Any of them who came home on a hospital ship sedated are probably under psychiatric care." He glanced at Richard. "At least those lucky enough to have survived their wounds."

"I don't need to be reminded of a son who never came home." She grabbed her scrolled headstone and shook it at the colonel like a pointer.

"Mrs. Leslie. You may not believe this, but I can understand... feel your grief."

Richard selected a more comfortable situation, but his mind refused to be transported out of the room.

Renford's voice cracked. "I, too, had a son who didn't come home. His ship was torpedoed, all hands lost."

Mrs. Leslie lowered her pointer and put it back on her lap. "No grave marker?"

"Yes, there is a stone, but he's not under it." He paused, probably for effect. "A sailor accepts that possibility just like a paratrooper accepts the double if not triple danger he may encounter."

She shook her head. "Why can't we settle our differences without sending young men to fight?" Her chin didn't quiver but tensed with recognizable determination. "Why'd you require me and my daughter to come today?"

"I hope *invite* was the word I used." His sudden glance pulled Richard out of his race car and brought him back to the table.

"This week Richard celebrates his first anniversary home from the war. I thought a gathering of those who love him would be appropriate." His expression, one of victory. "That you do love him is evident by your presence here, by your accepting him back into your family."

"Of course he belongs at home. At least until he finds a wife to take with him to his own place. Sometimes I worry that might not happen."

"There aren't women in his circle of friends?"

"Many. He hangs out in bars and drinks and dances and God only knows what else, but never brings a girl home to meet his mother."

Renford didn't respond before Richard acknowledged her glare. "Ma, I'm not ready to settle down. There's too much stuff going on. I can't even keep a job."

"You aren't making delivers for Mr. Kelley any longer," the first break in the colonel's countenance. "I thought the matter got settled at the trial."

"He quit that job weeks ago," a wave of her hand, flippancy in her tone.

Richard had never seen an expression of success dissolve so quickly as on Lt. Col. Renford's face. "We talked about the problem I had after the incident in the back alley. I nearly killed that guy."

"But you're still on good terms with your old boss?"

"Yeah, we play cribbage at The Rusty Scupper a couple times each week. He set me up with a couple of construction jobs but they fell through."

"Why haven't you mentioned this before?"

"I never thought of the Army as an employment agency?"

"I'll look into the GI Bill for some vocational training options. In the meantime, let's celebrate your successes."

"I ain't dead and I haven't killed anyone. Yeah, let's celebrate."

"Rita, we've been doing what adults seem to do best, blabber on and neglect the young people. How different is your life since your brother came home?"

"I had to give up my bedroom because Richard needed the one with two windows."

"That's not the reason, at least not the entire reason I sleep in the attic." Richard regretted not accepting Rita's two-window explanation, but all attention zoomed in on him. "Sometimes I have nightmares and wake up…"

"He screams, but he doesn't like it to have his mother come to comfort him. I don't mind, but he wants privacy." She gave the psychiatrist a wistful glance. "Isn't there something you can give him for bad dreams?"

"Have you been taking your medication, Richard?"

"Usually, but I forget sometimes."

"He doesn't forget. He comes home drunk and hardly makes it to his room." Nearly in tears, Rita continued. "I'm sorry, Richard, but I want you to get some help."

"I can see we still have some unresolved issues. I'd like you to start coming here every week like when we first started these sessions. Since you are between jobs right now, I'll see if we can boost your disability back to at least fifty percent."

Richard squirmed. "How about meeting every other week? That way I can spend more time looking for work. Frank can help me." He brightened. "As a matter of fact, he offered me another full time job just last week."

"And you first mention it now? I'd been home praying you'd find something since your disability got cut back."

"You'd be praying a whole lot more if I took that job." A brief rush of pride. "Frank wants me to be his body guard. He's earned a few enemies in his business, and he thinks my size would confuse anyone who might attack him."

"He'd use you for bait?"

"They would be less tempted to shoot him, but move in close because they would think I'd be easy to overcome."

"I don't want my son part of the mob."

"You didn't want me to be part of the Army either, but here I am."

"You were wise to refuse the job, and not just because of the danger. It would set your treatment back to when the war ended. I want to see you a week from today to work through some of these issues. I will check into the GI Bill."

"And don't forget to raise his disability pay. He doesn't make enough to cover his share of the rent."

Renford stood at attention. "Mrs. Leslie, I will do everything I can for your son, but he has to cooperate. I would like to see you—and his sister—on a regular basis, maybe once every month. We will work as a team to bring this son back to you minus the damage the war has caused."

Chapter Six

Richard chose the same seat at the table as the previous week, this time not flanked by mother and sister. The colonel's office unavailable, his secretary vague about the reason—some urgent meeting or some remodeling project—an obvious spur-of-the-moment fabrication. Strangely, he felt comforted. With home life, social encounters, and job prospects on the decline, he needed a reminder of military camaraderie to raise his spirits. If he hadn't been denied reenlistment, he could be serving in a building such as this. But, if another war should break out...

Lt. Col. Renford interrupted Richard's WWIII followed by a female wearing an Army uniform. "Richard, I'd like you to meet Lieutenant Jansen."

Richard stood at attention but redirected his salute to shake the woman's outstretched hand. "Hi. Just call me Nancy."

"Yes, Ma'am."

"Nancy," she stressed and gestured for Richard to sit, taking the chair to his left. "I wouldn't even be in uniform if I had known Ted wanted me to meet you."

Lt. Col. Renford camouflaged a grimace with an exaggerated smile and remained standing. "I asked Lieutenant Jansen to attend our session because she has some suggestions that might be helpful." He glanced at the female officer. "Go ahead...Nancy...and I'll rejoin in a few minutes." He walked out leaving the door open.

"Nancy?"

"Yes."

"Are you and—Ted—always this informal, or just with the crazies who come here to get their heads screwed back on proper?"

"A good question. I did time in the field, European theater, and had my fill of pulling rank. Being a WAC officer in the combat zone, I felt the need for protocol. Here I prefer just being a woman and a psychologist. As for that other part of your question, I am honored to work with soldiers who were crazy enough to jump out of airplanes."

Nancy could have told him to fly out of this third story window and he would have obliged.

"What I gathered from Dr. Renford's notes, you are experiencing some very common post combat traumas; nightmares, restlessness, and occasional anxiety attacks. First off, I want to assure you this is quite common. Also, you feel rejection from having your reenlistment denied."

Elbow on the table, she raised an open hand. "How am I doing so far?"

"You left out an angry mother and a sister who no longer respects her brother."

"No, what I left out—what we're going to work on—is your perception that you don't quite *fit in* like you did before the war."

"Things weren't that rosy back then either. I joined the Army to escape problems."

"That, too, is quite common. The difference being, back then you were just a teenager, but you've since become an adult. You now have tools to work with that are not usually available to young people. Some call this common sense."

Lt. Col. Renford entered followed by an aid carrying a tray of teapot, cups, and containers with sugar and cream.

He said, "Your mother is an English lady who taught you to drink tea rather than coffee. I'll need your approval of the Army's brewing skills before we invite her and Rita back."

The aid left, and Renford filled the three cups. "That Kenai grass you described doesn't grow in Minnesota, but it's too cold outside to sit on the lawn anyhow."

Nancy asked, "You take sugar and cream?" Ignoring Richard's indecisive nod and with the grace of his mother at half her age, she dipped a small mound of sugar into his tea and blended some cream with a single hand motion. "I often wondered why coffee became the drink of the military." She repeated the process with her cup and lifted it to her lips. When she set it down, Richard's gaze locked onto the red smudge on its rim.

Renford interrupted Richard's stare. "Have you told Richard your, shall we say, suggestion?"

"No, we were just getting acquainted. But now might be the proper time." She faced Richard. "I understand you like to dance."

***

Richard rode the streetcar back from his session at Fort Snelling, his on-and-off-again car parked in back of Trumel's Automotive, the voucher for dance lessons from Nancy and, he chuckled, *Ted*, in his coat pocket. He stepped off the streetcar at 354 Selby Avenue and paused in front of Arthur Murray Dance Studio and savored the wisp of a memory.

Eight years earlier, he'd recently returned home ending two years of court mandated country living at the Munson family farm, his second placement in Wisconsin. The first one nearly got him sent to Redwing, Minnesota's version of Boy's Town.

Instead of enrolling at Harding Junior High School as he had promised his mother that morning, he and the older sister of Rita's best friend spent the afternoon peddling magazine subscriptions.

A cluster of adults lingered in front of the newly franchised Arthur Murray Dance Studio. He and Patsy swayed to the music piped out to the sidewalk. Two thirteen-year-old kids dancing, obviously a studio promotion, attracted attention. At just the right moment, they handed out magazine subscriptions, suggesting those endorsed by Arthur Murray himself. They had their best sales that day.

Two years later—he had just returned from sheep herding in Montana—Patsy told him about Glen Miller coming to St. Paul. They hopped onto the back of a University Avenue Streetcar and jumped off at Midway in front of the Prom Ballroom celebrating its grand opening. Only sixteen at the time, they were turned away at the door. No matter, they had but thirty cents between them. The remainder of the evening they sat on overturned trash cans near the ballroom's back door listening to Glen Miller's band.

Whatever happened to Patsy since the war? He hadn't thought to ask Rita.

Richard studied the Army's voucher, unbelieving his good fortune. He briefly envisioned swirling Lt. Nancy around the dance floor, but thought better of it. Maybe Patsy would take dance lessons with him. If she couldn't afford Arthur Murray, he'd teach her the steps at Frankie and Johnnies. He could stop there on his way home and ask if she still lived in the area.

That evening Richard left the bar in time for dinner, and sat with his mother 'til midnight listening to Big Band Sounds broadcast from *Prom on the Midway*. Tomorrow he'd sign up for dance lessons at Arthur Murray Dance Studio, compliments of the U.S. Army. He would have to find another dance partner; Patsy had married and left town.

Chapter Seven

"Would you care to dance?" Richard had assessed the crowd at the Prom-on-the-Midway, and he selected the less than beautiful but stately brunette sitting with two girlfriends. Throughout a full dance-set, they hadn't left their table.

Blood-red fingernails freed a cigarette from its monogrammed compact. "I'm not sure that's a good idea." Long slender fingers inserted it into an engraved cigarette holder.

"Come on. I just finished six months of lessons, and I'd like to try out some of these new Latin dance steps."

She replaced the cigarette. "Okay, you asked for it." Rising, her unfolded legs boosted her to over six feet tall, Richard gawking into her buxom bosom. "A Samba or Rumba, maybe even a polka, but I don't think we should do any close dancing."

"Okay with me." His hand on her waist, Richard walked her out to an opening on the dance floor. After a few practice steps, he twirled and dipped, and they promenaded into the crowd. Two or three turns around the dance area and couples began to step aside, clapping and cheering. The trumpeter stepped from the bandstand and blasted his sound their way as they gyrated to his rhythm.

"Whew! I think I need a rest. Come to my table, and I'll introduce you to my girl friends. I think Trish would love to do a slow waltz." She led him by his hand. "I would too, but not with all these eyes fixed on us." At the vacated table she said, "They must be out on the floor."

"Yeah, I saw them." He had noticed them dancing with each other.

"Maybe you're not ready for a break. Don't let me cramp your style." She reached for her purse. "I'll just wander off to powder my nose."

"Your nose looks just fine." He pulled her chair from the table. "I'll sit with you for a while."

"By the way, I'm Mary Lou." She allowed Richard to seat her. "What's your name?"

He pushed her friend's drink aside and sat beside her. "Richard."

"Friends call you Rich or Rick?"

"Not unless they want to piss me off."

"Well, *Richard* it will be. Do you have a last name? I certainly wouldn't want to get that one wrong."

"Leslie." He detected a smirk and added, "It's a Scottish surname. My father was a direct descendant of the Crawford-Leslie family in Aberdeen shire."

Mary Lou's expression turned somber. "*Your father was?* Has he passed away?"

Richard blushed. "That's a long story." He forced his eyes out of the blank stare they so often locked into. "Listen." He grabbed her hand. "They're playing a slow one. Let's do this set, and then I have to catch the streetcar back to East Seventh Street."

Mary Lou snapped open her purse and inserted her cigarette compact. "Just this one, and then I will give you a ride to whatever is so important at East Seventh."

Richard promenaded her, improvising moves that avoided his face squashed between her breasts. "Frankie and Johnnies."

"What?" He twirled her.

Back face-to-face, "Where we're heading after this dance. I want to show you off to my friends."

"Just the ride."

He twirled her twice more.

With her face to the ceiling and his hand flat against her back, she said in a husky voice, "I'm not ready for the *friends* part."

He pulled her close and stopped in mid step. "Okay, then a quick stop at White Castle and a walk through Phalen Park. I have a story I'd like to share with you."

"You do know how to capture a lady's curiosity."

***

From the stack of Jap bodies, some still writhing, a sharp staccato voice screaming its complaint to the Emperor or possibly a long since dead ancestor. Richard clamped his ears. He couldn't look and didn't want to hear.

"Richard."

"I did it, Ma. For Edward." The bodies slithered single file toward him like eels in slimy ooze. "I had to," his explanation short of an apology. "It's what I trained for." He grabbed an arm and it broke loose from the body like off some strange sea creature. "You knew it was my duty." One by one the bodies paused and stared, then parted to pass on either side of him. "Ma demanded it."

He yelled. "For my brother." He tried to count as Ma had demanded, but numbers kept dissolving into the slime. *Name them—count later.* "Geronimo. Jenkins. Edward." *Not names! Numbers! Ma only needs to know how many. Count backwards.* "One hundred, ninety nine, maybe only twenty or thirty. I tried, Ma."

"Richard, wake up."

"I tried to keep track, Ma, but they keep coming too fast."

"You're having a nightmare."

Richard opened his eyes, and he clawed at the layer of burned flesh that clung but wasn't his. Streams of fire arc and splash into an enemy bunker, running and screaming, naked bodies turning black.

"Your sheets are sopping."

"Get away from me. You're not my mother. She wouldn't, couldn't." He checked his swing in time.

Her hand covering her face, she hadn't stepped back. "Richard, there's a man here to see you."

"Ma?"

"You were having a nightmare."

Panic. "What did I say?"

"What I didn't want to hear but you needed to remind me." She removed her apron, peeled back the sheets clinging to his torso, and covered his heaving chest. "What have I done to you?"

He fought back sobs. "It's not our fault, Ma. The war…" He rolled over and buried his face in the pillow, wishing he would suffocate.

"There's a man downstairs waiting to talk to you, but first there is something I must tell you."

He sat up and his body began to shake uncontrollably. He reached for the fallen quilt and wrapped it around his shoulders. "What does he want?" He stood, a corner of quilt draped on the floor. "Is he MP, Ma?"

"No, he's civilian. I told him to come back later, but he insisted he would wait—allowed time to wash your face and get dressed."

"I'll make him go away. He should listen to you. This is your house." He strode toward the door, his body rigid. "I'll kick his butt out."

"No, I want you to hear what he has to say. But first there's something you need to know. About your father. Probably the reason this guy came all the way from Scotland."

He considered the Scottish Highlanders he encountered in the islands, bagpipes and all. Part of a British regiment. "Was he in the war?"

"No, he's a lawyer for the Leslie Clan. That's all he would say until he could to talk to you."

"What do I have to do with some law in Scotland?"

She sat on the bed and motioned with her hand. "Come, sit." She breathed deep. "Your father…" Her jaw tightened and her chest heaved. "Your father claimed he belonged to the Crawford-Leslie family back in Scotland. Said they owned the Rothie House, a castle in Aberdeen shire. I never believed him, but now with that lawyer in my kitchen, I'm beginning to wonder."

"Why me? Shouldn't he be talking to my father." *I have no grandson* raced through his mind. Facing his grandmother's maid, the shrill voice from another room—he clamped hard on the image and returned to Ma and the incredible information she decided to lay on him while trying to recover from a nightmare, and a hangover.

Her voice broke. "I wonder...think maybe...he passed away. The family would have to contact you if he died." Her body stiffened, "With your older brother...Edward... gone." She took two deep breaths and swallowed. "You, Richard Lee Leslie, would be the next in line. At least in that branch of the family."

"What would they want with me?"

"I have no idea, but I thought you should know these facts before talking to him."

"Tell him I'm sick and can't talk, or that I've gone crazy—that would be closer to the truth."

"Stop talking like that. He won't tell me anything, and he needs to catch a train to New York later today."

"Tell him I'll be down in a few minutes."

"I don't want to talk to him unless you're with me."

"Okay, let's go." He pulled the quilt tight around his upper body.

Lifting the trailing edge his mother said, "Just like the King of Scotland."

***

"You're royalty!" Mary Lou tapped the cigarette pinched between thumb and finger throughout Richard's narration and inserted it into its holder.

"Don't stop now. What did the guy come all the way from Scotland to tell you?" She glared. "The suspense is killing me."

Richard hadn't intended to tease or enhance by withholding details of his ancestry, not the reason he brought her to Phalen Park in the first place. That urge had subsided half way through the telling. He regretted sharing with his new friend the carefully selected parts of the encounter with his mother before confronting the clan lawyer. Mary Lou, a New York model, she admitted after beer and White Castle hamburgers, could never understand the situation between him and his mother. He lost interest in telling his own story.

"You can't fill me up with these gut-bombs and not admit that you are royalty."

Richard helped himself to one of her cigarettes and lit both from a book of matches. "Hardly royalty, just a family clan."

"You tell me what the lawyer said, and I'll make up my mind if you're a blue blood or not." She blew smoke into the star-lit sky.

"My father hadn't died, and I couldn't tell if my mother felt relieved or disappointed. He ran out on us when I was five, and never bothered to even meet my younger sister, Rita."

"Then how did you get involved?" She ejected her cigarette from its holder onto the moist ground and let it smolder.

"My older brother got killed in Italy, and apparently our cousin, heir to the castle, died there too, about the same time. The cousin was the only child of my father's brother, and his parents were desperate to continue the lineage. The Leslie Castle is located in Aberdeen shire, historical seat of Clan Leslie, located a few miles from Aberdeen. The core of the castle dates to the 14th century."

"So when your father dies, you get the castle?"

Much too eager and missing the point of his sharing an intimate part of his past with a girl who danced well. "My father signed off as an heir and I did too." He glanced up at the harvest moon veined by the naked branches of the Elm tree against their backs.

Her gaze moved between his cigarette and the one she tossed. "Was that a tough decision?"

"No. The Leslie clan had fallen on hard times, and they needed an American with cash. That certainly isn't me." He pointed to her Lincoln parked on the grass. "I have trouble finding streetcar fare to get where I want to go."

Richard stood and drew a distasteful draw on his cigarette. "The terms required my living in Scotland. I left St. Paul once and it turned out very bad. I don't ever want to leave again."

His cigarette sparked like a firefly as he tossed it. "It's getting late and your friends will be worried about you."

With a swipe of her arm she brushed aside empty beer cans and food wrappers, and reclined on the car blanket they'd spread out for their picnic. "I don't want to go just yet."

"I can't leave you alone out here." A quick glance back at the moon. For a moment he had returned to Montana and all that happened since then disappeared. He settled on his back alongside her.

She leaned over and kissed him on the lips. She whispered, "Being shorter than me has its advantages," as she unbuttoned her blouse and removed her bra.

"Hey, you two."

A face leered much too close, but Pvt. Richard Leslie swatted at it and muttered. "Leave us alone. I waited a long time for this date, and me and the lieutenant plan to spend the night."

"Is that you, Leslie?" All interrogation melted from the voice. "You and your lady friend can't sleep out here, against park rules. And her car is parked illegally."

Richard jolted awake and got to his feet.

A confused expression appeared on the boyish face of the officer. "I'll tear up the ticket if you both leave now." All authority evaporated.

"I don't want any trouble." The young cop held out open palms. "I'm leaving now, but I'll stop by later." He backed away. "With support." He paused at Mary Lou's car, removed the ticket from the windshield, and drove off in the patrol car.

Like from a cocoon, Mary Lou peered out from the blanket Richard had wrapped around her naked shivering body after she fell asleep. Dressed, he intended to watch over her, but must have dozed off. Her husky voice, "What was that all about?"

"Cops think I'm a bad ass. Just the young ones. The older cops brought me home many times when I was a kid. They know I won't use my weapon against them. Especially not a St. Paul beat cop."

"What weapon? You aren't carrying a gun, are you?"

"No. I hate guns. Had too much of them in the army."

"You said weapon."

"My hands are considered lethal."

"That ain't all of you that's bad. Come here soldier." Mary Lou unwrapped the blanket, her nakedness an invitation to enter.

He shrugged and stared off into the distance.

She scowled and snuggled back into her cocoon alone.

The silence felt oppressive. Why won't she get dressed?

I a tone meant to tease. "Did you know that you talk in your sleep?"

A shiver of fear. "What did I say?"

"I couldn't make out the most of it, but you called me *Lieutenant*, and I think your dream was quite pleasant. Who was she?

"Just a female officer I dated in the Islands," *and had sex with after she killed a Jap sniper when I had my back turned.* "When you get dressed, I'll walk you to your car."

At the car she tossed her blanket, bra, and silk stockings into the back seat and said, "Want to know how you got my attention?" She attempted eye contact. "Your reaction when I stood at the Prom. That I was much taller than you didn't faze you in the least."

"I faced a Jap from the Imperial Marines. He was even taller than you."

Her expression dumbfounded, "Surely not a dance partner."

"Let's just say, when the music stopped only one of us was left standing."

Chapter Eight

Lt. Col. Renford filled three teacups and sat across from Richard and Mrs. Leslie. "I'm sorry Rita couldn't attend our session today. I'll make a note to schedule our next family meeting after school lets out." He moved the sugar and creamer closer to Richard's mother. "She's a senior this year, I believe."

"Yes, and I wish Richard would go back to finish high school." Mrs. Leslie lifted her cup and breathed in the aroma. "He had so little left."

"Three years, Ma. They'd make me retake the entire tenth grade."

"You could do it in less than three years." She faced Renford. "The principal let him skip ninth grade."

"That was because my country school in Wisconsin already covered all that stuff." Not ready to rehash this family argument, Richard shot a quick glance at the colonel behind a veil of steam from his raised cup.

Renford acknowledged by interjecting, "It's edifying that some rural schools excelled. We hear so much about others less accountable."

Back on a comfortable track, Richard said, "Mrs. Munson, the lady where I lived during my seventh and eighth grades, taught at the one room school house half a mile down the road. She helped with my homework after I finished my chores. She stressed reading for comprehension. Everything I want to know, I get from books." He caught the colonel's glance and then lowered his gaze. "Even the Army's manual for paratroopers."

"Required reading, no doubt, when in training." Renford blundered right into Richard's trap.

An opportunity to shock. "Apparently my drill instructor hadn't read it. He reneged when I challenged him to a duel under the rules of combat."

Renford raised his hand palm out. "Perhaps something we can discuss at a future session. I doubt your mother cares to hear those kinds of details."

A pseudo-benign smile. "Tell us, Richard, what's been going on in your life lately?"

Richard nearly blurted *horseback riding with a New York model*, his most recent secret kept from Ma. More fun and much healthier than useless and painful sessions with Renford.

Renford glanced from Richard to his mother. Not getting a response, he answered his own question. "Between dance lessons and employment at that freight company, Richard's been too busy to meet every week."

Richard anticipated Renford leaking this bit of information, and braced himself against Ma's reaction.

She faced the colonel. "His life of *wine, women, and song*, has become *wine, women, and dancing*. An improvement, but his staggering into the house night after night concerns me."

Not the response Richard feared. He expected Ma's demanding where he went on those days he'd ask for cab fare to get to Ft. Snelling.

"Ma, I'm twenty two years old. I don't need a curfew." Now he'd endure another lecture. *Living at home you follow house rules.*

Renford took a different approach. "Perhaps, when you save enough money you can rent your own place, or even buy one through the GI Bill."

The suggestion caught Richard off guard. He had no interest in going out on his own, but Renford wouldn't get off the topic.

"My gosh, you've lived away from home much of your young life, totally independent on that sheep ranch in Montana when just a teenager."

Richard blurted, "And jumping into combat when twenty." After all, he had been wounded and needed a safe place to heal.

"I've agreed to skirt issues involving combat, and I don't think we should begin today in front of your mother."

"I work and I dance. Maybe have a few drinks. You asked what's happening, and that's about it."

His mother scowled. "The freight company calls you whenever they got something to unload at the warehouse. It's not steady work."

"I shuttle trucks around the yard and sometimes make deliveries. George, my boss, likes how I handle their pre-war Reo with the chain drive. I told him I would drive it all the way to California and back, if their other trucks couldn't keep up with freight orders."

Renford interrupted. "That might not be wise for a number of reasons."

Not for discussion. He stared into the clock while the voices of mother and psychiatrist continued their lopsided conversation. His mind delivered him to different place.

***

Richard spurred ahead of Mary Lou's mare, and they rode single file through the narrow streets of Swede Hollow. He pulled up alongside her when they crossed the gully and stopped near the mouth of a cave He dismounted and lashed his reins to a branch. "The horses will stay put while we explore."

He held her mare's halter, and when he reached to take the reins, Mary Lou kicked at him, foot still in the stirrup. "Are you suggesting we crawl into that hole in the ground like a couple of Neanderthals?"

"You were excited about the adventure last night at the ballroom."

"While you swung me around the floor, yes, but out here astride a ton of horse flesh presents quite a different perspective." She flashed a flirtatious smile. "Now if I were straddling a man one tenth as heavy, that would be my kind of adventure."

"Two hundred pounds."

"What?"

"One tenth of a ton would be 200 pounds."

"You did the math. Good for you Einstein." She gazed down at him. "Don't be so literal. I meant it as a joke."

Not sure why, he felt let down.

"If I get off, how will I get back on without that little stool we used at the stable?"

"I can boost you back up."

Her silent stare felt interminable. He intended to expand their activities beyond dancing, but wondered if horseback riding had been such a good idea.

"Okay, I'll be a sport. Stand back, I'm coming down, but not into the cave." Her gaze traveled between Richard, the ground, and each foot still clamped tight against the horse's sides. She froze in the saddle.

"You dismount the exact reverse of how you got up there." He tugged on her right pant leg. "Slide this foot loose and swing it behind the saddle."

A couple of her knee slaps against the belly of the horse and Richard struggled to keep it from plodding forward. He released her shoe stuck in the stirrup and guided her leg across the horse's back. With one foot still in the stirrup and the other on the ground she whispered, "Help?"

Richard released her foot and lashed the reins. He made a broad gesture.

"This area's still called Swede Hollow, but a bunch of Mexicans have pretty well taken over." He pointed north. "You get a good view of Schmidt Brewery and the Hamm Mansion from down here."

60

"That's the second time you said *Mexicans* with that certain inflection." She brushed the dust from her slacks. "You don't like them, do you."

Richard had never considered if he liked or disliked the residents of Swede Hollow. "They just happen to be the latest group to settle there. The Irish were here before them, came after the Swedes left." He reached for her hand. "If there are any Americans I dislike, it would be the Irish. My Ma's English." As if that settled the matter.

She accepted his hand and followed his lead. "All good and well, but keep me away from that cave." She peered into the abyss. "Who knows what creatures lurk down there."

"Bugs, snakes, crickets, and one giant lizard." He squeezed her hand. "Let's go."

"If I get bitten, I'm holding you responsible." The cave darkened and, as they progressed, its only source of light source grew smaller and smaller. "That's it. No more daylight, and I'm out of here."

"Wait." Richard stepped into a niche and pawed the ledge until he found the candle in its holder.

A flash of light and an unstable and oversized shadow jiggled on the adjacent wall.

"Richard!" Her shriek awakened a flutter of wings, their shadows attacked the wall monster. "Richard, that's not funny."

As if leading a funeral dirge, he approached, the candle flickering in front of him giving his face a ghostly appearance.

"Now, cut that out." Anger had replaced fear in her voice.

"Sorry. I didn't mean to give you a heart attack."

She began to pound his chest until hot wax splattered. "Damn you."

"Hey, it was only a joke."

She stifled a giggle. "I peed."

"Huh?"

"Right here, in my pants, I pissed." She grabbed his arm and turned him toward the entrance. "I want you to ride like the wind and get me clean clothes."

He faced her. "I...I don't know..." His mind reeled. "I can...you can have my underwear."

"Don't be ridiculous." She took off her slacks and stepped out of her panties. "You can keep these as a reminder of our *last* time together." She fitted them onto his head, and broke out laughing. "Serves you right for frightening me."

Richard peeled the silk garment from his face, then pressed it to his cheek. "You didn't wet yourself."

"No, but the expression on your face was precious. I would have peed if I had thought of it in time, just to teach you a lesson." She unbuttoned her blouse. "As long as I'm half undressed anyhow..."

Panties in one hand and a flickering candle in the other, Richard cowered. As with dancing, the female shouldn't take the lead. He hadn't brought her to the cave for sex.

She unsnapped her bra and grabbed her panties back. "At least have the decency to drop your pants." She opened his belt buckle. "And my butt isn't the one that will touch the cold floor."

Why not oblige? With his pants caught at knee level and trigger finger stuck through the loop on the candle holder, he beckoned with his head.

"Follow me to a place where neither of us has to lay on the ground." He shuffled into the darkness, a dancing glow from the flame reflecting off moist walls.

She laughed. "Okay, Little Jack Horner. Where's your corner?"

He didn't like the image. "Just a few more steps."

"If that candle goes out, you better be ready with a match. My Ronson's still in the saddle bag."

Around the bend under a narrow shaft of light sat an army cot. Richard set the candle on a ledge amid beer bottles and fast food wrappers and let his pants drop to his shoes. "Me and Virgil—you're gonna have to meet him soon—created that skylight. We noticed water dripping when it rained, so we bored a shaft through the overhead limestone."

"I'm obviously not your first sexual conquest in this horrid little love nest."

"That's not why we did it." Suddenly the area felt contaminated. We want to get a permit to grow mushrooms down here. Problem is, nobody actually owns property in Swede Hollow. In the gully near the creek some Mexicans…" He decided not to state a disclaimer. "… created a community garden, and they respect each other's produce. I'm not sure how the honor system would work inside the cave. Could be some vandalism."

Mary Lou shook her clothes loose from the ball she'd been carrying and started to dress. Sarcasm in her voice, "You turn a girl off as easily as you turn one on. I loved you on the dance floor. I'm starting to hate you down here."

Standing in his shorts, an image of a dead Jap flashed through his mind. "I'll take you back to the stable." The kill—her kill—had aroused the female officer who accompanied him into the jungle for sex, but left him feeling as wretched then as he felt now.

Riding side-by-side out of Swede Hollow, Richard said, "Are we still on for tonight? We don't need much practice, but we have to be absolutely sure of ourselves next week at the contest."

Mary Lou nudged her mare ahead, and Richard allowed her to lead all the way back to the stable. Either she hadn't heard him, or she avoided his question. Richard signed for use of the horses—he'd be shoveling shit for a month to cover the rental.

As he held her car door open, he again asked about dance practice, dreading her response.

"I'm afraid I won't be able to join you for the contest." She slid behind the wheel staring into the windshield.

Richard clung to the open door dumbfounded.

"Come inside and sit down so I can explain."

"I can hear you from out here." He kept an escape available.

"My dance partner, José Mendez, is coming in from Guadalajara, and I paid the entry fee in his and my name." She thumped the steering wheel with her palms. "I'm sorry, Richard, but José and I made this commitment a long time ago."

"You never told me about José."

"And I never asked about your girlfriends. We just hit it off on the dance floor and had some sex."

"Let me guess: Your Mexican friend is over six feet tall and weighs about one tenth that horse you rode today." He gave the door a slight shove and pressed it until the latch clicked. He turned and walked away.

Chapter Nine

The cave incident unfolded without conscious thought. Alone with Renford—his mother refused further invitations—Richard's shield had evaporated, didn't protect his ego like during past sessions. He felt naked as if his pants were again around his ankles.

"How did that make you feel?"

For the first time after three years of on-and-off-again counseling, Lt. Col. Renford's question often asked just to annoy, Richard surmised, suddenly seemed sincere. Being jilted by a dance partner felt shitty, but he couldn't admit it. He merely shrugged, as if such a response was obvious.

Renford continued, "What did you do with those unpleasant feelings?"

"I wanted to shoot the Mexican Hat Dancer."

"But you didn't." An extended pause. "What held you back?"

"Well, he wasn't with us at the time, and I didn't have a gun. Two pieces of luck for him."

"Maybe you had a chance to cool down. Some time to think about consequences?"

"I doubt it." Renford hadn't a clue as to his deepest, darkest secret, or—Richard's mind swirled—had the psychiatrist led him to this self discovery and was now suggesting a solution? No matter; the strength of his Scottish roots could control whatever situation arose. He'd avoid the issue until the questioning took a different tack.

"What kept you from taking drastic measures?"

Richard had already lost count of the clock's ticking before Renford accepted the challenge and changed the subject.

"Did you go to the Prom Ballroom the night of the contest?"

Yes.

***

Mary Lou uncrossed her legs. "Richard, I...I."

Before she could stand, Richard put his hand on her shoulder. "Don't bother to get up." Across from her, a man with olive-tone skin, red silk shirt bloused and opened to his waist, got up from his chair, Adam's apple eye level, Richard assessed the situation. *Nothing he couldn't handle.*

He lowered his gaze to an astonished and still-seated *vixen*, Virgil's term for Richard's New York model. "I just wanted to wish you and— he shot a glance at the Mexican daring him to make a fuss—your dance partner good luck."

Mary Lou scanned his military dress uniform. "Did you reenlist?"

He faked a confused expression. "No." He turned his back to her. "I just couldn't find anything colorful enough, so I went drab." His adversary avoided eye contact, but Richard faced him long enough for Mary Lou to react to the contest number pinned to the back of his shirt.

"I see you decided to join the contest after all. I'm happy for you."

"Made the decision at the last minute." Mexican José Mendez safely seated, Richard faced his ex and unfaithful dance partner. "Got lucky. Number eighteen, exactly the number of months I spent in the South Pacific. Not a record but a good average."

"Where's...who's your partner?"

"I haven't decided yet. According to the lead judge, first time anyone ever signed up without a partner." Richard scanned the room as if looking for one.

"His son was a paratrooper. Not my unit, but men who jump out of airplanes form a kind of bond." His gaze settled on the two girls who, no doubt, came to watch their friend show off. "Didn't even charge me the entry fee."

Mary Lou, her composure restored, beckoned to her dance partner who moved closer to her side. "I would like you to meet José Mendez. He came all the way from Guadalajara, Mexico, to participate in this contest."

José offered a slight bow and Richard stood at attention.

"I see your girlfriends came to show support. I never did get to slow-dance with Trish like you suggested. I think I'll go over and make it up to her."

***

When the psychiatrist removed his glasses and set them on the desk, Richard worried his account of the evening might not be believable. Was he being dismissed?

"First prize!" Renford slapped his desktop as if at a neighborhood bar and someone told a lusty joke. "And the two of you never even danced together before. That's unbelievable."

His self image restored, Richard filled in the details. "I told Trish that I felt bad never asking her for a dance. My timing was perfect. An announcement over the loudspeaker explaining the change of order; I would start the contest, assuming I could find a partner."

Lt. Col. Renford's face no longer resembled that of his psychiatrist.

"I had noticed her style while she danced with the other girl who was the better dancer, but Trish was a perfect follower. I had an instructor like that who could anticipate even my beginner's bad moves."

"Are you and Trish going to continue dancing?"

"Nah. The entire bunch left town. Wherever Tommy or Jimmy Dorsey's bands are performing, they show up and collect trophies. Trish and the other friend just tag along on Mary Lou's tab."

"You don't sound disappointed."

"Good riddance." He squirmed as if his shorts had bunched. "Frankie introduced me to this nice quiet girl who sometimes shows up with her sister."

"Frankie?"

"Yeah, the female half of *Frankie and Johnnies.*

"I didn't realize they were real people who owned the tavern. Tell me about this girl. What's her name?"

"Norma. I'm not sure of her last name."

"Just on a first name basis?"

"She's getting divorced and hasn't decided about a name change."

"She a good dancer?"

No.

***

"You don't like to dance, and you nursed that same beer all evening. What *do* you like?"

A wry smile. "I like White Castle hamburgers."

Richard beckoned Virgil to their table. "Let's move the party to the cave in Swede's Hollow. You and whoever else is interested commandeer some beer from Frankie, while me and Norma grab a bag of White Castles."

Norma tugged Richard's arm, and whispered, "I'll have to leave pretty soon. My sister, Gladys, is coming to get me. Besides, I need to say goodnight to my kids before they get tucked in.

He faced Virgil. "Forget it. Go back to your dart game." He turned to Norma. "Kids? You got kids? How many?"

"Two, a boy and a girl."

"I like kids. Got a bunch of nieces and nephews." He downed his beer and set the mug on the bar. "Tell you what. Instead of beer at Swede's Hollow, you, me, and Gladys will grab some White Castles and find an empty bench at Phalen Park. You got that much time." Her continued grip on his arm, an answer to all his unasked questions. "I want to meet your kids. Not tonight but maybe some time during the day, when they're not napping."

***

Lt. Col. Renford's glanced at his watch and grimaced. "Have you taken Norma to meet your mother?"

"That might be a bit touchy. A divorcee with kids. I'm going to wait for a while. Ma doesn't even know Mary Lou left town."

"She aware you two won the contest?"

Richard curled his lip into a smirk. "I gave Trish our trophy to rub in Mary Lou's nose. Never told Ma anything about it, just that I'd won a contest."

"Maybe you should keep her more informed about what's going on in your life."

"She'll ask questions that I can't answer. I'll just wait and see what happens."

After a moment of silence, Richard stood and walked out of Renford's office.

Chapter Ten

Brakes screeched, gears ground, and forty thousand pounds of trailer forced the semi an additional football field before the '39 International shuddered to a stop. With his hand fisting the knob on the shift lever, Richard willed his heart rate lowered to at least to match the rhythm of the chugging engine. Eight hundred feet of bridge, the guy pumping gas at Kingman had told him, six hundred of them suspended over the gorge.

He'd crossed that bridge once before with a different rig, that load turned into a disaster. Still shaken after the accident, the dispatcher back in St. Paul advised Richard, "If you don't get behind the wheel immediately, you'll never have the courage to haul freight cross country." Richard agreed and vowed to never pull another load.

But with no word from Norma since she disappeared months ago, he broke down and signed on to the load now paused at the bridge he hesitated to cross. The pay had tempted him, and the constant up and down shifting to keep an even tachometer reading took his mind off losing the woman he hoped to marry.

He made 135 parachute jumps earning him chronic back pain, fell from a bridge construction in Minnesota developing vertigo, and tumbled from an out-of-control semi roaring down the mountainside; a trio of events that should have cautioned him against trucking through the mountainous western states.

His truck idled at the approach to bridge, California in sight.

71

"Are you sure you want to drive a rig all the way to California?" Virgil's bowling ball hugged the edge of the alley two-thirds of the way down and curved back. He yelled, "Strike."

Richard, ball in hand on the adjacent lane, said, "I just gotta get out of town for a while." So far in the game he'd matched strike-for-strike. The head pin hit square, seven and ten pins wiggled but didn't fall. Missing his spare, he plopped down on a chair and grabbed his beer.

Virgil held up his bottle of Hamms. "Here's to the first long haul of your new trucking career. That's trucking with a 't' not an 'f'." He chuckled. "May you never drive your rig off the edge of the earth."

As Richard clicked bottles, a surge of exhilaration tinged with fear swept over him, reminiscent of sharing a quick butt just prior to jumping into combat.

Virgil held bottle to bottle until Richard pulled his back and then chugged. "What's your mother say about your decision?"

Richard rubbed the rim and took a swig. "She doesn't like my being away, but it would be steady work."

"You got disability. What the hell. You don't need full time work."

Richard peeled off the *LAND OF SKY BLUE WATERS* label. "If I want a wife and kids, I need steady work." He stared at the naked brown bottle.

"You haven't heard from Norma?" Virgil stepped to the ball return.

Richard positioned himself and aimed his ball. "Going on four months. I got no idea what went wrong." He released the ball, pins scattered, but his voice barely registered, "strike." He stared at the fallen pins. "I hinted that she and the kids should join Ma and Rita and me for Thanksgiving, but she stopped coming to Frankie and Johnnies before I had a chance to ask."

"She's got family." Virgil toed the line. "You have no idea where they live?"

"Clammed up every time I asked. Told me she lives with her sister, Gladys. Her brother still comes to the bar once in a while, but he doesn't know where she went, or, I suspect, won't tell."

"Strange family." Virgil rolled his ball and grimaced. "I think the mystery is what attracts you to her.

***

Cars honked and a few trucks blew their horns as they swerved around Richard's stalled rig blocking the suspension bridge. He barely noticed.

"Glad you could get away from the shop for a few minutes." Richard accepted the Hamm's Beer Virgil handed him and broke the cap loose against the wall of the cave. "I needed to talk to you before I went home to Ma."

Virgil took a second bottle from the bag. "When did you get back from your California trip?"

A long gulp, his first taste of beer since two weeks ago at the bowling alley where they toasted his new job. "Just got off the train and came here."

"Train? Where's your truck?"

"Bottom of a mountain pass, or it was until they towed it away." Richard stared into the half empty bottle. "Lost the brakes. Had to jump and let it go."

"At least you're still in one piece. What did your boss say?"

"Haven't gone to see him yet, but by our third telephone conversation he'd calmed down. The Las Angeles County Sherriff convinced him the runaway wasn't my fault. Even threatened to cite him for faulty equipment, would have charged him with manslaughter if I'd been killed."

"Guess you weren't cut out for that line of work."

"My boss instructed Dispatch to schedule me with another load soon as I got back."

"Crazy." Virgil shoved the empty bottles into the bag. "I gotta get back to work. See you tonight at Frankie and Johnnies."

He hadn't thought to ask Virgil about Norma. Had he betrayed her, needed his friend and beer more than he wanted her?

That evening, Frankie huffed, "You had your fling and she ran off. Get over it."

He got drunk but didn't *get over it*. With Norma it was more than just sex. He loved her and wanted to be a father to her children. Had she thought otherwise, fearful of abuse, like from that louse she married? *Maybe it's best this way*, he lied to himself. *If it was meant to be, she will return*, his Ma's opinion he'd scoffed at but tried to accept. He might change his mind and attempt another trip out west to help him forget.

He left the bar early and went home to his empty bed but couldn't sleep.

***

Through the cab's side mirror, Richard caught a glimpse of a truck closing in from behind, brakes smoking, but no attempt to steer around his rig. The driver pulled up close and got out. A good Samaritan wanting to help or a tough guy hot to chew his ass? Richard rolled down the window. If he stepped down, a second driver might not be capable of crossing that bridge.

"You got engine trouble?"

"Just cooling the brakes after coming off that steep hill."

"They ain't smoking, just smelling a bit. Should be good to go." The guy pulled out a pack of Luck Strikes, shook two cigarettes loose, and handed one to Richard.

"I'll block traffic from this side so no damn fool tries to pass you on the bridge. It feels a bit narrow out there." Richard took the cigarette and accepted a light from a stick match.

"Thanks."

Gears jammed into low range, eyes focused on the broken white line, Richard popped the clutch with a full open throttle. The truck crawled forward, and the tachometer red lined. He gritted his teeth. Determination, his only reliable tool, brought him to the California side of the bridge. Still in granny gear, the rpm's dropped as the International climbed the switchback of curves to the rim of the gorge. He made it across.

A glance back at the truck leading a string of cars, and he caught a glimpse into the abyss. He wanted to escape, jump out like on his last California trip, but his truck wasn't moving. Cars shot past him followed by the trucker who pulled over and slowed. Richard waved him on, not wanting to explain his actions.

Next challenge, the pass where he had lost his last load. He doubted the desert had repaired the gash at the base of the mountain where his truck had veered off the roadway. He wouldn't stop until he'd reached his destination, unloaded, and located a place to sleep.

***

"No!" Richard shouted from inside the motor inn room. "For the last time, I don't want *company*."

The same sweet voice or a new one, he couldn't distinguish from outside the paint-blistered door. Red toenails fitted through the gap at the threshold, and strong scent of vanilla permeated. The two-dollar-a-night roadside inn offered amenities he hadn't negotiated. Two days and still no return freight back to Minnesota.

Come morning, he'd call his boss. This company truck would be coming home empty, empty like his life had become without Norma.

***

"You're shivering. Here, take my shirt." The cave at Swede's hollow kept out the October wind, but not the damp air.

"Come home with me. Ma wants to meet you and your kids. She'd be the perfect grandma for them."

"I can't let my husband know that you and I—you know—are having sex. He'll get the judge to award him my kids."

"Tell me who he is and I'll take care of it."

"I don't want that. He agreed to a divorce, and the judge told me not to give him any excuse to change his mind. We both know what he meant by *any excuse.*"

"We meet at Frankie and Johnnies, we spend an hour or two at Phalen park, and Gladys or your brother takes you away. It's driving me crazy. At least tell me where you and Gladys live. I don't even know if you have more family than just two kids and a sister and a brother.

"I really like you, feel safe when I'm with you." She grabbed and kissed his hand. "When my divorce and other issues get settled, I promise to meet your mother and sister."

***

Lack of sleep, lack of booze—Richard had agreed to stay sober throughout the trip if the dispatcher guaranteed a turnaround of two days or less—he'd doze and wake up. *Other issues?* Child support? he assumed, but now the unknown loomed in his mind. Mental health issues? He certainly could understand what that meant, but what in her life could have caused enough stress to drive her crazy? She's not depressed as his mother suggested, just too shy to come to the house.

Old nightmares flared; falling, not out of an airplane but off of bridges, off ledges of tall buildings, from trees, just falling, never hitting the ground. Three combat jumps, his only fear, getting shot on the way down. One slip on wet steel, dangling from the bridge by a safety tether, awaiting the ladder truck from the fire department, and he developed a fear of heights.

"Get right back up there," the foreman ordered, "or you'll be afraid of heights forever." Vertigo, his psychiatrist diagnosed, solution in agreement with the foreman. Another job to walk away from.

And another, if the dispatcher hadn't found a return load by morning.

Chapter Eleven

Hot and wet and slippery, shiny gallon cans of sliced carrots exited the steam oven, received tin lids crimped around the edges, and clustered at the end of the conveyor. With gloves already sopping, Richard slid four sealed cans off the platform into an opened box, folded the tabs, and loaded it onto a waiting forklift. He raised his voice above the idling engine. "If you lower the fork a couple inches, I can just slide the box over, won't have to lift each one."

A cross between a sneer and a jeer appeared on the operator's face, and she continued to make his job more difficult.

"Hey, I asked nice," as he hoisted and slammed the box into place.

"What's the matter? Boxes too heavy? Must weigh all of thirty pounds."

If only she were a man. "There's no reason to make our jobs more difficult. I would do the same for you."

"But I've already have an easy job. You can't make it better." She peered around the stack growing taller on the lift.

"I could share my lunch with you." *After I spit on the peanut butter.* She backed away and yelled. "Show me what you got."

Richard ignored her, pleased that George, who pulled his fork lift into her spot, cooperated. His dribble of tobacco juice would blend nicely with the peanut butter he offered to share. In similar circumstances, George would be satisfied with just a fresh chew.

Load completed, Susie—he doubted it was her real name—returned and raised the fork half of a foot above the platform. Richard restrained his anger and hoisted each box without comment.

Chin settled on the knuckles of both hands, she said, "I asked what you got in your lunch box."

"Spinach. Like Popeye, I need strength because someone is on my ass."

"You compare me to Brutus? How awful."

"You're certainly not Olive Oyl. She looked out for her man." Another box filled and hoisted.

"I hate spinach." She reduced the gap by a couple of inches. "But I would accept dinner tonight."

"Okay." The lift lowered, Richard slid the last box on top the load, and she backed away. George, brown liquid dripping off an unshaved chin, eyes trained on Susie, nearly slammed into the platform.

When Susie returned Richard said, "I just talked to George, and *he* agreed to take you out to dinner." The lift rose a full foot above the platform. "Just kidding." It dropped a few inches. "George turned you down."

***

Skirt hemmed to the knees, gum snapping, the blond teen skated up to the Ford's window on the driver's side. "Whacha gonna have?"

Susie reached across and tugged on Richard's sleeve. "George would have bought me a chocolate shake and fries."

Richard rolled his eyes and faced the waitress. "You heard the lady."

"And you?"

"Spinach."

"Huh? You crazy?"

Susie slithered around the shift lever that jutted up from the floorboards and settled her chin on Richard's shoulder. "You don't got spinach?"

She nibbled on his earlobe. "Just fill a dog dish with lettuce. He can munch on that."

"We got hamburgers, hot dogs, and fries. Don't got no lettuce, for sure no spinach."

Richard swatted Susie away from his ear. "I'll have a hot dog and fries."

Two quick snaps. "Anything to drink?"

"Got what I need in the trunk."

Susie sat up straight. "Cancel my shake."

***

Two Ft. Snelling security guards escorted Richard, his private's uniform bloody and tattered, into Lt. Col. Renford's office. "Fresh from the drunk tank. Thought we'd dry him out a bit before delivering him as requested." They plopped him onto the chair and departed.

Richard glanced up, caught Renford's glare, and clamped his hands to his head with a vise-like grip.

Renford stood. "What are you doing in that uniform?"

Unsure who asked, his situation still blurred, Richard threw the officer a salute from his chair.

"Soldier, you are to stand when in the presence of a superior officer until put at ease."

"Yes, Sir." Richard staggered to his feet and repeated his salute.

Renford held Richard at attention almost to the point of collapse, then sat and said, "At ease."

"Thank you, Sir." He peered down at the chair gauging its placement and, with both hands grasping the arms, dropped onto the seat. He refused to grimace at the jolt of pain when his body made contact.

"Now that we completed that little performance, tell me what this is all about."

Richard chased cobwebs. "I don't know. Guess I thought I was back in the Army." Fog cleared the way for throbbing pain. "Ma tried to stop me, but Rita said, 'Go ahead and make a fool out of yourself.'"

Renford pulled a file, thicker Richard noticed, and began to read. "Mother's frantic calls reported at local police station and at this office. Son recently returned from a seasonal job in Wisconsin acting erratic." He glanced up. "No apparent alcohol abuse at this point." He placed the file between them. "When did you begin to binge?"

"Not until a few days after I hitchhiked home." He wished he were someplace else.

"No car. No job." Renford stood and intercepted Richard's view of the clock. "Things are starting to look quite bad." He sat back down. "You got fired?"

"Worse, kicked out of Wisconsin forever." His eyes glossed over. "Didn't know they could do that."

"Well, they can't, but they can make it miserable if you ever cross the state line. What did you do?"

"Remember how I threatened I might kill someone just to prove something."

"Go on."

Richard made eye contact and quickly dropped his gaze. "It wasn't intentional, just an accident."

"With your car?"

Richard buried his face in his hands and his body heaved. He nodded between sobs.

"Another car involved?"

Richard shook his head. "She was riding with me."

"Were you drunk?"

"Maybe a little. We met at the canning factory in Barron, Wisconsin. Vegetables destined for the Army."

Bright shiny cans dulled to military brown mimicked the last couple of weeks of his life. Deep sobs and Renford shoved a box of tissues across the table. Richard blew his nose.

"She came on to me my first day on the job. I took her to a drive-in, the kind where gals scoot out to your car on roller skates."

Tanks and jeeps and C47 airplanes emerged and faded in the recesses of his mind. He stood, yelled "halt," and aimed an imaginary M1 rifle at a car that ignored his command.

Lt. Col. Renford barked, "Now's not the time to relive the war."

"Huh?"

"You're mimicking a rifle, thankfully not aimed at me."

Richard focused on his outstretched arms and then at his target, a German POW he had killed in the line of duty back at Camp Pendelton. He willed his arms to relax, but his hands continued to clutch his rifle.

"Please sit down. Now let me get this straight. The girl who died was not the one with children that we talked about."

"No."

"What happened to that relationship?"

"She ran away."

Renford did a drum roll with his fingers on the desk. "From what I gather, you didn't *kill* anyone. However you're probably responsible for the death of a young lady and you'll definitely face certain consequences."

"Like getting kicked out of Wisconsin." He sat, "I can handle that."

"True, but her death is something you will need to face the rest of your life."

"I didn't do it intentionally."

"You put yourself in a situation that bears the responsibility. Did she have a family?"

"She lived with her mother, but we didn't get along very well."

"What happened to cause friction?"

"She complained about losing her job at the ammunition plant when the war ended. I told her what I thought about that." Richard paused for a reaction. "Then she complained about returning veterans taking all the good jobs." Still no expression of understanding Richard expected from a fellow soldier.

"I don't suppose you are in communication with her."

"I told her I was sorry for her loss at the police station, but we haven't talked since then."

"You'll need to do more."

"I can't change what happened or make her feel better about it."

"She'll grieve and remain angry, even if you express your concern and admit to your part in the girl's death. You can't do much to change that. But it might help you get over your guilt."

"What should I do? Invite her to lunch at my mother's house? I can't visit her in Wisconsin."

"A letter describing the positive aspects of your relationship with her daughter might help each of you."

"It'll make her mad and make me sad."

"That would be a good start toward acknowledging your repentance."

"I'm already beating myself up over it."

"Then possibly as a positive action toward improving your emotional health."

"I gave up driving. From now on, public transportation or return favors with friends who own cars. Like Virgil, for instance."

"You might want to reduce your alcohol consumption, or even cut it out all together."

"I already cut back." Wide opened eyes met his gaze. "I mean before my relapse yesterday."

"Records indicate you stayed drunk for at least three days, and your face and bloodied uniform suggest a brawl or two."

"All right, it was a serious break down, and I'm paying the price with this splitting headache. And having to face you is no easy matter either."

"I may be the least of your problems, and just maybe our times together might bring some light back into your life. However, I am committing you to the hospital for observation, at least for the next forty eight hours. I sincerely hope you won't fight with me on that, because we're running out of security guards who are willing to restrain you without using excessive force. You probably have an idea of what that means."

"My mother…"

"I'll call her as soon as we are done here and arrange transport for her to visit you in the morning."

"Tell her to bring something for me to wear. Civilian clothes. I want to burn these."

Chapter Twelve

"You're getting married?" Lt. Col. Renford stood outside the door to his office briefcase under arm.

A month since his last session, Richard enjoyed the shock his announcement caused. "I came early not knowing how complicated my change of status from single to married would be. You know the military, hurry up and wait."

Renford unlocked his door, reached and turned on the light. "Either Norma returned or you gave up waiting. For your sake, I hope this isn't a rebound relationship."

"Norma came back to me."

"There has to be some missing pieces you're not sharing."

"She had my baby."

Renford checked his wrist watch. "I have some open time before our scheduled appointment. Come in."

Richard hesitated. "Ma and Norma are having tea at the café."

"They'll be fine for a few minutes." He motioned for Richard to sit while he hung his coat behind the door. Shuffling a few loose papers on his disk, he said, "She hid her pregnancy from you. Why would she do that?"

"Norma didn't want anyone but her family to know she'd given birth." Richard flashed a glance at the clock and then focused on his folded hands.

Emil scarcely raised his voice above a whisper.

"Norma had your baby."

85

Richard released his neck-hold, and the patrons at Frankie and Johnnie's shifted their attention back to conversations before the altercation between Richard and his girlfriend's brother.

"My baby?" After two children, she should have known how to avoid getting pregnant. It's the woman's responsibility. "When?"

"Last January. Toward the end of the month."

Richard's mind struggled with the numbers until his mother's comment interrupted his calculations. *I want to meet this girl who you tell me doesn't dance. Bring her to our house for Thanksgiving dinner.* He couldn't admit he hadn't seen her for what? Three or four weeks?

Richard realized that Norma had struggled through the second half of her pregnancy without his support. He'd need to make it up to her somehow. "I want to see her."

***

Emil took a cautious step back. "Listen, if she wanted you back in her life, she'd say so."

"What kind of baby?" Emil's grin almost broke their truce. "I mean a boy or girl?"

"Ma named her Lorraine, you figure out the kind."

Richard felt the crowd staring, but a quick glance across his shoulder indicated no one cared enough to stop their usual chatter. "Her ma named her?" Something not right about that. "I have to talk to Norma."

"It's not what she wants."

"I got the right to see my own child. Talk to her mother." He raised a fist, but *Lorraine* had melted his impulse to threaten her uncle. "Emil, I need you to help me to make things right. I wanted to marry your sister before she got pregnant. She agreed, but asked me to wait until her divorce came through."

"I'll tell her what you said, but she'll be mad at me for even talking to you."

***

Richard could sense Renford's piercing gaze but continued to study his hands. He gave his practiced response. "Norma didn't want her former husband aware she'd had an affair before their divorce finalized."

"Obviously, her divorce became final, if you're planning to marry." Renford paused but Richard continued to avoid eye contact. "She must have realized the child couldn't be hidden forever."

"She left the baby girl at the hospital for adoption." He raised his hand to his face and brushed away a tear.

"Where's our baby?" Richard stood in the doorway and scanned Norma's small apartment. "Your other two children?"

Norma averted his gaze. "I told Emil that our meeting here was a bad idea. He could have given me a ride to Frankie and Johnnies."

"Too many busy bodies. We need to discuss this matter in private." He struggled to remain calm. "Where are all your children?"

"They don't live with me." Norma clutched the back of her kitchen chair but didn't suggest they sit.

"You lost custody?"

"They're in Wisconsin with my parents."

"They haven't been with you since your divorce?"

"Not since I left my husband and moved in with Gladys. My divorce came through before I had the baby."

"Didn't you want your children with you?" He took a step forward.

Norma shrugged. "Not enough room here for kids, and no one to watch them. We both have day jobs."

"I want to marry you and bring our family together." A wide gesture and he moved in closer.

Norma cowered. "You don't need those problems. I don't need them either." She turned away. "I left the baby at the hospital for adoption."

"You gave up our baby?" He clasped her shoulders as if to force the truth out of her.

She shook her head. "When Ma found out I had a baby, she made me stop the adoption process and told me to bring the baby to Wisconsin." She faced him but averted eye contact. "Said she raised eleven of her own and could handle another one."

"I want to marry you."

"Pa yelled. 'You *will* bring my grandchild here. She belongs with family.'"

"Marry me and we will be a family." He dropped his arms to his side and searched for yet failed to meet her gaze. "We talked about marriage, even set a date—sort of." He held out his hand "I agreed to wait until your divorce was settled."

Their eyes met long enough for Richard to sense fear and sadness. "I want to take care of you."

Norma lowered her head and began to teeter.

He moved close and put his arm around her. A childhood image of him sitting on his shoeshine box, defending his location on Seventh Avenue from bigger kids trying to take it from him. "You *will* marry me!" He'd lock horns with her father about the baby. "And we will take Lorraine home with us."

She nodded but kept her gaze lowered.

"And your other two." He put his arm around her waist as her body went limp. "We are a family."

***

Renford broke the silence. "I'm so sorry to hear Norma didn't want the baby."

Eager to explain, Richard's voice reached an unnatural pitch. "Norma's mother insisted she claim her child just before the six week waiting period expired. She offered to help raise the baby girl. Named her Lorraine."

He paused and took a deep breath. "I asked Norma to marry me and she consented." His attempt to smile failed. "We'll have to live with my mother until I find work." Shamed, he lowered head.

***

Back in the car, Emil asked, "Return to Frankie and Johnnies?"

"Take me home." Richard thanked his future brother-in-law and whistled along the walk and up the stairs to report his good news to his mother.

She glanced up from her knitting. "You're home early. Did the health department finally close down that pub?"

"No, Ma, it's still open." He remained standing. "I decided to get married."

"That's nice. Did anyone agree to marry you? I hope that model from New York didn't come back."

"Norma agreed to marry me." He refused to react to his mother's sarcasm. "She's the gal I told you about last summer. The one you wanted to meet but never got the chance."

"Did she run off to New York, too?"

"No, she went into hiding to have my baby." He needed to control the conversation.

"She had a baby! Your baby?"

He nodded, allowing the information to sink in.

"A girl from the bar disappears for nine months and returns with a baby, claiming it's yours."

"Ma, the baby girl is my child. We would already be married, but Norma had to wait until her divorce was finalized."

"Then why did she run away?"

"She got scared, Ma. Thought I wouldn't want her with another child."

"Another child?"

"She has a son and a daughter from her previous marriage."

His ma clapped her hands. "I have another grandchild. My only son has given me a granddaughter." She set down the needles and reached out.

"A ready-made family."

Richard lifted her from the rocking chair and pulled her into his arms.

"You love this woman?"

"Very much."

"Well she loves you, too. I know this. She came back to you. It was meant to be."

"Ma, she makes me happy."

"When can I see my granddaughter?"

"Lorraine, our daughter, is staying with her other grandparents, along with Norma's other two children." His voice lowered. "Norma put our baby up for adoption, but her parents in Wisconsin agreed to raise the child."

"Sounds like they're raising all three children. I want my granddaughter here with me, with you and Norma. They can keep the other two." Her eyes pierced. "Richard, make that happen."

"All three of you plan to move in with your mother?" The inflection in Renford's voice didn't betray approval or disapproval.

"Ma wants me and Norma and our daughter to live with her. Norma feels we should include her other two children, actually made it a condition for our getting married."

He'd have to deal with his mother on that issue when he brings all three to her upstairs duplex. "I, we'll move to our own place when I find a permanent job."

"Your second chance after the accident with the trucking job didn't pan out?"

PVT. RICHARD LEE LESLIE

"They fired me because I drove back without a load." His resentment began to rise. "I had to fight to get paid." A flash of anger returned and he shouted, "*They* violated the terms of our agreement."

Renford studied some papers on his desk.

"Dunwoody Technical Institute in Minneapolis has an opening in automobile automatic transmission repair. If you're interested I can sign you up through the GI Bill."

Richard brightened. "Virgil said automatic transmissions are the coming thing. General Motors introduced it with their Oldsmobile even before the war."

"I can assume you are interested?"

"I know where Dunwoody is. The cross town street car line goes right by it."

I can help you change your status to married, but first I would like to meet Norma. And the children if they are with her."

Renford went to his filing cabinet. "I'll locate the information from Dunwoody while you go and get them."

Richard stopped at the PX to buy cigarettes before telling his mother and fiancée that his psychiatrist wanted to see them. Norma didn't even know the extent of his dealings with Renford, only that he approved the monthly disability checks. Explaining that the money would stop once he found full time work had been truthful, but he doubted he could ever hold down a regular job. Five years since he returned, he hadn't kept a job longer than a few months.

Learning a skill at Dunwoody and the responsibility of a family could change all that. However he fought back the urge to run away, or at least return home without introducing Norma to Renford. He told the cashier at the PX to keep her filthy cigarettes. He didn't need them.

"Colonel Renford, this is my fiancée, Norma Thompson." Richard respected Norma's wish not to use her married name. All would change that afternoon.

91

"Pleased to meet you, Norma, and hello again, Mrs. Leslie." Renford indicated Richard's mother take the center chair of the three clustered in front of his desk.

Had the conference room been occupied, or had Renford intended to squeeze them together, or… Richard wondered…separate him from Norma?

"First, I want to congratulate the future bride and groom on their decision. When is this happy occasion taking place?"

Richard glanced at the clock but held his focus on their discussion. "This afternoon, so we don't have much…"

I instructed Lieutenant Jansen to prepare the paperwork for changing your marital status and to assign you a slot at Dunwoody as a GI." He glanced from Richard to Norma. "I'm sorry. You haven't heard the good news. Richard, fill them in."

"I said I'd look into it."

"That's wonderful, an answer to a mother's prayers." She patted Richard's knee.

"A lot of changes in a short time span, but all of them appear to be positive." Renford singled out Norma. "Richard tells me you have three children, one of them his. I assume they will live with the two of you."

Richard squirmed when Norma didn't respond. "Was that a question, Sir?"

"Yes, I suppose it was."

"When we're done with the J.P this afternoon, Norma and I are driving to Wisconsin to discuss the children with her parents."

Direct at Norma. "Oh, they don't live with you now?"

Richard blurted, "Her parents are looking after them until we…" He had blundered into the trap set for Norma.

"What will be your living arrangements after the wedding?"

Renford's question tossed out like a pop fly to the infield for anyone to catch. Richard sensed his mother's resentment toward Norma's older children but hoped she'd keep her feelings to herself.

Mrs. Leslie's voice filled the silence. "Richard, Norma, and the baby can move in with me. The older ones would be better off out in the country with their grandparents."

"Norma, how do you envision the situation after you're married?"

Richard glanced at the clock with no intention of fading from the conversation; he needed to glimpse Norma's expression. Fear? Anger? Hurt?

Almost pleading, Norma whispered, "I want my son and daughter back with me."

"You gave them up."

An argument he had hoped his mother would never express in front of the woman he intended to marry. "Ma, Norma never intended to leave them with her parents."

"Just until she got pregnant and snared a husband."

A tap on the door and Lt. Jansen entered, pre arranged, no doubt. "I have the paper work ready for signatures, if I can steal Richard away for a few minutes."

Richard remained glued to his chair. Without his presence, Renford will have control over his mother and wife.

"Lieutenant Jansen needs your signature, Richard." On impulse Richard jumped to his feet as if Renford had called him *Soldier.*

"Yes sir." He glanced back but realized the hopelessness of his situation.

Richard raised his voice above the clacking of the street car heading back to St. Paul. "What did you two discuss with Colonel Renford after I got pulled out of the room?"

"As long as you continue the auto repair program, I will allow Norma's two children into our home. He agreed to increase your disability to cover a family of five."

***

Richard touched his bride's arm and she pulled it back. "When I complete the program and find a job, we will move to a place of our own."

"Colonel Renford suggested…"

"Ma, Colonels don't suggest. They give orders."

"So be it. Until you earn your own money, Norma and I will handle your finances."

"So, what's new?"

"Everything is new. Whatever you've been accustomed to will be different."

"I wasn't pleased with my life anyhow. I welcome the change." He faced his fiancée and wondered, will she? Norma accepted his outstretched hand.

Chapter Thirteen

"Make yourself comfortable. Colonel Renford will be here in a minute." A young and cute and civilian secretary directed Richard to sit on the leather sofa, a new piece of furniture since his last visit. Lt. Col. Renford's unoccupied chair and the polished mahogany desktop glaringly void of his usual jam-packed file unnerved him. Why had he been seated before his psychiatrist arrived?

"Would you like coffee?" She faced Richard and brushed her hand across the pleats in her skirt.

"I quit because Ma always said coffee would stunt my growth."

"Maybe you should have given it up sooner." She blushed, but held her ground.

Richard liked her spunk. "I'm taller than you." A memory clicked like a hunger pain. "Do you dance?"

"Hold on. Let's settle the business at hand first. Since you are no longer a growing boy, would you like coffee?"

"Are you going to have a cup with me?"

"Drinking with the client is hardly part of my job description."

Richard wanted to ask what time she got off work but said, "No, to the coffee. But when the lieutenant colonel gets done with me, I may change my mind."

"Now a full-bird colonel. Colonel Renford's been promoted."

A rising resentment he couldn't understand. "I'm not required to salute anymore." He tugged on the collar of his bowling shirt. "See? No uniform."

"I'll be right outside this door, if you change your mind while you're waiting."

Richard detected a slight puckering of her lips and followed her shapely pair of legs leaving the room.

Expecting to be chided for a year or more of missed meetings, he felt mildly aroused. Sex with Norma after they married hadn't blossomed as he had hoped.

Colonel Renford entered and approached Richard, his hand extended. Dumbfounded, Richard accepted the handshake and attempted to stand, but a firm hand on his shoulder convinced him otherwise. "Stay seated."

Renford sat alongside Richard rather than across the desk. "We haven't had a chance to talk for, oh gosh, over a year. Not since your marriage to...." He glanced toward the desk where Richard's file normally sat. "Norma." He crossed his legs. "I assume things are going quite well, since you hadn't taken advantage of the Army's mental health program."

Richard drew a deep breath. "Well..."

"The reason I called you in...." Another glance toward the desktop. "We have some business to wrap up." He uncrossed his legs. "I'm sorry to say, I won't be available to you after today."

"You mean I've broken free from the Army's hook?" Richard's gaze roved between the empty chair behind the desk and the full colonel seated next to him. "I'm not so sure that's a good idea." The connection he'd avoided for the past year made him feel insecure.

"Oh, you'll have access to professional help, if you decide you need it. Just not with me."

"How come...? But, who...?" Wasted breath, considering Richard's experience with the military's usual withholding information. "Yes, Sir," an impulsive response.

"We've come a long way together over these past six years, and I can attest that you've been successfully rehabilitated and integrated into civilian life."

He made eye contact. "Perhaps I should ask about your employment success before I state such a claim."

"I've been fired twice and walked off the job once." An admission Richard had intended to keep from the colonel, but his world had just gone topsy turvy.

"What went wrong?"

Another victim of this chaotic world? "I suffered through job interview after job interview, thanks to the employment service's need to feel helpful, landed a couple of jobs any monkey could have done, and... ."

There was no other *and* except that he got fired or walked off each job within weeks. "The foreman on a construction job could have gotten all of us killed the way he handled explosives. I tried to tell him—."

"In the Army you acted on orders that could have gotten you killed, but in civilian life you resent being told what to do."

"Yes, Sir. I've thought about that."

"And what conclusion about making a living have you arrived at?"

"I have taken on two part time jobs, both on my terms. I'm the short order cook at a breakfast café, the only other employee a waitress/cashier. I also drive taxis a few afternoons and evenings. With both jobs, I don't have to answer to a boss who uses me as his ego boost."

"Apparently, my job assessment still stands. How is home life going?"

"Norma's pregnant again and Lorraine's been shipped off to Wisconsin because she got on her mother's nerves. Ma can't get along with my wife, so she moved to my sister's duplex. I have two jobs and we can't make the rent."

"I'll make a note of these problems and have the V.A. mental health department get in touch with you."

"With Ma gone and Norma not working, I'm more concerned about my disability status lowered to fifty percent."

"I'll see to it."

"Sir?"

"Yes?"

"Might I ask why you are no longer assigned to my case?"

"A fair question. As you probably know, since Ft. Snelling had been decommissioned, we function as a veteran's administration, and we maintain the Military Intelligence Service Language School. Because of our involvement with the United Nation's police action in Asia, my multi-linguistic skills are needed overseas."

"The Koreans?" The war he'd be fighting if the army had allowed him to reenlist. Maybe his life would have been better.

"Our allies, the Japanese."

From out of nowhere, a wave of Japs wielding bayonets and yelling *bonzai* began their attack. Richard screamed, "Incoming!" and wedged himself between cushion and arm rest. He awoke restrained to a hospital bed, on either side Ma and pregnant wife, but no baby daughter.

A voice with no discernible face. "I perused Richard's medical file and reviewed Dr. Renford's recommendations. We'll start our sessions by working on what triggers Richard's outbursts." Clip board pressed to his chest, and a hand clasping his patient's shoulder, the voice continued. In about twenty four hours you'll be released to go home."

Triggers? Richard had no intentions of ever returning to Ft. Snelling.

Chapter Fourteen

Richard experienced a moment of euphoria feeling Norma's approval, even her encouragement. The woman in the long red gown had asked him to dance claiming she, too, had been a contestant here at The Prom Ballroom, when Richard and a stranger from New York won the trophy.

"You certainly haven't lost your touch," came her breathless voice as her face brushed past his.

"You aren't doing so bad yourself."

"Why haven't I seen you here since the contest?"

A twirl, his hand secure against her arched back. "Busy, I guess,"

They promenaded booth-side and parted, she yelling, "I'll be back after the next set. Got that one promised."

"You sure you don't mind me cutting a rug with other women?" Richard asked his wife. Not expecting or getting an answer, he sat alongside her, across the table from her sister, Gladys, and her husband. "That gal is trophy material."

Gladys nodded and her husband's attention remained glued to Richard's disappearing dance partner.

Richard made the decision to treat Norma to an evening out, not just drinks and dancing to the juke box at *Frankie and Johnnies*. Bringing Gladys and her husband along was Norma's idea. He agreed, knowing they would sit with her if he had an opportunity to dance. She rarely danced and since her recent pregnancy, their third since he met her, she stopped altogether.

Back in bed sometime after midnight, "Why not? You can't get pregnant if you already are."

"I just don't feel up to it."

Richard never insisted on having sex, but usually his wife cooperated. A terrible waste, not having to worry about making a baby.

"Are you ready for another child?" Norma asked.

She didn't say *another mouth to feed* and he was grateful. "As many as you want."

"I don't do this on my own, you know."

"You're supposed to tell me when it's a bad time."

Norma drew a deep breath as if preparing for an argument. "You come home from the bar all hyped up, and I feel it's my responsibility to calm you down, to help you sleep."

"If you got pregnant every time I can't sleep, we're heading for one mighty big family."

"You tell me drinking helps. I wish there was some other way."

The perfect opportunity to tell her about his recent invitation. He began, "You know how much I like riding horses."

"Whenever you spend an afternoon riding, you and your buddies celebrate 'til the bars close and then continue drinking and eating White Castle hamburgers in Phalen Park until wee hours in the morning. That doesn't help you sleep."

"This will be different. It will take a month of planning." He pushed himself against the headboard to a sitting position. "At least a month. I've been asked to join the Jesse James gang as they reenact the Northfield bank robbery."

His voice nearly falsetto, "I get to play Bill Chadwell who lived here and suggested the gang pull off a robbery in Minnesota. Bill gets shot and falls off his horse. That's why they want me. I know how to fall without hurting myself."

He slid down onto his back and stared at the ceiling. "I'll have to save up money, but the reenactment won't happen until September seventh, the eightieth anniversary of the shooting. Two weeks before my birthday." A detail that might shake a few bucks loose from the two women in his life who controlled the purse strings. "The whole town of Northfield is getting ready. They budgeted twenty thousand dollars."

Richard faced his wife, she sound asleep. He rolled over and began the raid. He never made it beyond Bill Chadwell, Clell Miller, and Bill Pitts shooting their way across the bridge into Town Square.

***

The alarm went off at 4:30 and Richard doggedly swung his legs over the edge of the bed, feet searching for his slippers. He had an hour to get ready and walk ten blocks to the Payne Avenue Café; a mere hole-in-the-wall breakfast-only eatery, but it held his future. Norma couldn't appreciate his vision, especially since he gave up driving taxi to accept this low paying job.

"If business is bad and you don't make expenses, you get nothing."

"I know I can make the business profitable. Joe promised full partnership when that happens." A bit of truth slipped through his defenses. "At least I don't have to face that sneering dispatcher who doled out one-day cab leases when a regular driver didn't show. To him, he was handing out candy to a bunch of low life street kids."

His argument had fallen on her deaf ears, but his mother took a different view. "You always had a knack for cooking, more so than most of my girls. Maybe this is the opportunity you've been waiting for."

Waiting was the operative word. Other than the beer route that ended in near disaster, he hadn't managed to stay with any job longer than a few months, none that he even considered as a career.

***

"Cooking is a skill, maybe even an art." Richard, the only customer at the time, had encouraged Joe, the despondent fry cook. "A true chef performs for the customer even with his back turned. That can become an advantage, like the magician quietly setting the scene and then, presto, the magic happens and the audience is awed."

"Maybe you can see it that way, but I can't." Richard had opened a door to an opportunity.

"Here's the deal," Joe began a few days later, while Richard swiped his toast across the plate to mop up the remaining egg yolk. "You just wasted another trip downtown only to find all the cabs had been taken for the day."

He paused as if Richard needed to be reminded. "Right?" the final twist of the knife. The cook loosened the bow in back, lifted the apron's loop over his head and handed it to Richard.

Richard said, "That's the kind of thing I've been suggesting. Customers expect to be messed with." He pushed his plate aside. "Now hang it over my head like a bib, set the pot in front of me, and tell me to refill your coffee cup for once. People love to be part of the action."

"I wasn't entertaining you. I was making a serious proposal."

The deal was confirmed with a hand shake, details vague about compensation, a percentage of the take at the end of each week. To seal the pact, a verbal promise of full partnership if Richard could turn the business around.

The café became his domain. A businessman at the verge of bankruptcy would have to attribute the café's turnaround to Richard's culinary craft. Partnership would be inevitable.

***

Spatula in hand and Jesse James' gang on his mind, Richard almost wished the flow of customers that morning would give him a break to fantasize the reenactment.

Twelve noon, on the dot, Virgil sauntered in and glanced up and down the empty row of stools. "Any of that mud left?"

"A bit strong. Just about to toss it out and clean the pot. Had to hide it until the last hanger-on took the hint that breakfast was over." Richard filled two cups. "Flip the lock and switch off the neon. We've got something to discuss."

"Can't take too long. Pa only gives me a short noon break." Virgil glanced at the glass enclosed case. "That a Bismarck left over."

Richard handed it to him. "Use a napkin. I don't want to dirty another plate." He ducked through the narrow opening under the bar and sat alongside his friend. "I told Norma about the reenactment last night."

"What did she say?"

"She didn't say no. I think we got a deal. Tell the gang that I'm in, as long as it takes place on a Sunday. That way after I close at noon on Saturday, I'll have the afternoon and evening to get ready."

Virgil sipped and grimaced. "The only character left to fill is Bill Chadwell who falls off his horse. You sure you can handle that."

"A horse is a lot closer to the ground than an airplane." Richard didn't mention the matter of a parachute. "I learned to roll as I hit the ground."

"You were nineteen years old back then,"

"I'm still under thirty, at least until next month." He expected that argument from Norma, not his best friend."

"Come down to the shop at closing time, and we can head up to White Bear Lake to rehearse our parts. The rest of the guys are probably up there already."

***

Richard awoke from his nap on the couch and approached Norma in the kitchen. "Where are the kids."

"Outside or in their room. I felt you needed your sleep after last night."

"Appreciated." A quick glance at the oven. "I won't be eating here this evening." He tried to sound casual. "Virgil and I are heading up to White Bear after he gets off work."

"What's up there?"

"We're practicing for the shoot out."

"The OK Corral?"

"Very funny."

"No, really. What are you two up to?"

"We're part of the reenactment of the James gang robbing the bank down in Northfield. Remember, we talked about it last night." He broke eye contact and peered at his wrist watch. "I gotta go. Should have told you to wake me, but Virgil won't leave without me." His kiss goodbye was intended more as a distraction than just a farewell.

"You need money?"

"Took an advance from the till. Having a good week. Joe will be pleased." He grabbed his hat from the peg near the door. "Goodbye. Don't wait up."

***

Richard, portraying Bill Chadwell, calmed his horse at the entry to the bridge as planned. The mare whinnied and pawed the ground, sensing action, annoyed with having her ears plugged against gunshots. Clell Miller and Charlie Pitts —Virgil and a guy he worked with—didn't take these precautions, but they didn't have to make a timed fall. He wanted no surprises.

Richard, his reenactment group, and the townspeople including visitors, knew the outcome, but not Bill Chadwell back on September 7, 1876. Richard tried to erase the entire twentieth century from his consciousness. Except for the falling off his horse. Norma, his mother, and his kids who could comprehend the danger pleaded with him not to proceed.

"Fall onto the horse's neck and gallop out of town like Charlie Pitts did." Norma, inadvertently using the original gang member's name, brought a smile to Richard's face. "If your body has to land on the ground for the townspeople to mull over, get off the horse like Clell Miller did." She corrected, "Like Virgil Trumel, for God's sake."

"That's not the way it happened." Moments before the action, an improbable reenactment of Corregidor flashed through his mind. Would it be watered down to protect the sensitivities of the audience? A second flash, *Norma might be right.* But it was ten minutes past two and the shooting had begun, the cue that they were to begin their historic charge.

Clell Miller, Bill Chadwell (alias Bill Stiles) and Charlie Pitts (alias Sam Wells) thundered across the now-concrete bridge for the eightieth consecutive time, or as many times since the first reenactment. Reaching Town Square, struggling to control the agitated horses more startled by the shouts from crowd than gunshot they'd prepared for, Richard, according to the script, fired multiple shots into the air. *No one is to be killed,* Jesse's directive during the planning stage might just go by the wayside.

Except for the shot that knocked Chadwell off the saddle, Richard, true to his character, had erased his mind of the entire outcome other than the futility of the attempted robbery. At the scene, two citizens killed and two of Jesse's gang killed.

After the posse chase—reenactment only to the other side of the bridge—the rest of the gang either killed or jailed, except for Frank and Jesse. The biggest irony, a heist yielding a paltry twenty six dollars and thirty-one cents.

The conclusion of this escapade—something Richard attempted to selectively forget—something the original three gang members had no notion of or they might not have participated. Common sense suggested that by time the rear guard appeared, law enforcement could not have yet arrived. None of the robbers expected armed citizens, the element that thrilled the crowd gathered to watch the enactment.

***

The fatal shot, the fall; through the roped off area Richard glimpsed the frail frame of his wife running toward him. *Go away. You'll wreck the scene,* but he couldn't tell her because he was dead.

"Oh, Richard, I warned you."

His head lifted, but he couldn't move his eyes. *Killed instantly* the script read.

A man's voice, "Ma'am, you'll have to come back. Other actors are coming to retrieve the bodies."

"He's my husband, and you crazy people killed him."

Richard felt the man's foot nudge his back sides, and he struggled to remain dead.

"See, he's only pretending to be dead. Now please go back behind the ropes."

"Wait 'til you get home," produced an ever so slight twitch from the deceased bank robber.

***

Richard's part in the Northfield incident buzzed among the breakfast crowd, as he allowed—even accentuated—his leg to drag as a result of the fall.

"What happened to you?" the perfect opening for a recounting of the reenactment, and he entertained the group.

Noon came too soon to Richard's notion, although the single customer who occupied the same stool all morning continued to express interest in Richard's retelling over and over to customers who came and went.

"That's quite a knack you got."

"Just a practiced ride. Not much skill."

"No, I mean a knack to keep the place full all morning."

"Joe, he's the owner, and I got a deal going, and I'm working to a full partnership."

"Joe never mentioned partnership when I purchased his café this weekend, but he practically guaranteed that you would continue as chef."

"I don't understand," but the confusion was beginning to clear. His pulse quickened.

"Well, here's the deal. You can continue with a percentage of the day's gross, with a maximum take of say, twelve dollars. Not a bad take for a morning's work."

The new owner left his jaw vulnerable. "What say you?"

Richard untied the bow in back, slipped the loop over his head, and strung it over the new owner's head. Had it been around Joe's neck, Richard would have tightened it before he walked out.

Chapter Fifteen

O sole mio. Life was good.

"Bet you're the only kindergartener who gets dropped off at the school in a fancy Yellow Cab." Even in casual conversation, Richard would identify the taxi company that overlooked—or failed to check—his past driving record, for the second time. He had quit the company without notice in order to build Joe's breakfast café into a successful eatery with a promise of earning full partnership. When the business flourished, the owner backed out of his commitment by selling the cafe.

Richard avoided meeting with the café's former owner fearful of losing his temper, and Joe reciprocated most likely out of fear. The satisfaction gained from teaching him a lesson wouldn't be worth going to prison, probably for a long stint.

Richard struggled to regain the dispatcher's trust by checking in at the cab company every morning, hoping to secure an available cab for the day. Although always sober, sometimes he nursed a slight hangover from the evening before, but never indulging in *the hair of the dog* while cleaning and filling coolers early mornings at the Third Street Bar, his most recent part time job.

A decade of recovery from his war experience and a family—wife and five kids—Richard felt good reason to spout opera. Lorraine, the daughter who brought him and Norma to the altar, started kindergarten. Lorraine, the daughter that Norma rejected—he could find

109

no milder term to describe the mother-daughter relationship—began her first away-from-home experience.

"O sole mio-o-o." Sour notes descending down the "C" scale. Had his little girl noticed?

He reached across to pat her head; she glanced back and smiled unaware of the sadness that interrupted her father's crooning.

Twice before he had shielded Lorraine from her mother's rejection, once as an infant and again as a toddler, sent to her Wisconsin grandmother, the last time returning with welts across her backside.

"I was naughty so Grandma told me to fetch a willow branch." She added as if more explanation was needed, "From out by the garden." No trace of tattling but a statement of fact from a two year old.

Many times Lorraine would take mini breaks away from their home, the government housing project, to expand her play area beyond its immediate back yard. A child's call to an adventure or an escape from… . Richard shook off what he considered his failure to help Lorraine blend into the family, again, the kindest word he could use to describe the rejection she certainly sensed from Norma and her two older children.

One of the child's secret places, an unofficial landfill down the street from their apartment, probably caused her illness.

"Hepatitis can result from contact with rusty nails or decaying vegetation," the doctor explained.

Richard sensed, *Parents allowing their unattended children to play in the city dump*, the doctor's more honest interpretation.

Unaware that the disease was contagious, Richard allowed their daughter to sleep with him and Norma. Lorraine recovered, but they wound up hospitalized. For three weeks, their five children lived with Norma's sister and husband.

"Hepatitis often hits adults harder than children," that same doctor announced, his shaking head silently expressing, *these people*!

"You will also have a greater chance of recurring episodes, perhaps years from now."

"Off you go." Richard reached across his daughter's lap and pushed open the passenger door. "Have a good day at school. You can walk home with your brother and sister." His eyes traced the footsteps along the sidewalk until the brick building swallowed his little girl.

Seventy five dollars and a tank of gas interrupted an impulse to ditch the cab and return to the Third Street Bar and finish the cleaning tasks left undone that morning. A beer would taste good. Norma had given him the cash to lease the cab for that day, and she would expect it plus his profit back that afternoon. Some days he barely caught enough fares to refill the tank and give Norma back the money.

Only one jackpot in three years of on-and-off driving. A guy wearing a tweed suit, eyes hidden behind dark glasses, expressed an urgent need to get to Eau Clare, Wisconsin, to conduct business with another fellow who could have been his twin.

"Wait," an order from the passenger seat, brief case clutched as if it contained battle plans.

"Hey, I gotta keep the clock running."

The guy pulled a wallet from his suit jacket and peeled out a hundred dollar bill. "Will a 'C' note work for you?"

"If there's another one when we get back."

"Let's see what the clock says."

Nearly one hundred dollars left after expenses and giving Norma what would have been a better than average profit for the day; only half of that amount still in hand after an evening at The Third Street Bar drinking and playing pool, his skill with the cue adding to rather than subtracting from his pocket money. Two more nights of drinking, all that remained of the trip to Wisconsin was the retelling.

Across the street from the St. Paul Hotel, Richard awaited his first fare for the day. Leaves floated onto the windshield while Richard relived the weightlessness following the snap of his chute breaking free fall. He erased the memory of the carnage below and relished in the nothingness of mid air suspension. He needn't ever hit the ground running as his eyelids drooped, and the sleep he'd been shorted the past evening blended into his dangling mid air.

"You up for business?" The soundless leaves gave way to a hand-slap on the windshield.

"Yup." Richard jerked awake as a man dressed in a black with a splash of red and a white collar continued to tap on the passenger's side half open window. "You caught me in my morning meditation," as he reached across to open the door. "You can sit up here, Father, if you like. No company rules against it."

"I believe I will. Maybe I can help you reconnect to your higher power that I so rudely interrupted."

"Me and God got an agreement. He takes the back seat if someone needs a ride." Richard glanced over his shoulder about to explain his figure of speech, but then chose to let the priest believe he meant God actually sat back there. "Where to?"

"The Cathedral."

"That makes sense." Richard flipped the timer and shifted into gear.

"Am I that transparent?"

"N no," Richard stammered, struggling with the image. *Transparent?* "I'm not Catholic, Father."

"If so, might not there be a slight contradiction referring to me as Father."

Richard still struggled with *transparent* as if his passenger were some sort of spirit, "I give rides to all clergy. If the pope got into my cab, I'd say, 'Where to, Your Holiness?'"

"I doubt you will encounter Pious the Twelfth here in St. Paul, but possibly a bishop or two."

The red sash! It must mean something. A bishop? Richard stifled an urge to salute. "How should I address you, being a bishop."

"I was hoping you wouldn't notice. *Father* will do nicely."

112

"Well, I'm a military man. If I get the rank wrong, it's goodbye weekend pass. "

"A veteran of the World War Two, I imagine. Maybe Korea, or possibly both?"

"Just the big one. Got busted up and they wouldn't let me reenlist." Richard puffed his chest. "Five Hundred and Third Parachute Regiment. Three combat jumps in the Philippines." Not the sort of information he openly shared with strangers, but, what the hell, some of that money from Sunday's collection plate for a big tip would be nice.

"You have earned my respect, soldier." The bishop's turn to boast. "Marine captain, served as chaplain in Iwo Jima. We've seen some difficult times. But I was never forced to shoot anyone."

"Toughest part, until you come to the conclusion Japs aren't human beings."

"Yes, that indoctrination did make the task somewhat easier. How are you coping now that we realize the Japanese are also children of God?"

"I try not to hate them, but I won't go so far as *God's children*. Not with what some of them did to American soldiers."

Richard pulled up in front of the Cathedral, stepped out, and rushed to the passenger door finding himself face-to-face with the bishop.

"I'll need a ride after my meeting in about an hour. I'm hoping you'll be available."

"I could wait. Not much business this time of the day anyway."

"Yes, please wait, and keep the clock running. I think our bumping into each other was a kind of intervention."

"You mean God put you into my cab?"

"I tried to avoid wording it that way, but yes. We might be very beneficial to one another."

***

"Gave a bishop a ride today." The urge to brag to Virgil at the Third Street Bar opened their conversation. "Nice Guy." Richard deigned to pass judgment on a fellow soldier who achieved success after the war. "He blessed the marines and fed them communion before they faced the Japs on Iwo Jima." *Enemy*, the bishop had suggested as a way to take focus off their nationality.

Maybe in his cab, but not in a bar with buddies. "Most of them got shot up anyway. You know the marines, glory seekers." That shift of focus felt good, and he enjoyed his friend's shocked expression at gruesome details of war.

Virgil raised his empty glass toward the bartender and gestured two more beers. "Bet he stiffed you on the tip."

Richard motioned his intention to pay for both refills, and the bartender noted it on a slip of paper kept in the cash register. "No, the bishop had me wait an hour and paid clock time. Got a good tip, and he wants to meet with me again."

"Where, behind the altar at the Cathedral?"

"In my cab. He wants me to pick him up tomorrow afternoon to take him someplace. Didn't say where."

"Mystery man." Virgil reached into his pocket. "I'll get the next one."

"No more for me. I think I'll head for home. It's been a long day."

***

Richard rushed through his early morning chores at the bar and grabbed a bus to the taxi dispatch downtown in time to see another driver take off with his intended cab.

"Sorry, all the regular drivers showed up this morning." The dispatcher's disdain oozed past his forced smile, and Richard fought the urge to knock that grin off his face. He hated wimpy men with big egos flashing their authority.

Neither returning home nor going to the bar appealed to him. He walked the downtown streets reflecting on his boyhood explorations, his money-earning schemes, and his ducking down alleys to avoid the cops. *Irish*, the most of them, his English mother lamented after they brought her wayward son back to their apartment long after curfew. So too, the Catholic priests. Was the bishop one of them? More than likely. Richard relished in the mutual respect he developed with the Irish cops and now with the bishop.

The dome of the Cathedral loomed. He hadn't intended it as a destination, at least not until later that afternoon, but there it stood. Was his new found friend inside? Probably not because he was a *visiting prelate*. Richard chuckled at the title. Probably back at the hotel or touring some of the city's Catholic churches. Or eating breakfast. He felt the wad of bills Norma had handed him as he left the house and decided he was hungry. He headed up Seventh Street toward Mickey's Diner.

The diner, a converted Pullman railroad car, entertained its third breakfast shift since midnight, actually those same street people who had been pushed out by the breakfast regulars had filtered back to resume nursing cups of coffee and possibly a sweet roll. They would obediently leave but return during the afternoon lull. In winter especially, this pattern offered temporary reprieve from sub zero weather. Richard sat at the counter and ordered a full breakfast, after which he'd explore more of his city careful to avoid the numerous neighborhood bars.

"I didn't get a cab today." From the bench in front of the Cathedral, Richard met the prelate's gaze that shifted toward the street. "I'm only a part time driver, whenever someone doesn't show up for the morning shift."

"A bit difficult to support a family without predictable income."

"That's another story." Richard avoided addressing the man in black with any of his titles.

"We can sit right here, and I'll explain what I intended for us this afternoon." The bishop's hand disappeared into the folds of his cassock and pulled out a pack of Lucky Strikes. "Would you like one?"

Richard declined but wished he hadn't.

"A rare specimen, a GI who doesn't smoke." He pulled a deep drag and released a cloud. "How did you manage that?"

"Cigarettes were for trading, not for smoking. I used to smoke a little—still do when... ." He decided not to mention drinking. Here was his chance to portray the kind of family-man image that eluded him.

"Probably when you get together with army buddies over beers."

The bishop's guess was half right; he had barroom friends but he avoided fellow war veterans.

"I was hoping you could take me to Fort Snelling to browse through the cemetery. I knew some good men who reside there."

"You can still flag a cab. Every driver I know would appreciate a fare that big."

"No. If you're free, I'd rather talk to a veteran who survived Dante's Inferno."

"I guess that's a Catholic version of hell." His hell at the moment was a need for a cigarette.

"Your faith condemns bad people to something different?" Polished black shoes ground the cigarette butt into the sidewalk.

"I never hung around churches much as a kid. But when I was sent to a farm in Wisconsin the lady of the house took me with her family to a Lutheran church. I suspect hell is hell no matter which denomination you belong to."

"And war is war, and declaring a truce doesn't always bring peace to the warrior." Back into the cassock for the pack of Luckies, he shook a few loose and presented it to Richard. "How bad are the nightmares?"

Richard accepted the cigarette and the light, answered through a puff of smoke. "Bad."

"I'd be surprised to hear otherwise. How do you cope?"

"I survived the army's complete five year psychiatric package no worse for the wear."

"Meaning?"

Richard regretted his flippant response. He had felt better during that time. Couldn't hold a job but getting up in the morning to face the day didn't feel so desperate. A mother and sister offered less stress than a wife and kids. "I thought it worked at the time. But now I'm not so sure."

"Can I help?"

"You already have." He glanced toward the church. "I won't convert."

"Last thing in the world I would expect." A sly grin. "At least not the first thing. How can I help you cope?"

"With my nightmares?"

"Life in general."

"I'd be happy just to be rid of the bad dreams."

"Tell me about them."

"Nothing to tell except that I wake up screaming, sometimes attacking my poor wife." Richard's tension relaxed. "Last week while napping on the couch Norma, she's my wife, chased the kids to their rooms because I had been shooting a make believe pistol like some kid playing cops and robbers."

"Were you back in the war?"

"That's the scary part. I was shooting some strange guy right here in St. Paul. I guess he must have bugged me or something."

"Maybe just the way he looked at you?"

"It was only a dream."

"It's called resentments. Might not even have a cause. Just a flare up at someone for no apparent reason."

"That must be it. Norma woke me. She knows how to gently stroke my arm ready to pull away if I start to swing." Tears blurred his vision but he continued. "I killed a guy in my sleep and it scared me stiff." Richard appreciated the silence while the bishop, as in a game of chess, pondered his next move.

"I'm leaving for Baltimore in the morning. Perhaps I can schedule you to take me to the airport."

"If I get to lease a cab. If not, I'll have one of the regular guys pick you up. The St. Paul Hotel where you flagged me yesterday?"

"Awakened you, I believe. Are you up for a little walk?"

"That's mostly how I get around these days."

"Walk with me to my hotel. I have something I'd like you to have."

The St Paul Hotel, its edifice quite familiar from downtown explorations as a kid, its austere lobby not so familiar or comfortable.

"I'll have you wait here while I locate the item I'd like you to have."

Richard's five foot seven frame stretched, head lifted; he had entered the building having business with a bishop, not to clean the spittoons, assuming there ever were any in this building. He chuckled at his time warp, and returned to his present circumstance, left standing as an obstacle for elegantly dressed men and women to walk around.

His father's image came to his rescue, last seen through the eyes of a five year old child. He'd dress for work—railroad conductor's uniform, tie and all. Richard stood his ground even encouraging everyone's attention. But the truth of his situation imposed, a taxi driver without a cab awaiting a bishop who took pity on him. He bolted toward the door.

"Can I help you?" One of the bedecked desk clerks abandoned his post and blocked Richard's exit.

"Gotta check on my cab." He glanced toward the elevators. "If the bishop comes down before I get back, send him out to me."

Yeah sure expression evaporated as the robed cleric sashayed toward them. "Evening, Your Holiness. I believe your cab is awaiting you."

"Thank you, but first Richard and I have business to attend to." He gestured toward a couple or ornately carved chairs. "Here in your elegant lobby." He touched Richard's elbow and walked him away from the astounded hotel employee.

In the bishop's hand, Richard eyed what resembled his certification to drive taxi prominently displayed in his cab. "If that's the ten commandments, I can tell you right now that I broke every one of them." This was not true. He never cheated on Norma, but decided not to interrupt the bad guy impression he'd given of himself. Lately, he wallowed in negativity.

"A different kind of commandments, not list of rules but behaviors that might assist in maintaining peace of mind, possibly an aid in keeping the commandments God passed down to us through Moses."

The Serenity Prayer

Grant me the serenity to accept the things I cannot change, courage to change the things I can, and the wisdom to know the difference.

Living one day at a time, enjoying one moment at a time, accepting hardships as the pathway to peace, taking, as He did, this sinful world as it is, not as I would have it, trusting that He will make all things right if I surrender to His Will, that I may be reasonably happy in this life and supremely happy with Him forever in the next.

Reinhold Niebuhr

Richard tucked the card in his jacket pocket. "I have to go home and explain to Norma about not leasing a cab and not coming home either."

"I hope to see you tomorrow about eight o'clock."

"I'll do my best."

"God go with you." The bishop's hand crossed his face and Richard felt blessed.

Part Two

Chapter One

Fifteen years after the incident that nearly destroyed our family, I decided to check the details surrounding the crime my father committed back in July of 1962. That spring, I had completed my elementary grades, and I eagerly awaited starting a new school in fall. However, Richard Leslie wouldn't be delivering his daughter in a yellow taxi on her first day of junior high as he had when I began kindergarten; as if he had kept that taxi job—or any job—throughout my elementary grades. Dad's angry outburst early one Sunday morning changed all of our lives forever.

Married with a family of my own, I owed it to my two children to have facts about their grandfather's mental breakdown separated from idle gossip. With my seven-year-old-daughter in tow, I headed to the public library to locate archived newspaper articles describing the incident.

My gaze settled on the first headline until my eyes watered and blurred my vision of the microfiche. Secrets that had been whispered when I was a teenager and became a taboo subject by the time I married were horrifyingly true. I snapped the off-button and the headline dissolved; no such switch could make the reality disappear.

I requested printed copies of the only two articles I could find concerning my father's actions and hustled my daughter out to the car. My husband, babysitting our son at home, had to leave for his afternoon shift at the post office, and I needed time to absorb the details of the shooting and consider what effects the articles might have had on my father's trial.

ST PAUL PIONEER PRESS

July 2, 1962
Man Runs Amuck in Loop
Wounds Two with Pistol
Victims in Fair Condition
By Donald Giese
Staff Writer

A gun wielding, 36-year-old man ran amuck in St. Paul's Loop early Sunday and wounded two men in a wild shooting spree.

Richard L. Leslie, 36, of 664 Otsego St. who police said was positively identified as the gunman was subdued by passerby and police in front of the Greyhound Bus Depot Ninth and St. Peter Sts. after a violent struggle.

His victims, Robert Beck of 587 Summit Ave. and Charles Schoephoerster, 37, of 1077 De Soto St. are in Ancker hospital recovering from bullet wounds.

Both men were reported to be in fair condition Sunday night.

FIRST SHOOTING

The first shooting occurred at about 1:10 a.m. in the Little Chef café, 443 Wabasha St. where Leslie, unemployed, was sitting at the counter eating a ham sandwich and drinking coffee.

A cook, Gerald Fuller, 36, of 106 N. Smith Ave. said Leslie had told him his wife had left him and that he was "going to hurt somebody real bad."

"He kept saying that over and over," Fuller said.

As Leslie sat at the counter, he was approached by Beck, an employee of Jackson Ambulance service who handed Leslie a card advertising his firm.

Leslie knocked the card to the floor. Beck picked it up and handed it again to Leslie.

POINT BLANK

Then, according to witnesses, Leslie got up, pulled a .22 caliber revolver from his pocket and fired point blank at Beck, wounding him in the chest.

"He was five feet away when he fired," a witness said.

Leslie then "waved the gun wildly and ordered everyone to stand back," according to one patron, and then ran out the door and went north on Wabasha St.

Schoephoerster, also a patron in the café crowded with customers at the time, followed Leslie out in the street.

He approached Leslie near the bus depot and told him to "take it easy." Leslie pointed the gun at him and fired. Schoephoerster ducked before the gun discharged and was struck in the right shoulder.

Schoephoerster, staggered back to the café, where he was observed bleeding from the shoulder by Patrolman Ray Betts. He shouted to Betts, "My God. I've been shot. He went that way."

TAKES CAB

Leslie then jumped in a Yellow cab driven by Leonard Currey, 45, of 892 Rondo Ave. and poked the gun in Curry's ribs telling him to get going.

When the cab was blocked by another car Leslie jumped out of the car after a struggle with Curry.

Meanwhile Robert Warn, 32, a Radio Cab driver, had seen Schoephoerster shot and ran toward Leslie after he got out of the cab. The 250-pound Warn hit Leslie with a left and downed him.

Warn, 549 Topping St. and two other men then pounced on Leslie until Betts and Patrolman Joe Renteria came up and helped in the struggle.

PLACED IN THE SQUAD

Police Sgt. David Weida, supervising uniform officer on duty at the time, arrived and Leslie was placed in Weida's squad car. It required six men to get Leslie in the car and four to restrain him during the trip to headquarters.

On the way, officers said, Leslie kept screaming "Everyone tries to push me around, I'll kill some more, including you."

He was placed in a maximum security cell where he continued to rave. At 3:15 a.m. Capt. Burton Pond, in charge of the station, decided to have Leslie examined.

"When we opened the door to his cell he came charging out making animal-like sounds." Pond said. "It required five of us to hold him."

Leslie had perhaps given a clue to his violent intentions earlier, police said, when he provoked an argument with George Throne, 18, of 1410 N. Snelling Ave, over a song Throne was playing on the jukebox in the Little Chef Café. Throne said Leslie challenged him to a fight and that throne told Leslie he'd meet him outside in 45 minutes, figuring he'd cool off by that time.

Detective Lt. George Barkley, head of the homicide division, said following the shooting Leslie could "easily have killed a half dozen people."

Police found Leslie's gun in front of the bus depot. In his pockets they found 63 cartridges. The revolver, a foreign-made weapon was fully loaded. From the cartridge cylinder they extracted one shell with a deep firing-pin imprint on it. The trigger had been pulled. The firing pin had been activated. The shell had not been fired.

"Somebody walking in the Loop last night had Old Lady Luck riding on his shoulder," Barkley said.

I realized that *Old Lady Luck* applied to *all* the victims; the two left alive, some hypothetical person as the writer implied, *and* my father. The wounded men healed; those *walking in the loop* remained unaffected except for stories to relate to grandchildren, but Richard Leslie's problems compounded.

By day two, the emphasis changed from victims to heroes, and, of course, a villainous monster. Mercifully, the public's appetite for drama of this kind diminished, and a third installment couldn't be found, however reprints of the articles appeared in outlying newspapers whose readers thrived on inner city crime.

ST PAUL PIONEER PRESS
July 3. 1962

2 Cab Drivers Assist
In Gunman's Capture

by William Riemerma
Staff Writer

Two St. Paul cab drivers were key figures in Sunday morning's capture of the gunman who had shot two strangers near the Greyhound bus depot.

Leonard Curry, a Yellow Cab driver, struggled with the armed man to prevent him from making a get-away in his cab. Robert Warn, a 250-pound Radio Cab driver, took over from there and flattened the gunman with a left hook.

After the shooting his second victim on the sidewalk, Richard Leslie, the 36-year-old gunman, got into the front seat of Curry's cam band jabbed a gun into his ribs."Hurry up and get going," he told Curry. Curry, 45, of 892 Rondo Ave, had made up his mind he wouldn't leave downtown if he could help it and got a break when a car in front blocked his path.

The nervous Leslie then started waving his gun out the cab window.

Meanwhile Warn, 32, of 549 Topping St. had seen the sidewalk shooting and had tried to cut off Curry's cab.

Seeing Leslie jump out of the cab, Warn got out of his cab and ran to the scene of the struggle for the gun.

He planted a left on Leslie's face and downed him. Leslie screamed, "Everyone is against me," and tried to get up, but Warn and other bystanders pinned him to the ground until police arrived.

Warn said as soon as he saw the shooting he went after the gunman "before he could shoot someone else."

"If I was going to get shot I wanted it to be downtown where help is quickly available," Curry said.

"I didn't want to be out in no-man's land with that guy."

***

I felt a chill travel up and down my spine; the reality of what my father had done pulled one direction and my betrayal of Dad's privacy another. *Let sleeping dogs lie,* my family's view on the issue, but what if that monster inside my father were to reawaken—if his drinking could somehow nudge it back to life? Resentments, the *sleeping dog* in my father's past, would snarl at the end of its restraining chain whenever he got drunk. Never fall-down drunk, just enough to quiet the chaos in his head and enable him to sleep. So he said, but he couldn't deny a simmering anger and his lack of patience with anyone or anything that got in his way.

I felt compelled to dig deeper, as if answers might be found in the dusty archives at the Ramsey County Court House.

Chapter Two

The earliest dated document retrieved by the clerk in charge of Ramsey County Court Records offered no surprises, but the words *STATE OF MINNESOTA against RICHARD LEE LESLIE* glared out at me. According to the complaint filed in District Court by Attorney William B. Randall, the resources of the entire state had been summoned to condemn my father. He would have the fight of his life.

State of Minnesota, ss.
COUNTY OF RAMSEY

DISTRICT COURT
SECOND JUDICIAL DISTRICT

STATE OF MINNESOTA
against
RICHARD LEE LESLIE

INFORMATION

I, WILLIAM B. RANDALL, County Attorney for said County, hereby inform the Court that on the 1st day of July , in Year 1962 , at said County, Richard Lee Leslie -did-- then and there being, did wrongfully, unlawfully, feloniously and wilfully make an assault in and upon the person of one Charles Schoephoerster, with a weapon likely to produce grievous bodily harm, to-wit: a gun, a more particular description of which being to this informant unknown; and did then and there with said weapon wound the said Charles Schoephoerster in and about the body, he, the said Richard Lee Leslie, being then and there armed with said weapon,

Unfortunately, none of the transcripts of Dad's court proceedings had been released to the public domain, but the following document states the results of his first appearance in court. A second page or possibly more had been withheld for some unknown reason.

ROGER STORKAMP

State of Minnesota }ss.
COUNTY OF RAMSEY.

MUNICIPAL COURT,
CITY OF ST. PAUL,

THE STATE OF MINNESOTA

Against

Richard Lee Leslie

State of Minnesota }ss.
COUNTY OF RAMSEY.

Before the Municipal Court, of St. Paul, in Ramsey County, and State of Minnesota:

I, ROBERT E. OTTE, of said Municipal Court, City of St. Paul, in Ramsey County and State of Minnesota,

do hereby certify that *Richard Lee Leslie*

was on the *5th* day of *July*, A. D. 19*62*

brought before said court, charged upon the oath of *George Barkley*

with having, on or about the *1st* day of *July*, A. D. 19*62*

in the County of Ramsey, and State of Minnesota, wrongfully and feloniously

Committed the offense of *Assault 2nd*

contrary to the form of the statute in such case made and provided and against the peace and dignity of the State

of Minnesota, (see complaint hereto attached) and after examination—having been waived—had in due form of law

touching the said charge and offense, the said Court did, on the *5th* day

of *July*, A. D. 19*62*, Adjudge that said offense has been committed,

The small print at the bottom of the page referred to the complaint, and indicated Dad's waiving the right to a trial. *(see complaint hereto attached) and after examination –having been waived.*

Dad had been charged with second degree assault, but he decided to give up the fight and accept the decision of a judge. This didn't sound like my father. However, only four days after the shooting, I assume he was still shaken and frightened. After rushing out of his cell like an animal, as the newspaper graphically portrayed him, a doctor should have prescribed some medication to calm him, but I suspect the police treated him as the caged animal he supposedly imitated.

Had the court railroaded Richard Lee Leslie into giving up all rights to defend himself? The next document squelched my eagerness to picture my father as a victim as well as a perpetrator.

ROGER STORKAMP

STATE OF MINNESOTA
DISTRICT COURT
COUNTY OF RAMSEY
SECOND JUDICIAL DISTRICT

State of Minnesota
ORDER FOR MENTAL EXAMINATION

vs.

AND APPOINTMENT OF EXAMINER
Richard Lee Leslie

The above named defendant appeared before the undersigned on July 6, 1962, to be arraigned on a charge of assault
in the second degree as set forth in the information of
the County Attorney Ramsey County, Minnesota, dated
July 5, 1962. Present in court besides the defendant was
his attorney, Thomas Moore, Public Defender, previously
appointed to defend the defendant in said matter, and also
present was Stephan Maxwell, Assistant County Attorney.

Both Mr. Maxwell and Mr. Moore represented to
the Court that they had grave doubts as to the mental
capacity of the defendant, and moved the Court to consider making a determination of the defendant's mental
capacity pursuant to MSA 361.18.

Upon the request of both defense Counsel and the
County Attorney that the Court make a determination
of the defendant's mental capacity and upon the review
of the circumstances surrounding the commission of
the crime for which defendant was charged.

IT IS HEREBY ORDERED:

That a mental examination of the defendant be made by the Court on July 16, 1962, at eight o'clock a. m., and that Walter A. Carley, M.D. is hereby appointed the assist in such examination.

Ronald E. Hachey (RS) District Court Judge

***

A court appointed attorney, Thomas Moore, in conjunction with the district attorney agreed to request Dad's mental status be tested. No doubt, he collaborated and secured this decision prior to advising my father to not contest the charge. Had Dad been aware of the behind-the-scenes discussion about his mental health before waiving his rights?

"It all went so fast," he confided years later when the adults in my extended family discussed the experience, sometimes within earshot of their children. Perhaps I was the only sibling to pay attention then, certainly the only one to pursue the matter fifteen years later

On July 24, 1962, eighteen days following his mental examination, the court summoned Dad back to face Judge Ronald E. Hachey, a name whose mention continued to rile Dad fifteen years later.

STATE OF MINNESOTA
DISTRICT COURT
COUNTY OF RAMSEY
SECOND JUDICIAL DISTRICT

State of Minnesota
ORDER OF DENIAL OF COMMITTMENT

vs

AND ORDER TO STAND TRIAL
Richard Lee Leslie

WHEREAS, on July 5, 1962, the County Attorney of Ramsey County, Minnesota, filed an information charging the above named defendant with the crime of assault in the second degree, which said act allegedly occurred on July, 1962, at said County, and

WHEREAS, Mr. Stephen Maxwell, Assistant County Attorney, and Mr. Thomas Moore, Public Defender, attorney of the defendant, requested the Court to make a determination of defendant's mental capacity pursuant to MSA 631.18 to determine whether or not defendant was mentally ill to such an extent that he would be unable to defend himself at the trial of said matter, and

WHEREAS, on July 6, 1962, it was ordered that examination of the defendant be made in court, and Walter A. Carley, M. D., was appointed to assist in such examination, and

PVT. RICHARD LEE LESLIE

WHEREAS, such examination was made in open court on July 16, 1962, at which examination were personally present the undersigned, the court reporter, the defendant and his Counsel, Thomas Moore, who represented him and had represented him in all prior appearances, Stephen Maxwell, Assistant County Attorney, Walter A. Carley M. D., certain witnesses who testified relative to the happening of the event, and also Eugene P. Daly, Chief Attorney of the Veterans Administration, who had with him all the medical records of the defendant and which records were made to the Court and Dr. Carley during said examination and

WHEREAS, there is attached hereto and incorporated herein by reference as fully as if set forth verbatim a report by Walter A. Carley, M. D. which the undersigned hereby approves and adopts,

THEREFORE, THE COURT FINDS:

That the defendant is not now insane nor is he an idiot nor an imbecile under the terms and definitions of MSA 631.18, and is found to be able to well aid in his legal defense.

IT IS ORDERED:

The matter be reinstated on the calendar for trial and such other further disposition as the Court may order.

Ronald E. Hachey (RS)
Judge of the District Court
Dated July 24, 1962

I skimmed over the *WHEREAS* statements and focused on the conclusion.

> *THEREFORE, THE COURT FINDS:*
> *That the defendant is not now insane nor is he an idiot nor an imbecile under the terms and definitions of MSA 631.18, and is found to be able to well aid in his legal defense.*

> *IT IS ORDERED:*
> *That the matter be reinstated on the calendar for trial and such other further disposition as the Court may order.*

That Dad recovered rather quickly from his outburst of anger, wouldn't surprise anyone who lived with him. He never shot anyone before, but we tolerated his ranting and storming about the house and neighborhood knowing that only a simmering of anger would remain come morning.

Hopefully, bringing his VA psychiatrist into the court proceedings would shed light on the root cause of his emotional breakdown. Dad had been wounded emotionally during the war, still carries those scars, and I feel he's not out of the woods yet. Back then, the future looked very gloomy.

My father had been declared sane enough to stand trial, but what about his frame of mind when the shooting took place? The next document from the stack resolved that issue. The court approved a second examination of Dad's mental state a couple months later on September 21st.

PVT. RICHARD LEE LESLIE

STATE OF MINNESOTA
DISTRICT COURT
COUNTY OF RAMSEY
ECOND JUDICIAL DISTRICT

State of Minnesota

vs

ORDER
Richard Lee Leslie

The above matter having come on for hearing at the regular Criminal Calendar, in the above Court, on September 4, 1962, Thomas E. Moore, Public Defender, appearing for the defendant, and Stephen Maxwell, Assistant Ramsey County Attorney, appearing for the State; and the defendant having moved the Court for an order appointing Dr. Walter Carley to conduct a mental examination of the defendant to assist defendant in the trial; and defendant further moving the Court that the reasonable charges of Dr. Carley for said examination to be paid out of the District Court Fund;

Now, therefore, upon all the files, records and proceedings herein, and argument of counsel, and a showing to the Court that defendant is destitute;

IT IS HEREBY ORDERED, that Dr. Walter Carley is hereby appointed to conduct a mental examination of the defendant to assist defendant in the preparation of his defense and that the reasonable charges of said examination shall be paid out of the District Court Fund.

Dated this 21st day of September, 1962.
Leonard J. Keyes
District Judge

The resultant psychiatrist's report sent a cold chill down my spine.

STATE OF MINNESOTA
DISTRICT COURT
COUNTY OF RAMSEY
SECOND JUDICIAL DISTRICT

State of Minnesota

vs

File 20920
Richard Lee Leslie

This matter came on again for further trial on March 6, 1963. Appearing in court were the defendant and his attorney Mr. Thomas Moore, and Mr. Albert Ranum representing the County Attorney's office. Mr. Ranum made a short reference to the evidence, which was followed by a statement in behalf of the defendant by Mr. Moore.

Upon all of the files, records and proceedings had and filed in said matter, evidence adduced by the various witnesses during the course of trial, and examination of the exhibits introduced for the Court's consideration, and more particularly Exhibit 1 of the defendant, being a record from the Veterans Administration at Fort Snelling, Minnesota, arguments and statements of counsel, and after due consideration of the same, the Court finds that the defendant, Richard Lee Leslie, was on the date of the offense alleged in the information, namely, July 1, 1962, insane; and it is the further finding of this Court that the defendant is found to be not guilty of the crime as set forth in the information of the Ramsey County Attorney dated July 5, 1962, for the reason that the defendant was on the date of the offense found to be insane.

Insane! Not *out of control* or even *temporary insanity*, but the naked truth. Dad had gone insane, and who's to say it might not happen again? Fifteen years of mood swings since that diagnosis, usually before and after bouts of drinking, hadn't sunk to a level even close to what I would consider insanity. He never awoke without full memory of the night before, justified by—never apologized for—some slight from someone who offended his sensibilities.

Dad had not been abandoned by the military he served so heroically in the Philippines, but why didn't the court assign him to a Veteran's hospital? Dad had two opposing explanations: Hachey rushed his decision before transportation arrived to take him to St. Cloud Veteran's Hospital or the VA driver failed to show up.

Without the transcript of the trial/hearing, no proof exists to support the Military's involvement other than documents the Veteran Administration supplied to the Hachey Court. In Dad's view, he returned to his cell awaiting a ride to St. Cloud Veteran's hospital. Instead, he was *fenced into* the back seat of a Minnesota Highway Patrol vehicle and, "...unloaded after dark and signed off like a piece of cargo at an institution for criminally insane."

The underlining and double underlining of key phrases in the next document supported his view that Judge Hachey would have preferred sentencing prison time rather than mental institutions. He chose the most secure facility for Dad's recovery—incarceration!

It is the order of this Court that the defendant be committed to the Minnesota Security Hospital at St. Peter, Minnesota, for safekeeping and treatment, it being the further finding of the Court that from all of the evidence the defendant has been found to have had homicidal tendencies. The defendant to be confined in said institution or such other institution for the same purposes as herein set forth as by law provided until the further order of the Court.

Dated March 6, 1963.

(S) Ronald E. Hachey
District Judge

"Hachey had it in for me," Dad often complained. I thumbed through the reaming dozen court documents and hospital records pertaining to my father's lock up time and ultimate release would hopefully settle the matter of Hachey's supposed interference.

If they support Judge Hachey's interference, I would feel compelled to share those results with him and admit my prying into his personal history, a decision I hadn't yet made. Dad hadn't had any legal problems for over a dozen years, half that time claiming his full release from psychiatric care.

Any document proving Dad's rehabilitation might ease my mind of some overlooked detail suddenly arriving at his door step by way of a parole officer or worse yet, the Military Police. Or a new brush with the law.

Dad openly displayed a pistol—*to keep the peace*—kept in a drawer under the till where he bartended, and I know of one incident where he pulled it out to threaten a group of Hells Angels who came to cause trouble. The issue was settled without gunfire, and they all sat down and got drunk instead. It was one of Dad's favorite stories.

When I asked if he could legally own a gun, he said, "Never been told I can't protect myself. Besides, the gun belongs to the owner of the tavern."

I reminded him of the rifle and shot gun he kept for hunting in North Dakota. He only shrugged. I refrained from mentioning his alcohol consumption might, in my opinion, trigger another relapse into the war. I have a distant memory of Dad napping on the couch, blasting an imaginary pistol at supposed Japanese soldiers. Mother chased us kids off to our rooms.

I set the hospitalization documents aside while I reconciled what I discovered with other memories from my childhood and teen-aged years.

Other than three or four escorted trips to the court house, Dad remained in the county jail for nine months. I recall bringing him clean socks once and was granted a few minutes alone with him. I never got to see his cell, and I don't know if he shared it with others awaiting trial.

Although I only saw my father once in a year and a half, I felt connected by lending Mother my baby sitting money for bus fare to visit him in jail and later at the hospital. When I wanted a new spring coat, she refused to help pay for it. I reminded her of what she owed me.

"That money went to your father, not me. Get it from him."

I refused to allow her to drive a wedge between my dad and me. "Then take it out of his military disability check," I demanded.

"I need that money for rent and food."

I complained that my older siblings got supplies and spending money from their father's monthly support check, and she told me that was none of my business.

From then on, I removed myself emotionally from the family. I turned down offers to babysit neighbor's kids and refused to take care of my baby sister. Early each morning I would leave the house and not return until after dark. I flaunted my independence. The emotional gap between my mother and me sprung wide open, and healed only slightly after I ran off to get married at age seventeen.

I doubt my digging into her husband's past will bring us closer, and it might irritate my father.

Already in this deep, I feel compelled to continue.

Chapter Three

Like a jack-o-lantern's missing teeth, gaps occurred within the flow of communication between Judge Hachey's Court and three treatment centers; St. Peter Hospital for The Criminally Insane, Hastings Mental Hospital, and St. Cloud Veterans Hospital. The first two letters in this regard from Judge Hachey gave me some relief knowing that the Veterans Administration hadn't abandoned Dad, but they raised my anger directed at the Judge.

Hachey's letter dated April 10th referenced Dr. S.B. Lindley's letter of April 5th requesting Dad be transferred to St. Cloud Veterans Hospital. A month had elapsed since Hachey's order on March 6th to commit Dad to the more secure facility at St. Peter. In Military parlance, that could be considered a rapid response, but if they had represented Dad in person at his hearing rather than reacting after the Court's decision, the results might have been dramatically different.

***

April 10, 1963
Dr. S. B. Lindley
Hospital Director
Veterans Administration Hospital

Re: 5100/136 c 7 476 079 Leslie, Richard L.

Dear Dr. Lindley:

I thank you for your letter of April 5th and your willingness to help the above named Richard Leslie. In order to facilitate the procedures used within the Veterans Administration Hospital, I would be more than willing to lift or remove any restrictions now in force and effect except for the fact that we have on our hands what I consider to be a person possessed of serious shortcomings.

Based upon the evidence adduced at the hearing last year, I found Mr. Leslie to have had homicidal tendencies, and further felt that he should be confined under maximum security conditions for safekeeping and treatment. Under those circumstances, it had been the practice of our courts to order commitment of the individual usually to St. Peter, and that release should not be affected until the Court was at least notified. In those instances, a further hearing or study of the matter is made, and then the individual is released to society or some other disposition made at that time.

I take it by the contents of your letter that you prefer that the Court lift all restrictions and that Mr. Leslie be retained in the Veterans Administration Hospital of such time as your care and treatment deem advisable, and that his release to society, when reached, be effected without any contact with the Court. The wording of my commitment order is an attempt to keep the matter under the attention of the Court to be in the position of making further disposition at the conclusion of the patient's care and treatment.

It is not intended that the order be so worded as to compel hospitalization beyond the point of medical necessity. What it intends to provide is that in the event of hospitalization, care and treatment are provided, that the Court be advised as to the date of the intended discharge, and that the Court have some discretion as to the disposition of the mater following the care and treatment. Under the circumstances, I prefer not to lift any of the restrictions now provided and to respectfully point out that this Court has no objections to care and treatment available at the Veterans Administration Hospital, leaving to your staff the entire question as to the duration thereof, but to refer the matter back to the Court at the time of contemplated discharge.

Several possibilities would be available at that time; for instance, the Court might determine that he be returned to St. Peter or that he be released to society or, finally, that some other disposition for his benefit as well as the members of society be put into force and effect. In any event, it is not contemplated that the order requires that the patient be hospitalized and confined beyond the point of medical necessity I am filing a copy of this letter in the court file for further references.

Ronald E. Hachey (RS)
Judge of the District Court

The administration from the Veterans Hospital apparently made another request on April 29th to have Dad transferred, as referenced by a second response from a somewhat agitated Judge Hachey a full month later. The Chief Registrar at the VA fared no better than Dr. Lindley, the facility he represented receiving a subtle rebuke from the Court for his efforts.

May 29, 1963
Mr. George Daly
Chief Registrar Division
Veterans Administration Hospital
St. Cloud, Minnesota
Re: 5101/136 C 7 476 079 Leslie, Richard L.

Dear Mr. Daly:

Since receipt of your letter of April 29th concerning the above named Richard Lee Leslie, I have again made a review of the files, proceedings, and records in an effort to determine whether or not Mr. Leslie should be hospitalized at the Veterans Administration Hospital at St. Cloud, Minnesota. I would be disposed to encourage such a plan for immediate action if it were not for the fact that I am in doubt as to the propriety of permitting Mr. Leslie to be released at large in the immediate future.

This is in no manner any reflection upon the program at the Veterans Administration Hospital, but it does present a serious problem inasmuch as there might be some doubt as to the advisability of releasing Mr. Leslie in the near future.

Before permitting such as plan to be put into operation, my obligation at this end would require that I be assured by the medical authorities that Mr. Leslie is at the present time capable of being so treated including periodic releases from the hospital, from the standpoint of his own protection as that of members of our society.

Unless there is a clear showing to the contrary, I am inclined to leave Mr. Leslie in the hospital at St. Peter, Minnesota, until such time that I am assured to a reasonable medical degree that St. Cloud, Minnesota, for such treatment as you described in your letter of April 29th. Matters such as these are subject to periodic review, and should the time arrive when we feel Mr. Leslie is eligible for such care and treatment, we can again consider the matter.

Ronald E. Hachey (RS)
Judge of the District Court
May 29, 1963

Wading through these wordy documents, one can conclude Judge Hachey to be defensive of his position in Dad's case yet sticking to his original judgment. The Court, eager to forgive when Dad, as a teenager, opted to join the army to avoid a felony charge, showed no mercy for a damaged soldier back from the war it had sent him to fight.

Not for lack of trying, Dad never made it to the Veterans Hospital. However, before the end of the year, he had been transferred to Hastings Mental Facility. No official statements exist that explained how the transaction came about, but a letter from Dad's lawyer, E. C. Mogren of Law offices Mogren & Kuehn, did shed some light on the situation.

The attorney's letter survived, but the Hachey's response either got lost, hadn't been released to the public domain, or never got written. After his last two rejections, I suspect the latter.

Law offices
Mogren & Kuehn
1016 New York Building
St. Paul, Minnesota

November 4, 1963

Honorable Ronald E. Hachey
Judge of the District Court
St. Paul, Minnesota

Re. Richard Leslie, Incompetent

Dear Honorable Sir:

You will recall that the above named individual was committed to St. Peter's Hospital and you advised the writer that you would not wish to release him to go to Veterans Hospital unless you were satisfied that he no longer posed a problem and that some doctor would vouch for this. For your information I enclose the original letter of September 26, 1963, that I received from Dr. Robert Pfeiler, who is now the assistant medical director and who had charge of the case and apparently, Dr. Pfeiler feels that it would be proper to transfer Mr. Leslie to the Hastings Hospital and we are wondering if you feel that is proper under the circumstances or if there should be some provision for a transfer to St. Cloud.

Respectfully yours,
E. C. Mogren

PVT. RICHARD LEE LESLIE

***

Had Judge Hachey paid attention to the advice of Dr. Robert Pfeiler referenced in this letter, he certainly would have prevented Richard Leslie's clandestine removal from St. Peter a month later on December 3rd. I could find no information describing Dad's release, but for his colorful retelling the process. Again and again!

A sympathetic guard who befriended Dad instructed him to stuff all his belongings into a cardboard box and wait in his room for further orders. Around midnight, the guard opened Dad's door and gestured for him to quietly follow down the hall, past the strangely vacated security guard's station, and out the unlocked doors. Once tucked into the back seat of an unmarked car, the driver told him to duck down, and they passed through the outer gates. On the open road, he learned his destination, Hastings Mental Hospital.

Dad talked very little about his nine month stay at St. Peter, probably because he'd been drugged the entire time. His Psychiatrist at Hastings said he had enough Thorazine to knock out a horse, and she had to gradually bring him off it. I recall three of Dad's anecdotes about his St. Peter experience, two interesting and one unbelievable. A fellow inmate had been imprisoned since 1910 for stealing a horse, and Dad earned the privilege of working in the kitchen. The less than believable story, one of the men he had shot in St. Paul arrived at St. Peter as a patient, threatening to kill Dad. The kitchen assignment had been the warden's attempt to protect Dad from his former victim. The coincidence unlikely, I considered Dad's recollection the figment of an addled brain due to over-prescribed drugs.

When Hachey heard about the transfer, he summoned Dad back to court demanding to know who approved it. Again my father's account is all I have to go on.

Dad said his lawyer faced the bench and yelled at Hachey claiming the psychiatrist's recommendation had been on his desk for weeks awaiting a response. I assume Dr. Robert Pfeiler of Hastings Hospital made the diagnosis. (His name appears later as Director of the Department of Public Health who ultimately facilitated Dad's final release.)

Without proper guidance from the Court, the transfer had been based on this medical opinion. Whoever ordered and facilitated the move remained a mystery. An embarrassed judge acknowledged the transfer and chose not to rescind his assumed decision by default.

I could find no court document to support or refute Dad's account, but he remained under psychiatric care through Hastings' facility, Judge Hachey unaware that Dad received outpatient treatment a few months after his arrival.

Treatment through Hastings proved to be humane and effective. Rather than drugs, Dad received therapy and experienced an open policy on visitations. I nearly relented and accepted babysitting jobs to give my mother bus fare, but her brother offered to drive to the hospital for periodic visits. Dad earned his first one-day pass, December 25, 1963, perhaps the best Christmas we ever experienced as a family.

Dad's case worker had plans to spend the holiday with family in the Twin City area, and he offered Dad transportation home and back, and, I suspect, an opportunity to sneak a peek into our domestic situation. After a few more visits, Dad was released to outpatient care, requiring him to meet regularly with a local psychiatrist who reported his progress back to the medical staff at Hastings. A fact kept from the Court!

Our residence had changed during Dad's incarceration. A fire had gutted our apartment while he was at St. Peter, and our family, Mother and eight of us kids, moved to the Projects, a subsidized apartment, rent based on Dad's eighty percent disability pay from the VA. We had lived there temporarily when I was a toddler until Dad found employment with the taxi company, and shortly after I contracted Hepatitis B from the back lot and passed it on to my parents.

As soon as Dad switched from inpatient to outpatient, his level of disability raised from eighty percent to one hundred percent retroactive over the past three years. Apparently, the VA considered a family of ten to be more needy than one of just nine. With the new-found funds, Dad negotiated the purchase of a two story house in St. Paul and moved his family out of the Projects. Mother took a job and Dad stayed home tending a large garden and getting involved in some community activities.

My mother's behind-the-scenes efforts to get her husband's court release appeared in a letter from Walter Mondale's Office, he still being Minnesota State Attorney General just prior to his appointment to United States Senate in 1964.

William Randal, County Attorney, Ramsey County, State of Minnesota

Ramsey County Court House, St. Paul Minnesota.

October 30, 1964 October 30, 1964
Mr. Walter F. Mondale
Attorney General State of Minnesota
State Capitol
St. Paul, Minnesota

Re: Richard Lee Leslie

Dear Sir:

On August 7th, 1964, Judge Ronald E. Hachey received a letter from Dr. Smith in which Dr. Smith stated that it would be desirable to discharge Richard Lee Leslie from further treatment at the Hastings State Hospital. Dr.

Smith said that since Mr. Leslie must be referred back to the District Court before such a discharge is granted, they were asking that Judge Hachey advise them as to this decision in the matter.

Actually, a strict reading of M.S.A. 631.19 in the second paragraph indicates that one found not guilty by reason of insanity and found also to possess homicidal tendencies may be liberated when there is presented to the court the certificated in writing of the superintendent of the hospital where the person is confined, certifying that in the opinion of the superintendent: first, that the person is wholly recovered; and second, that no person will be endangered by his discharge. The case, State vs. District Court of Hennepin County, 185 Minn. 396, 241 NW 39, provides that if the certificate is provided to the district court, the district court has no discretion in the matter, but instead finds it mandatory to discharge the patient.

Therefore, I would suggest that the appropriate certification in writing be obtained and presented to the Honorable Ronald E. Hachey, Judge of the District Court.

Sincerely,

Paul E. Lindholm
Assistant County Attorney

cc: Honorable Ronald E. Hachey
    Judge of Ramsey County District Court
    1421 Court house
    St. Paul, Minnesota

An assistant attorney general from Mondale's office by-passed the Court and ordered Dr. N. E. Smith of Hastings Hospital to have Dad's psychiatrist prepare a certificate stating Dad's recovery and forwarding it to Judge Hachey. His letter shows that the judge remained under the impression that Dad still resided at the hospital.

Mr. Robert Pfeiler
State of Minnesota
Department of public Health
Centennial Building
St. Paul, Minnesota

Minnesota Security Hospital
St. Peter, Minnesota

Dr. N. R. Smith
Hastings State Hospital
Hastings Minnesota

November 10, 1964

Dr. N. E. Smith
Hastings State Hospital
Hastings, Minnesota

Dear Dr. Smith:

I received a letter last week from, Mr. Lindholm of the Ramsey County Attorney's Office, relative to the discharge of your patient, Richard Lee Leslie. I have not consulted with you on this case, but I assume from Mr. Lindholm's letter, that you feel that the patient is wholly recovered from his mental illness, and that he will not endanger the public or himself if he is discharged.

Mr. Lindholm is correct in his reading of M.S.A. 631.19. That law provides that if the Superintendent, (Medical Director), of the Hospital where the person is confined, (Hastings State Hospital), is of the opinion that the person is, "wholly recovered and that no person will be endangered by his discharge", then he may present to the Court committing the patient, a certificate in writing to this effect.

This certificate, which should be executed by the Medical Director who has now assumed the duties of Superintendent in this regard, must state that in the opinion of the Medical Director, the patient is wholly recovered, and that no person will be endangered by his discharge.

If you find in the affirmative on these two questions, then you should prepare your certificate for the signature of Dr. Zellar, and forward it to the District Court, to the Honorable Ronald E. Hachey.

Very truly yours,
Galen M. Cadle
Assistant Attorney General

Cc: Hon. Ronald E. Hachey
Dr. Hector Zellar
Dr. Robert Pfeiler
Mr. Paul; E Lindholm

Hachey had received copies of the back-and-forth communication between the Ramsey County Attorney Office and Minnesota State Attorney General, but we can only guess at his reaction. Probably still embarrassed by Dad's secretive transfer to Hastings, and possibly overwhelmed by the barrage of letters reaching his desk, Hachey caved in. After receiving the certificate of recovery from Dr. N.R. Smith of Hastings Mental Hospital, Judge Hachey ordered the county attorney to set a hearing date to legalize Dad's release. His letter shed some light on Dad's escape from St. Peter Institute for the Criminally Insane a year earlier.

November 20, 1964

Mr. Paul Lindholm
Assistant County Attorney
Court HouseN

In receipt of a communication from Dr. N.R. Smith, Chief of Service, Hastings State Hospital, requesting a review or a hearing concerning one, Richard Lee Leslie, who was originally committed to the Minnesota Security Hospital at St. Peter, Minnesota, and was released there from and transferred to Hastings State Hospital on December 3, 1963, by the Department of Public Welfare for continued treatment and rehabilitation.

At your convenience, will you make arrangements for getting the personnel together for such a hearing? Before setting a date, would you contact me to arrange for a convenient hour?

Very truly yours,
Ronald E. Hachey (RS)
Judge of the District Court

Judge Hachey's admission, "...released there from and transferred to Hastings State Hospital on December 3, 1963, by the Department of Public Welfare ..." solved the mystery of when the transfer took place and possibly who ordered it. Dr. Robert Pfeiler, Assistant Medical Director at Hastings Medical Hospital in 1963, had been promoted to Head of the Department of Public Welfare by the time of Hachey's letter nearly a year later. Either Dr. Pfeiler had been Dad's advocate all along, or Judge Hachey preferred to retroactively assign the transaction to Pfeiler from his new position. If the latter, Judge Hachey demonstrated a lack of respect for Hastings Mental Hospital as well as respect for St. Cloud Veterans Hospital.

I like to assume Dr. Pfeiler smiled when Judge Hachey released Dad, two and a half years later.

Either the county attorney or the judge delayed action as the order for Dad to appear before the Court hadn't been written until a year later.

PVT. RICHARD LEE LESLIE

STATE OF MINNESOTA
DISTRICT COURT
COUNTY OF RAMSEY
SECOND JUDICIAL DISTRICT

Richard Lee Leslie
File No. 20920

The Court having been advised by the Medical Director of the Hastings State Hospital that the above named defendant has received the full benefit of hospitalization and his condition is such that he is considered as recovered.

IT IS ORDERED:

That the Sheriff of Ramsey County transport the above named defendant from Hastings State Hospital to Ramsey County Jail to await further disposition of the above entitled matter.

Dated November 16, 1965.

***

When Judge Hachey got around to ordering the Sheriff of Ramsey County to transport Dad from Hasting State Hospital to Ramsey County Jail, Dad had been loose on the streets as an outpatient for nearly two years. When the sheriff pulled up in front of the jail minus his passenger in custody, I'm sure Judge Hachey learned the truth.

I am not aware how the matter got resolved, but I know for a fact that Dad didn't go to jail to await a hearing for his release that wouldn't happen for another year and a half. Apparently, Judge Hachey was none too pleased with the circumstances.

The last document rescued from the archives—the Court action ultimately releasing Dad not included in the public domain—was a motion originated from Dad's court appointed attorney addressed to The Hachey Court, not the other way around.

STATE OF MINNESOTA
DISTRICT COURT
COUNTY OF RAMSEY
SECOND JUDICIAL DISTRICT

State of Minnesota, plaintiff

vs.

Richard Lee Leslie
File No. 20920

PLEASE TAKE NOTICE, that on the 14th day of July, 1967, Terrence S. O'Toole, Attorney for Defendant, will move the above named Court, before the Honorable Ronald E. Hachey, Judge of the above , at 1:30 o'clock P.M. or as soon thereafter as counsel can be hard, to restore to capacity the above named Richard Leslie.

Terrence S. O'Toole, Attorney for Richard Leslie, does hereby move the Court to restore to capacity said Richard Leslie based on the grounds that the Medical Staff of the Hastings State Hospital, Hastings, Minnesota, had indicated he has completed his treatment and is ready to be returned to capacity.

Dated July 13, 1967.

***

Soon after, a ruling from Hachey's Court ordered Dad's discharge, another document lost to posterity. Frozen in my memory, Dad's legal rights had been restored within days of my wedding, a date that ended the confusion surrounding my legal name.

The Court released Dad four years after being assigned to psychiatric care through Hastings Mental Facility, nearly all of that time as an outpatient. His entire ordeal lasted five years almost to the day, the effects on him personally will remain the rest of his life.

My opinion, Dad's guilt having shot two men, his six months of jail time awaiting Judge Hachey's decision, and being locked up in an asylum for the criminally insane got his attention. According to my grandmother—Dad's mother—he finally admitted to having a problem, and he began to cooperate with his psychiatrist, something that he hadn't done when returning from the war. Grandmother attributes both blame and credit to my mother for trapping her son into getting married, but she changed her opinion when, as his wife, she supported her husband through those rough years.

From a young girl's point of view, I witnessed my father's behavior change from loud and aggressive to loud and passive. Dad will always express strong opinions, but he had learned to back away from any physical challenge. Perhaps the most noticeable change was his need for incessant chatter. When I hinted at his talking too much or told him outright to shut up, he quoted two rules set down by his psychiatrist, *count to ten before acting and always let your feeling out.* All other discussions between him and his psychiatrists remained Dad's secret.

Chapter Four

Groceries unpacked, I had rewarded myself with a Coke when the doorbell rang. Can in hand, I came face-to-face with my younger sister who had no reason not to be back in Illinois that I'd been aware of. Had she left Leroy? On-and-off-again relationships were common with my family but hopefully not dependable Mary Ann. She being nearest my age and my level of shared trust of all my siblings, any decision about sharing my stash of legal documents with family suddenly became more immediate.

"Come on in to my messy house. You've got some explaining to do." My usual short and to-the-point sister greeting. "I'll put some coffee on."

"Guess what." Allowing no time for any response, "We're moving to North Dakota." My reaction cut off in mid gasp, "Leroy bought a farm next to his Dad's. One hundred and eighty acres."

"That's nice." Since neither of us city girls had a clue of what an acre was, I assume she merely echoed Leroy's enthusiasm.

"It's a dairy farm."

With an image from Dad's nostalgic recounts about farm life in Wisconsin, I blurted, "Cows? Pigs? Chickens?" Replacing Dad with my sister in that picture didn't fit.

"Just cows. And a bull. Leroy don't believe in artificial whatever it's called." Spoken like a not quite yet farmer.

163

"With your kids?" A silly question, but I had trouble squeezing them into that developing scenario.

"Of course. They're excited about being with their other grandparents."

Our sons, born within days of each other, had strengthened our bond, but moving to Illinois soon after put some distance between us. North Dakota didn't feel that much closer.

Details of their decision exhausted by a second cup of coffee—and Coke, I approached my subject of interest. "Do you ever look back on those years when Dad had all his problems with the court?"

"Not without getting mad at Hachey all over again."

The importance of the research I eagerly pursued had suddenly dimmed, and might disappear entirely as far as family is concerned. It will have dead-ended with me; any of my siblings ever digging into the matter is unlikely. However, discussing the little our family knows, or think it knows, is still fair game.

"Dad's starting to drink quite heavy." *Continuing to drink*, but I needed a starting point for our conversation.

"He's welcome to join us in North Dakota. It's a big farm house and getting him away from St. Paul might be a good idea." Touching a nerve, she added, "Leroy would be a good influence on Dad."

My husband, Tim, until joining Alcoholics Anonymous, had an overwhelming influence over Dad, quite the opposite what Mary Ann suggested from her husband. I discouraged the idea. "Dad would never give up his job at Third Street Bar."

"Ma said that's temporary, just until he finds an automotive job."

"You know Dad's employment history. Always claimed to know more about the business than any of his bosses. He'd either walk away or get fired. After completing that course at Dunwoody Institute, he did have more knowledge about automatic transmissions than most." I shook my head in frustration. "Still that superior attitude."

"He did well with his beer and snacks route, until he stepped on some hoodlum's toes."

I left that false impression ride. The *hoodlum* was a local mafia boss who actually protected Dad's venturing into Wisconsin. They were old buddies. He even wanted to hire Dad as a body guard after the war. Dad refused, probably his best decision ever, and they often played cribbage until Dad met Mother. "He quit that delivery job after an attempted robbery. Some colored fellow picked on the wrong guy for drug money. When cornered, Dad will protect himself."

Mary Ann asked, "Is that when the NAACP got involved? I thought that was just one of Dad's stories."

"They defended Dad, even though one of their people got hurt pretty bad. Dad quit driving because he injured his back unloading beer barrels."

"So, he takes a job at a bar and gets involved with a motorcycle gang."

Away from St. Paul these past four years, my sister seemed well informed of family matters. My expression must have given away my surprise.

She explained, "Ma told me about some guy named Tiny and his motorcycle gang."

"Gossip hardly worth the cost of a long-distance call."

"No, not over the phone. Just yesterday, at home."

"In St. Paul? At Conway?" *Home* should refer to husband and family, not back with Mommy and Daddy. Or, maybe I'm just envious of Mary Ann's nostalgia for the place where we grew up.

"Yeah. Been back a week. I took Ma shopping and out to get her hair cut."

"Back a week already?" Trying to make light of her slight, I chuckled. "Catering to Mother's vanity."

As a child, I longed to run my fingers through her hair. She wouldn't allow me to get that close.

"What's with the gun? Ma mentioned a revolver, but didn't elaborate."

"Belongs to the bar's owner, keeps it hidden in a drawer near the cash register. A few weeks ago, Dad refused to serve one of Tiny's buddies because he was drunk and obnoxious. The guy must have stewed a couple of days before rousing the gang to rough up Dad a bit." A tidbit of information that should and did get my sister's attention. "Tiny warned Dad ahead of time, and they hatched a plan. When a bunch of motorcycles pulled up in front of the bar and the gang tromped in, Dad greeted them holding the revolver like he was John Wayne. In a calm voice he said, 'I'll serve you, but I don't want any trouble.'"

"Faking surprise, Tiny stepped forward and said, 'Oh Hell, let's just have a drink and let bygones be bygones.' They all proceeded to get drunk."

"Dad shouldn't be messing with guns, especially at a bar."

"I got on his case, too. He just sloughed me off. Claimed it wasn't even loaded."

"I'm surprised that Ma puts up with him anywhere near a gun, even if it's not loaded. She sold his shotgun while he was..." Mary Ann paused as if trying to find the right word. "Gone."

"Nearly gave it away, according to Dad. The guy took advantage of Mother because she didn't understand its real value." I accidently touched on Dad's superior attitude toward his wife and most other women. With Mother, I agree he's smarter, but she seems to have more common sense. Makes it all the more difficult for him to give up a good deal of control to her and his mother. I felt his defeat.

I changed the subject to another family trauma. "Do you remember the fire?"

Eyes lit up. "That kid could have gotten all of us burned to death. And what was his mother thinking? Shutting the closet door and leaving their apartment like nothing happened."

"The kid was a pyromaniac and she covered for him."

Mary Ann asked, "Were you home when it happened?"

A fair question. I was in junior high school and seldom hung around the apartment during the day, or even after dark, for that matter. "All eight of us kids were. Don't you remember?"

"I was only ten. But I can still picture Ma walking us to Aunt Rita's small apartment like a bunch of chicks following Mother Hen. Lucky Ma was there when the fire broke out." Mary Ann peered into her coffee cup. "Seems like she'd been gone a lot. Was she working?" Her attention focused on Mother rather than Dad.

"The job at Whirlpool came later, after Hasting put Dad on out-patient status. At the time of the fire, she kept herself busy trying to get Dad transferred out of St. Peter."

"And taking care of us kids." Mary Ann reminisced. "I remember moving to the Projects quite clearly. Less crowded than at Aunt Rita's, but the boys got the bigger bedroom, and four of us girls squeezed into the smaller one."

"We had lived there years earlier."

"I must have been a baby. How did we...?

I paused but Mary Ann failed to complete her question.

"When I got hepatitis from that filthy back yard and passed it on to our parents, Dad moved us back to the apartment on Seventh Street where we used to live with Grandma Leslie." Thinking about that place conjured many unhappy memories as a toddler. Grandma fighting with my mother and forced out of her own apartment. Mother leaving me unattended and I fell off the second story porch. My being sent back to my Wisconsin grandmother because Mother was pregnant with Mary Ann. I can still feel Grandma's swats across my butt with a willow switch.

"When did we move to the apartment on Ostego where that kid nearly burned the place down?"

"After a year or so on Simms Avenue."

Mary Ann's mood turned somber. "I remember moving often." She brightened. "Well, once Dad got out of the hospital, it didn't take him long to get us moved out of the Projects to our own house on Conway."

"Thanks to being put back on one hundred percent disability. He made the down payment with the three years back pay he received." The moment seemed right. "After nine months of lock-up at St. Peter, do you think Hastings' psychiatrists should have allowed Dad that much freedom so soon? He was barely there a month."

"No thanks to Hachey!"

"I suspect the judge made his decision and couldn't change his mind without looking weak." A deep plunge. "Dad could have gone haywire again and done something worse. Maybe even killed someone."

"Dad would never do that." Mary Ann voiced the opinion I'd shared until I read the newspaper accounts.

"That's what we thought that back then."

A childhood vision flashed of Dad asleep on the couch yelling and firing a make believe rifle into the air. Ma shooed us off to our rooms, said Dad was having a nightmare. Little did we know how his nightmare would become ours.

Mary Ann's opinion remained firm. "Well, he's a different man now." She reflected, "That part of my life is cloudy. I was still in elementary school. All I remember is crying myself back to sleep 'cause Dad wasn't there to tuck me in."

"You had Mother," a direction I hadn't intended for this conversation.

"Ma wasn't as affectionate as Dad."

"She let you brush her hair." There, it was out, my only childhood envy of any of my siblings. Mother had long soft hair but, like touching a hot stove, a second attempt didn't happen.

"Fixing her hair was my chore. We all had our jobs to do."

"I never thought of it that way." My leadership role in our family, belated but glaringly necessary, to stand up for my father as a counter to siblings who side in with our mother, or don't give a damn about either. Mute though it must be, I will maintain my opinion about our father's too casual treatment by his psychiatrist, a feeling I had resisted until researching the facts. He shot two men with little or no provocation. Location of the entry wounds indicted an intent to kill rather than just wound. Within inches, just one of the bullets would have changed Dad's charge from attempted murder to first or second degree, or an insanity plea that would have been taken more seriously.

My head tells me Judge Hachey's opinion was correct, and my heart sides in with those who diminished Dad's crime. Why hadn't I left the matter rest with family lore rather than dig into the facts? Consider the entire coverage of Dad's criminal act buried permanently, along with the curiosity of one snoopy daughter.

The conversation with my sister steered back to Dad spending time in North Dakota. I agreed to work toward that goal, if I can't get him to help himself without having to leave home.

Chapter Five

"Leroy needs all the help he can get."

"You'll just be in the way."

Dad's temporary move to North Dakota, another topic for my parents to argue about. Mary Ann got to Dad before I had a chance, and I'm not sure that's such a bad thing. At least everyone in the family—those who showed up for the barbeque at Phalen Park to see Mary Ann and Leroy off—seemed excited for him. Even Mother, who discourages Dad's impulsive decisions, offered just token resistance, agreeing to possibly join him when the heat in the city gets oppressive. I doubt she would miss him in any intimate way.

"Farms can't be that much different from when I was a kid working at Munson's in Wisconsin."

"Dad, they were farming with horses back then." I chuckled to lighten what could be a cold water splash on Dad's enthusiasm.

"A horse might not be a bad idea to ride the fence line." Leroy adjusted his suggestion in mid sentence. "I bought a pickup to handle all the utility jobs. You'll be busy in the garden with Mary Ann. A city girl, she'll need a lot of help."

I glanced at my sister for her reaction, the grimace I expected didn't show. "You ready to take on a garden?"

"Half an acre. Now that Dad is coming with us, I'm looking forward to it."

Leroy sidled closer to Dad. "This won't be anything like your dairy farm back in Wisconsin. No cows locked in rows waiting to have their teats pulled. I'm building a milking parlor."

"Parlor? Like their very own living room?" my tiny pinprick in Leroy's inflating balloon. "Maybe invite some neighboring cows over for an afternoon tea."

"Leroy's cows always come first." A glimmer of sadness written in her expression. "We won't even have a parlor in our house."

"Don't need one. What was the front room is now the office." He shot me a menacing glance. "Kitchens is where the action happens in farm houses."

"Apparently you've been to see the place." I faced Mary Ann. "Have you?"

"No need to." Leroy robbed Mary Ann the chance to express any hesitation. "She'll do just fine. You'll see when you come to visit us."

I snorted, "You stole my sister and now my father, yet you expect me to show up at your doorstep?" I maintained fake indignation, knowing it fooled no one except maybe Mother who has no sense of humor. To her the world was a dangerous place that required constant vigilance. Growing up among ten siblings in a one room converted chicken coop would make her defensive. Living with my father and eight children of her own kept her from becoming frivolous.

Mary Ann and her family including Dad departed, and my relationships simplified to one husband, two children, and some friends, mostly couples but for one or two women whose companionship I could claim as my own.

***

Dad returned that fall arms loaded with jars of tomato sauce for family and a head full of stories to share across the bar at Third Street.

Mary Ann claimed their home was alcohol free, except for 180 proof White Lightening, available in North Dakota.

Minnesota liquor laws restricted whiskey to half that strength and regulated when and where it could be sold. Leroy, on the other hand, regulated the White Lightening. Nightly, he and Dad toasted the day's work with a single shot of the stuff; fresh cream on breakfast cereal and malted milk shakes at bedtime had taken precedence over alcohol. Throughout the summer, Dad had developed a healthy tan, but an expanding belly. My sister did her part and now it's my turn.

"Dad, I would like you to join Alcoholics Anonymous. You already have two sons-in-law going and…" My practice speech didn't even convince the image in the bathroom mirror. I tested his reaction by taking his part.

"I don't have a drinking problem." I role played his defiance much too easily. His response wouldn't be that predictable. More like, "Who, Me?"

What argument could be used against such a stonewall? "Yes, you," would merely get him to dig his feet in. "Dad, I'm concerned about your drinking," or maybe, "Mother is…"

A wifely pressure might be effective, but she would never confront him directly. Just another nag from Norma? Like what? Leaving dirty socks lying around? Bad manners or personal hygiene? Or any other usual wife's complaint? Not my father. He had few, if any, socially unacceptable mannerisms. He remained a gentleman even when drinking. He may be opinionated and overbearing, but that fits my mother's complacency and docility like a glove. She could and would and did disapprove of his spending habits, but together with his mother they solved that problem after he got out of treatment. Mother continued to control their finances, with little left to nag over.

If I go to her, she'd protect Dad and deny any problem I might suggest. My siblings won't back me because they like him the way he is, even follow in his footsteps.

My grandmother could wield an influence over her only son, but she might feel I'm going behind his back. If she considered his drinking a problem, she'd have confronted him already. Maybe she has. Maybe she thinks my mother's control over the money keeps his drinking in check. She might not realize his resourcefulness with friends and influence with Mother. Once the bills are paid, Dad can talk her out of anything, always manages to get his way. Even with their meager resources, none of my siblings would deny their father beer money if he asked.

Besides, Grandma wasn't well; my aunt who cared for her suggested Grandma might be at death's door, but Dad refused to accept that prediction, at least in the near future. I can't complicate a sick woman's mind with Dad's problem.

I called my aunt to ask about Grandma's recent labored breathing. Dad's three sisters who share in their mother's care attribute her gasping for breath to anxiety caused by a fourth sister living near their father in California. During her last Minnesota visit, she spilled the beans that Grandma's estranged husband of over fifty years had passed away, not recently but four years ago. Grandma had vowed to see him into the ground, not out of spite, many in my family claimed, but because she still loved him and didn't want him to remarry. Her incentive to stay alive had ended. Whatever the cause, she was about to die and family rallied, all except the sister back in California.

I learned from my aunt that Grandma had been taken to Ramsey County Hospital in an ambulance. After a scramble to find baby sitters for when my husband was at work, I prepared to remain at Grandma's bedside until her inevitable passing. Grandma had never spent a day of her life in a hospital, and she'd resist ending her life in one. Hopefully, my presence at her bedside would offer some comfort.

Three o'clock in the afternoon two days later, Mother pulled Dad away from Grandma's hospital bed for a bite to eat and some coffee. I and two cousins—Grandma's grandchildren—remained. I approached my most favorite person in the whole world to say goodbye, not caring who heard me.

"I love you, Grandma," words I should have said more often. Grandma Leslie represented everything right and wonderful throughout my childhood. I was an infant when Dad rescued me from my Wisconsin grandma, and I assume Grandma Leslie bonded with me immediately. As a toddler, I clung to her during arguments between her and my mother. Without warning, Grandma, moved out of our apartment, but I found her new place a few doors down. I ran to her whenever I could escape, once falling off the upstairs porch. Apparently, my mother, pregnant with Mary Ann, couldn't keep a watchful eye on me. My parents decided to send me back to my Grandmother in Wisconsin. I 'm not sure what I hated the most, having to use an outhouse or being swatted with willow branches for punishment. Dad came to rescue me, and our family of six moved into the Projects, another story.

Grandma responded to my declaration of love with her eyes and a slight lifting of her chin, enough for me to believe she took an image of me with her into Heaven. A nurse came running as Grandma's throat produced a gargle loud enough to be heard outside the room.

She said, "Say your goodbye and bring the rest of the family back from the break room."

Someone, I don't remember who, ran to fetch Dad and his sisters, but I couldn't let go of Grandma's hand. When Dad burst into the room, I stepped aside. I had said my goodbye and he needed to be next.

"Is she gone?"

I nodded unnecessarily, not sure if he even realized my presence.

"Ma! Ma!" He stared into her face, but didn't touch her. "I should've been here." Then his sobbing began, interrupting anything else he tried to say.

I deciphered *horrible birthday present* among other regrets between sobs. Grandma died September 17, 1976, two days before Dad's fifty-first birthday. I'd seen him angry often, and when I visited him in jail, I saw him scared. But not until standing over Grandma's bedside did I see my father cry, and continue to sob through the funeral, reaching near hysterics at the grave site. Months later he'd break into a crying jag, mostly when drinking. I hated to see him use alcohol to wallow in pain. I needed to act.

I stopped by my parents' house to check on the two of them living alone. The moment seemed right. "Dad, I'm taking you to an AA meeting."

He grabbed his hat and said, "Let's go."

I dropped him off at the meeting where my husband and another son-in-law attended, and I waited—stood guard that he not leave and head to a local bar. I 'd been sitting in the car for over an hour when Dad's face appeared in the opened window. He pointed to a cluster of men still straggling at the back door of the VFW building. "That guy doesn't know his head from…" Dad threw up his arms in disgust, then opened the door and plopped onto the passenger seat.

"Aren't discussions at these meetings supposed to be kept private?"

"I didn't break anything confidential. We all know he's an ass."

"I hope your argument didn't involve the issue of who paid for the wedding, again."

"That guy tells everyone that he had to pay for his own wedding reception. He didn't contribute one cent. I wouldn't allow it. A father is supposed to pay for his daughter's wedding." He avoided my glare by staring out the window. Almost as an afterthought he added, "Especially a man's oldest girl."

Dad had approved my decision to marry but wouldn't even offer gas money for the drive to South Dakota where marriage was legal for seventeen-year-olds. "Need I remind you, he's still your son-in-law?"

"He's…"

I allowed silence for reflection, his and mine. Dad never waivered from his promise made to my mother before they married.

"Your children are my children, no matter who their father is." Such a wonderful and honorable statement repeated often still left open the question as to which set of the family I belonged. As a child, my life had been too complicated to bother with what might have been a trivial matter, since everyone, even teachers and school administrators, accepted my use of the Leslie family name. By the time I needed to apply for a social security number, I could legally use my husband's last name.

***

Dad spent a few summers in North Dakota, Mary Ann and I each claiming a degree of success.

When Leroy quit farming and moved his family back to St. Paul, he found Dad a job that suited his need to work alone, out from under the probing eyes of a boss who never seemed to know as much as Dad about running a business. As manager of a Fina Gas Station, no one bugged him as long as sales of gas and supplies made a profit. Men would come in to buy cigarettes and would leave with candy for the kids.

After losing the house on Conway for not keeping up payments—I blame my mother who diverted the funds, but that's a different story—my parents moved to a trailer house north of St. Paul. The knack for gardening started in North Dakota flourished at a vacant lot behind the trailer court. Ironically, he formed a co-op with Asian immigrants, the Hmong from Cambodia who were resettled in St. Paul after the Viet Nam war.

When I asked how he got along, he answered, "They ain't Japs."

Dad never told me what he felt when he first saw me, but he described in detail how he reacted when Norma told him about me.

"I had your baby," my mother's candid response when Dad asked why she had run and hid from him.

"I want to marry you and we can raise our child along with your other two," his promise made on the spot. We three children were staying with our grandparents in Wisconsin, my half sister and half brother temporarily, me destined to be permanent until my Dad changed my mother's mind.

Dad sometimes altered his version slightly, a trait he'd developed to enhance his storytelling skills, but the sequence of events remained constant. "Until Norma ran off, I thought we were getting along quite well, but even her brother and sister, who had sometimes accompanied her to Frankie and Johnnies, avoided me."

He paused and I bit my tongue to keep from breaking the spell.

"One day her brother..." sometimes Dad claimed sister..."showed up at the tavern and said that Norma agreed to talk to me."

"Were you excited to hear from her?" I asked.

"Yes. I loved her already back then, and I was hurt deeply when she left me without even a goodbye. For all I knew, she might have stopped divorce proceedings and returned to her husband."

Dad remained alcohol free and most of his social life revolved around the AA group, including his on-and-off relationship with his first son-in-law. Ultimately, a squabble between them divided the family, but I didn't care. Although my siblings split into two camps, Dad's marriage survived, as mine did not. I reverted to the obscurity from family begun in junior high, and not until 1990 when I introduced my parents to my new husband did I fall back into their clutches.

My mother died in two thousand and three and, after two attempts to move in with children in Minnesota, Dad spent the last eight years of his life with my husband and me in Las Vegas.

Part Three

Chapter One

While dining at Denny's or some other nondescript café, my significant other of three months nudged me one step further into making a relationship commitment. Laurie had been divorced over a decade, I about half that long.

She stared into her half empty coffee cup, but before I had time to assess what she might be thinking, she glance up and said, "Roger, it's time you meet my parents," like some sort of schedule she had to accomplish. "We can stop by their house next Sunday," adding, "If you don't mind."

"Sure." Much too quick to agree. "Why not?" Up until that moment, I questioned whether she actually had a family other than her two adult children. Whenever I asked about relatives, she said that I wouldn't want to know them. An actual or self-proclaimed orphan, I didn't care. I hadn't been eager to embrace another extended family, my own and that of previous in-laws were already quite extensive. However, after attending Easter services at St. Andrew's Lutheran Church—as a Catholic, I had already made that concession—we ventured to the trailer court where her parents owned a mobile home.

Her dad answered the door holding a portable typewriter. Laurie pecked his cheek and he disappeared back into the recess of the narrow trailer mumbling about some darn thing, I assume he meant the typewriter. She stepped over to her mother who stood rigid against the kitchen counter and gave her a hug. I had a moment to savor the aroma of cinnamon probably wafting off the apple pie on the cooling rack atop the counter, and to assess the situation. No sign of Laurie's older brother who moved back home with his parents, off his parents, Laurie claimed; the kitchen/dining area neat but modest, even by trailer house standards.

"Mother and Dad, I would like you to meet Roger Storkamp." She stepped back and faced her father who stepped from the hallway. "This is my Dad, Richard Leslie."

I shook his hand and we each agreed our meeting was *nice*.

"My mother, Norma."

I approached, careful to take my cues as to a hug or handshake or?

"Hello." Norma offered a weak wave of the hand, a not-ready-to-touch gesture.

I responded, "Nice to meet you."

Richard filled the conversation gap following an awkward moment. "Sit down and have some of my fresh apple pie." We squeezed around the horseshoe-shaped table taking up the front of the trailer. "It's the pie that's fresh, the apples I canned last fall."

Statement of fact or an attempt at humor?

"Dad shares a garden plot with some other people in the court."

"I got the apples from Pine Tree Apple Orchard."

I sensed condescension as if correcting his daughter. Apples come from trees, not from shared garden plots.

Norma asked, "Would you like some tea or coffee?" Apparently, we presented less of a threat when seated. Only Richard drank tea.

I found Laurie's father to be talkative but not overbearing as she had forewarned, and Norma restricted her expressions to lips curled into a half smile when I spoke directly to her. (I met her mother a year later and detected either some genetic predisposition or parallel lives of male subjugation, possible abuse.)

Our obligatory visit lasted just long enough for a cup of coffee and a piece of Richard's homemade apple pie topped with a scoop of

Schwan's Ice Cream. When Laurie suggested we leave, Richard made no protest but stood and allowed us to slide out from behind the table.

I followed her lead and extended my hand. "Nice meeting you, Richard." I approached Norma, still seated, with my hand outstretched. "You, too, Norma."

She accepted my hand and said, "Thank you."

On the drive back to Laurie's condo, I asked, "Does your father like to write?"

She chuckled. "Don't be misled by the typewriter. It's probably one of his many bargains. He loves garage sales about as much as gardening and cooking. And, of course, his AA, twenty years of sobriety."

Some shared interests, except the gardening. Richard's sobriety had nearly matched mine, although I'd stopped going to the meetings. I blurted, in my usual fashion, "You know the difference between drunkards and alcoholics?"

Laurie smiled and waited.

"We drunkards don't have to go to all them meetings."

After her obligatory chuckle, she said, "My mother would have taken that joke literally, probably telling you how important AA groups are to keeping sober." She added, "Don't you miss going to the meetings?"

"After my wife and I divorced, I just didn't seem to need them anymore."

Like her mother, Laurie seemed at a loss for comment. She didn't laugh. "Everyone in our family takes Dad's participation in AA very seriously."

The next gap in our conversation matched that at her folk's kitchen table, but this time Richard wasn't available to thaw the ice. Am I being chided for mocking some tenuous ritual, if interrupted her family would collapse?

Laurie cleared her throat. "I already told you about Dad's war experiences and how it has effected him even to this day."

"He seemed normal to me." I reminded, "World War Two has been over for forty-five years."

"That war, yes. But not the one Dad carries around with him that could erupt any time."

"Like how?"

"Like going on a rampage and shooting people. He did it once before."

"Huh?" Any loss for words comes out in a huff.

"Back in 1962, Dad shot two guys at Mickey's Diner."

Still trying to recover, I nearly whispered, "Dead?"

"No, but Dad was put away for a while."

"Then he's okay now?" I graduated beyond one word expletives.

"Yes, but even agrees the meetings help him keep focused."

"Focused?" I regressed.

"He can't remember any part of the incident, mind went totally blank. His psychiatrist told him to avoid situations that make him angry and talk out his frustrations."

"Sounds like good advice for everyone. Has it worked?"

"Too well. He has permission to dominate conversations."

My second encounter with Laurie's parents occurred at Laurie's condo in White Bear Lake, a suburb of St. Paul. She invited—pleaded with—me to spend an afternoon meeting with her parents. They had news to share, and she feared it would involve her financially, which happened quite often in the past. She and I had summer travel plans that might become compromised.

To the contrary, Norma had been awarded a settlement from Whirlpool for chemical damage to her lungs, and Richard purchased some land in Wisconsin that included an abandoned house and some out buildings. As soon as the house would be rehabbed, they would move to Wisconsin. Laurie's older brother, Bob, agreed to join them as a sort of guardian to aging parents isolated out in the country, a clue that Norma feared being alone with her unstable husband.

Richard's personality turned a one-hundred-eighty-degrees from soft spoken to bombastic, as Laurie had forewarned.

The realtor who drew up his contract, the contractor hired to make the house livable, the neighbor who plowed half an acre of garden, and the AA group that invited him to join would find out he wouldn't be taken for granted. He had scrutinized each and found them serious at their business, but they just might want to take advantage of him. He created this home for Norma and a place for grandkids to experience a taste of rural life as he had. Norma neither corrected nor supported his assertions. To my notion, he was shielding his ego from an impulsive decision already going bad.

Laurie interrupted her father and asked Norma, "What do you think of this move?"

Richard cut in, "She's the one who got me thinking about a home in Wisconsin."

Laurie shot him a glare. "I'm asking Mother."

"Go ahead, tell her, Norma." Permission granted.

"It's okay by me. It might be good for the grandkids to get away from the city once in a while." Not a strong endorsement.

Richard continued. "Bob will have his own room upstairs, and there are two more bedrooms for overnight guests. Kids might want to stay longer when school's out."

"I'm glad Bob agreed to move in with us." Norma's first comment without prodding.

"No son of mine will ever have to live on the streets." Richard offered a different slant to the arrangement.

Laurie grimaced every time her father leaned forward on the rocker and dug his heels into the carpet when he stressed a point. She attempted to change the subject, perhaps to save her carpet, and mentioned that I taught evening classes and would have to leave for work soon.

Richard exempted me in advance from his rant against teachers who wasted his and his children's time and taught them nothing. Paid too much and did too little. He recited from rote his exchange with a principal who had the affront to call him in to reprimand one of his kids. The principal admitted he and his staff made a mistake and apologized.

Heels pressed into the carpet, "I could see the problem. Kids in the upper grades had no playground. I got together with some other parents and presented my plan to the school board and to the city council."

I had become Richard's audience of one.

"There was this vacant lot, probably reclaimed by the city for back taxes, not far from the school." Heels back into the carpet, Laurie groaned. "People used it as a dumping ground, old tires and broken pieces of furniture stuck in high weeds. A bunch of us parents, kids too, brought rakes and hoes, and I used my power lawn mower. We made a ball diamond for students." He misread my sour expression and refocused. "Just for after school. We made sure they didn't skip classes to play ball."

He sat back allowing for recognition of his accomplishment.

I foolishly obliged. "When the community works together with the teachers, a lot can be accomplished."

"You know what?"

I had no way to avoid his coup de gras.

"Not one teacher out there with us working our butts off."

Norma stood, faced Richard and said, "We better go."

Disbelief, maybe even resentment, flashed across Richard's face, but he got up from the chair.

"Yeah, we got another hundred miles ahead of us." He lifted his hat, a leather western style, and brushed back the few strands of hair that had escaped the rim. His hat never left his head, at least not in my presence, even while eating.

I congratulated him for accepting a life changing challenge and wished Norma a wonderful future at her new home and thanked Laurie for inviting me to hear her parents' good news.

Parents safely out of hearing I said, "That sure was a whirl-wind visit."

"I should apologize for Dad, but I warned you about him. I doubt he realized or remembered that you are a teacher. I hope you can over look his rudeness."

I nodded my ascent and said, "Your mother certainly surprised me. She mustered the courage to confront him."

"Mother has more power in that relationship than appears on the surface."

I tested my theory. "The only other thing she admitted liking about the Wisconsin move was that your brother would be living with them. Could she maybe be frightened to live alone out in the country with your father?"

Laurie denied that possibility, explaining Norma's soft spot for her oldest boy. I dropped the subject realizing I might have crossed the line into a family taboo.

***

That summer Laurie and I tested my new Suburban as well as the endurance of our relationship by delivering a trailer load of birch tree products to customers throughout California followed by a second route along the gulf from Texas to Florida and back to Minnesota.

My birch business and a health issue—I had bypass surgery at the end of the summer—kept us from visiting her parents in Wisconsin until sometime after Halloween.

Richard's rural estate was located on a county road a few miles from Bruce, a small Wisconsin town on State Highway Eight. His two-story farm house fronted the road, and a short driveway led to a detached garage around the back and to their main entry through an enclosed mud room off the kitchen. Set back from the house stood a horseshoe-roofed barn, freshly shingled, that probably should have been torn down. A barb wired fence enclosed the buildings, and a total of seventeen acres abutted the river in back.

A menagerie greeted us; one Shetland pony, one Herford steer, a gentle St. Bernard dog and a vicious cur of no known breed, two turkeys, and random geese and chickens. And a grandson who, according to his parents, needed special grandparent attention more than he needed junior high school. Richard had pulled off his dream, but not without cost. He'd spent all of Norma's money, and their household income barely met the monthly expenses, especially with winter coming on. Laurie sensed a trap, and I covertly observed a business opportunity.

Richard had prepared a large batch of spaghetti sauce using tomatoes and assorted vegetables from his garden and meat from his freezer, allowing it to simmer for twelve hours. He served the sauce over pasta with corn on the side and cake for desert. He sent a fruit jar full of his tomato concoction home with us, but we had to pay for two dozen farm fresh eggs. We spent the afternoon surfing the hundred or so channels offered via a gigantic satellite dish in his backyard. This was my first glimpse of Richard with his guard down, no judgmental bombastic language, just a man in charge.

***

Our relationship having survived a summer of travel, Laurie and I agreed to give it a second test, my moving in with her. Richard and Norma frequently stopped to visit, always unannounced. They'd fabricate excuses to drive the two-hundred-mile-round-trip and didn't want to offend any of their *kids* by neglecting to say hello.

Richard vacillated between bragging and complaining, sometimes in the same context.

"My chickens are starting to produce eggs faster than I can sell them." A few sentences later, "People from town are lining up outside my door to get fresh eggs. I had to tell them to call ahead or they might be disappointed."

When I asked how well his produce went, he said, "They cleaned me out. Sold everything I could haul to market." A little later he'd complain that other producers were undercutting his prices. "I plowed I don't know how much stuff under rather than give it away at those prices."

Sometime he would bait me with outlandish statements. "The science teacher bought my four hundred pound pumpkin for demonstration in his classroom."

I bit my lip, but couldn't resist. "How did you get it onto your pickup, let alone into his classroom?" I didn't even tackle his exaggerated claim or why the teacher would want to have that. I blocked his muttered answer, if he even offered one.

I felt most uncomfortable when he brought up the subject of teachers or AA members, both groups, I felt, were attempts to draw me into his tirades. Teachers weren't paid enough, a dramatic shift from our earlier discussions, and certain people dominate AA meetings with their problems, his oldest daughter's husband one of them.

"You know what I mean," like our secret handshake as members of a clandestine organization.

I'd remind him, "I don't go to the meetings anymore." To his credit, he never badgered me into rejoining. I'm not sure he even heard or acknowledged what I said.

Apparently his enthusiasm toward country living had soured, and he needed to air his grievances with me, as if only another man could grasp the nuances. He colored his diatribes with "I know you would..." and, "You know that..." The more he tried to pull me in, the more I resisted.

He'd recite past dialogue with people, his part dynamic, their lines usually apologetic. If they dared to challenge him in his retelling, his voice would crescendo in rebuttal until Laurie would tell him to keep it down.

A few occasions I would say something like, "I know he or she made you mad, but they're not here now, and yelling at me isn't going to help make your point."

In response to Laurie's criticism he'd apologize and get meek. With my challenge he would just stress that the guy made him mad with his stupid whatever.

By the time Richard would get up to leave—usually after Norma's insistence—I felt exhausted. One time I rudely walked out of the room and stared at my computer screen until they were gone.

On one visit he admitted a cash flow problem, and I could sense Laurie's instant panic.

He said, "We sit around the house with nothing to do but put puzzles together, so I got to thinking." He pulled a brochure from his pocket. "Cottage industry." He tipped his leather hat that had become his trademark along with recent mutton chop sideburns and a moustache.

"For a two-hundred-dollar-investment this company will send material to make rag dolls of various sorts.

They will buy as many assembled dolls back as you care to assemble. Norma and I are both good with our hands, and I calculate we could make at least fifty dollars a month."

He looked to Laurie for approval, and I could guess what she was thinking. *A two hundred dollar donation.*

I made the bid I'd been mulling around in my mind since I first saw his gentleman farm. "How about a cottage industry that generates a hundred dollars a month with no initial investment?"

"Doing what?"

"Shaping birch twigs into various sizes of wreaths."

"How hard is it?"

"Quite easy, mostly using your fingers to fit twigs into a mold and making four or five ties. Small wreaths take less than a minute to make."

"And Norma and I can earn a hundred dollars a month doing that?"

"At least."

"Sign us up."

I glanced from Norma to Laurie, a half smile to a deep frown. Laurie's most likely reaction, *now you've invited them completely into our lives.* My reaction, a mutually beneficial arrangement and some common ground on which to base a relationship with Richard Leslie, Laurie's fear not unfounded.

Chapter Two

Richard's hypothetical two-hundred dollar investment to make rag dolls became my five thousand dollar investment to produce birch wreaths; quantities of plywood to cover the loft's rotted floor boards—barn's lower level reserved for the animals— and stairs to replace the rickety ladder, wreath-making molds and supplies, a pickup for Bob to scout wood cutters and purchase birch branches as raw material—he agreed if I allowed personal use of the truck—and various tools whose purpose I never quite understood; all the while *I told you so* occasionally escaping my wife's sealed lips.

Richard sorted material and assembled wreathes, and Norma drilled and strung small logs to form fences. Customer demand for wreaths remained strong, but Norma's fences had a limited market. She enjoyed earning money, and I hadn't the heart to discourage her production. Inventory grew. She gave most of her income to Bob, irritating Laurie and Richard, but it didn't bother me. My inherited mother-in-law had become my buddy, and I developed a working relationship with Laurie's father.

Richard and I discussed business matters as if we ran a major corporation. He became overly conscious not to offend my sensibilities, my politics, or my career as a teacher. However, he often stepped over the line into areas of sales and overall operation of my company.

The problem came to a head during a business trip to Las Vegas, where I leased a booth for the Silk Show at the Convention Center to display my products. My business partners, Laurie and her three family members, convinced me that Richard's traveling along would be good for both of us.

I felt manipulated, but in retrospect, I probably would have suggested it if they hadn't. I had a somewhat voyeuristic interest in the gruesome details of his experiences with special forces in the Philippines; segments of which had come out in bursts and then receded like the enemy cannon he reported to Captain So-and-So, who ignored Richard's warning. His most unbelievable scenario, Douglas McArthur centered in his rifle's crosshairs as the five star general waded ashore at Corregidor.

Before heading cross country, I purchased his return airline ticket.

Richard talked to me almost nonstop while riding in the Suburban, and to anyone who would listen at truck stops, restaurants, and motels. He opened up about his past. I'd ask a question, and he'd string events like beads in a rosary, until I'd ask for clarification on some aspect. On that tangent, he'd ramble until I'd redirect. Later, I regretted not recording some of our conversations, especially concerning his war stories. Apparently, he felt safe sharing them with me. Unfortunately, I discounted most because of his obvious exaggerations. I had no basis for criticism except when the body count exceeded the amount of ammo available

I smirked. "They must have stood in line to get shot."

"It was a bonzai attack," trumped my attempt to discredit.

Our expedition progressed without incident, interrupted by deliveries. In Des Moines, our first stop, I climbed atop the ten foot high load—my trailer was a flatbed with side rails—and threw down birch poles, twig bundles, and wreaths.

He dodged the first few items and said, "You hand the product to me and I'll stack it."

"That's not necessary. I usually toss down the complete order. We can stack and double check the count later." He ignored me, stepping into the line of fire.

"Oops." A wreath hit him on the shoulder. "Stand back."

"It's not good to let them pile up."

"They won't get damaged. I even stand on the wreaths up here." A flash of his methodical wreath making procedures and inventory precisely stacked and counted in his loft, as well as his orderly kitchen when cooking or baking, and I relented. "Okay, but be careful. I can't always see you from up here."

He paid no heed to my warning. Product got stacked and then restacked, an unnecessary step. I chalked it up to his meticulous nature.

I crawled down and began to fasten straps to secure the remaining load. I yelled, "Coming over," and tossed the strap across the top. "How does it look on your side?" Not a serious question, because I could tell if the strap landed proper.

"A little further back," he advised. "A little bit ahead…that bundle sticks out…this strap is twisted…you should oil these ratchets…you have enough straps."

Stay out of my way, something I would never say while I went about my business as I had for many years without help. Back on the road, I pouted and he read road signs aloud making comments like, "You don't say," or reading a *one way* sign, he'd joke, "We can only go one way." He'd talk to birds, trees, fences, and cattle. He's say things like, "How are you today Mrs. Cow?" or "Mr. Horse?" And most annoying, *beep, beeping* every time I'd pass a slow moving vehicle, or we'd disturb a crow eating some road kill.

I decided to introduce conversation. "Laurie tells me that you were quite a bowler."

"I missed my perfect game by one pin," and the incident unfolded frame-by-frame. Usually Richard's stories grew as he dramatized them, but this one started at the top. The small details or the exact dialogue he recreated to enhance an incident forty years ago annoyed me.

I resented his know-it-all attitude. I'd cringe every time he'd reach the "...and I told him..." part of an exchange or his "...had to admit I was right," conclusions. Sometimes he'd get caught up in his exaggerations, like the four hundred pumpkin from his *garden*. One narrative it got him fifty dollars, and in another he donated it. His most extreme over-the-top-exaggeration, getting paid a dollar per mile for driving a truck to California back in the forties.

I exclaimed, "Four thousand dollars for a week's work."

"Yes." He nodded and held firm.

"Why didn't you keep that job?" A slight jab at his inconsistent work record.

"Didn't want to be away from my family."

"Drivers today only earn twenty cents a mile." I pounded my point home. "I can lease a truck, driver and fuel included, for a dollar a mile."

He responded, "I had to pay my own expenses."

And coffee was a nickel a cup. I bit my tongue.

I understand he just wanted to entertain with a good story, but to me, he was boosting his ego. Rethinking my *older brother comparison*—Richard being fifteen years my senior—most of what he said and did annoyed me.

Not withstanding his exaggerations, he was completely honest with his failings in his past. Apparently years of counseling following his tragic relapse in the sixties taught him to release rather than repress.

Again, I could have used a recorder for years later when he finally agreed to let me publish his war memoirs. Up until then, he continued to follow orders to keep his regiment's existence a secret, fifty years after the war. He claimed the 503rd Airborne Regiment had been expunged from all military records, his cloud of mystery, another ego boost. I made a personal commitment to check this out the next time I had access to a computer.

In Phoenix, I delivered product to an Asian couple. When husband and wife came out of the house, he scrambled back into the truck and wouldn't step out, very unusual because he'd talk to any customer or passerby who'd show an interest.

After a few quiet miles of silence, he said, "Next time warn me who we're meeting."

"They were Vietnamese, not Japanese." I sensed the problem.

"I know, but tell me in advance."

I agreed and even apologized, although I thought he was merely making a point. I had yet to realize his ingrained reactions to Asians.

To change the subject, I said, "If you want to see an interesting natural formation, take a look outside your window." The road swung to the left, and I entered a suspension bridge. The deep gorge suddenly came into view from the passenger side.

Richard screamed and stressed his seat belt trying to climb across the center console. He remained frozen in that position until we reached the other side.

Embarrassed, he sat back and said, "I'm afraid of heights."

I knew about his experience falling off a bridge on a construction site, left dangling until help arrived, but I had no idea he'd developed vertigo.

I repressed my irritations with him until that afternoon when we arrived at the motel in Kingman, Arizona. Richard's sister, Margaret, whom he hadn't seen for forty years, lived a few miles out of town with her husband. They knew we were in the area, but hadn't offered to put us up for the night.

We checked in, and I suggested he relax in the lobby, while I separate out the product for display at the Convention Center. He ignored my suggestion.

He took a strap out of my hand. "Here's a better way to do it." I stood back and counted to ten, or more.

After many attempts to align the straps and pinching his finger in the ratchet, he said. "I better get in out of the heat."

I finished reworking the load and went to check if he was okay. I found him in the lobby talking to a totally engrossed elderly couple, describing *our* birch business, details of production, distribution and, of course, the Vegas Silk Flower Convention. I slipped past them, on to our room, and took a shower. When I returned, I found him dozing on the lounge chair, but he snapped awake when I approached.

"Are you interested in dinner?"

"Well, I better eat something, but I'm kind of tired."

"There's a McDonald's across the street." I hesitated, knowing his need for sit-down meals, in restaurants served by a waiter, at his home served by him or Norma. Laurie's parents never stayed for dinner at our place when we lived in Minnesota.

"Sounds good. Let's go."

Our first of many fish filet sandwiches over the years, often eaten in the car.

***

The security gate already open with a lock the size of a small baseball mitt dangling, I decided to enter Margaret's fenced-in yard. Other than six tall torpedo-shaped cedar trees masking her trailer home, the two-and-a-half-acre lot consisted of natural desert terrain. I could easily turn around and not have to back out onto the road, always a consideration when towing a twenty-four-foot trailer. I could have left it back at the motel, but hooking and unhooking took too much time. I needed to get to Vegas.

A woman whose facial features matched my passenger, greeted us from the front step. She and Richard hugged briefly.

"Margaret, I'd like you to meet my son-in-law, Roger Storkamp."

My startled reaction—hopefully not noticeable—not caused by Margaret's appearance but hearing Richard state our relationship. I usually introduced Richard by name, leaving our relationship vague or mentioning he was Laurie's father. I had a ninety year-old father-in-law from my previous marriage who was a contemporary with my deceased father. I resisted Richard taking either of their places.

I shook Margaret's hand. "Nice to meet you."

She led us into their front room and stepped aside. I might have contained my reaction when introduced to Margaret, but I couldn't hide my shock when I saw her husband. It had been Richard's turn to not prep me about whom we were meeting.

Richard approached and shook his hand. "How are you doing, Bob?"

"I'm good, still the same guy who married your sister, with some minor alterations. Who's that with you?" Two clouded eyes searched for me.

"I can see some movement when you stand in front of the window." He held out his hand. "I'm Bob Attencio."

I hesitated to approach.

"You must be Lorraine's new fellow. I'd come to you, if I still had legs."

"I'm Roger." I shook his hand and melted. "

Bob patted our joined hands and pulled me closer. "May I touch your face?"

I shall never forget the warmth that man exuded. I knelt, about to be knighted, as his fingers explored my features. All anxiety evaporated.

"Laurie—I know her as Laurie but her family still calls her Lorraine—told me about your health issues."

"I only met her once. She was just a child, and I still had my sight and at least one working leg."

Margaret had directed us to chairs across from Bob, while she sat off to the side at the kitchen table, as if we had come to see her husband.

Richard faced Bob and said, "I'm diabetic, too," and continued to enumerate his other health problems. No one was allowed more physical ailments than Richard. Margaret, a stoic, who I learned later never complained, nodded politely.

When I realized that Bob and I carried on most of the conversation, I felt a need to redirect. Between Richard and Margaret tucked behind the kitchen table, forty years of silence continued.

I wandered to the side of the table opposite Margaret, able to maintain eye contact with all three of them. "Richard tells me you are the older sister assigned the task of caring for him as a child."

Richard started to retell the incident, as if we were still the twosome driving out here. "Margaret used to carry me on her hip. I was five and she was ten."

I interrupted facing the older sister in this scenario. "Wasn't he heavy?"

"He was just a whippersnapper of a kid. Got under Ma's feet in the kitchen, so I'd drag him across the tracks and set him down along side the road."

"I was fascinated with the old cars that drove by."

"But they weren't old back then, were they?" I couldn't let any fabrications go unchecked.

"Farmers came to town with Model A Fords and a few Model T's."

"We'd wave and hope they'd blast their horn at us." Seventy years just slipped past Margaret. "Truckers and Engineers too. Our father was a railroad conductor."

Three way conversation flowed smoothly, as I sat back and absorbed their history, especially when it included Margaret's second husband whose eyes appeared to locate whoever was speaking.

Occasionally I'd hear, "And you know what...?" a comment usually directed at me. Perhaps their forty-year estrangement required an unbiased observer as a backboard to bounce off their personal histories.

Margaret dutifully dropped out of the conversation to prepare lunch. We ate, said our goodbyes, and began the final leg of our journey to Las Vegas. Richard needed no prodding to reminisce all the way to the Hoover Dam where he as everyone else stood in awe of its grandeur.

He said, "I worked construction on that dam."

As a nine year old I cruelly considered but bit my tongue.

***

One day prior to the Silk Show, Richard and I checked in at the Stardust Hotel and unhooked the trailer in their truck lot. I jammed product inside the Suburban, and on the luggage rack I strapped a quantity of ten foot poles used to construct my display.

I dreaded Richard's interference, while I built easels and tripods and trellises with the poles.

I bypassed the official loading dock to avoid their hefty charges and lugged my material from my vehicle to the assigned ten-by-ten foot booth. Richard carried the wreaths and bundles he had prepared especially for this occasion, but he agreed to stay indoors and rest when I went back for a second load.

By the time I returned, he had collapsed onto a chair. No one bothered to turn on the air conditioner, and the temperature inside the convention center exceeded that outside in the glaring sun. He refused to drink warm water, so I doused his neck and walked to the refreshment station to buy chilled bottles. He took a few sips and asked to go back to the hotel. I agreed but insisted he stay in the lobby around people rather than alone in our room.

By late afternoon, I had assembled my display and returned to find Richard happily playing a slot machine.

"Feeling better?"

"Yes, but I'm very hungry."

He held our place in the buffet line, while I went to the rest room and washed my face and hands. No one seemed to notice my dirty sweated-in clothes and sneakers.

Richard attended the booth with me each day until lunch time, when I drove him back to the hotel. The last day of the show, I sold my display, and we celebrated with a steak dinner at William B's, no wine since we were recovering alcoholics.

The next day I dropped him off at the airport and continued on my way to California.

***

By 1997, Richard and Norma were netting over $3500 a year, and I was able to turn a profit. However, Laurie's fear also materialized.

Early one evening, I came home to find my wife and her parents seated around our living room wearing somber expressions.

Laurie approached, brushed a kiss on my cheek, and faced her father. "Well, here he is. You can ask him." She wandered into the kitchen.

Richard planted his heels into the carpet. "Eagle River County has a new regulation for the construction of cesspools."

"Are you thinking of replacing your present one?"

"It's so full of sediment, I have to get it pumped way too often. Costing a fortune. But the darn county won't let me just dig a new one. I gotta build a mound above the natural terrain and create a drain field around it." He studied the track he had made in the carpet. "Should get it done before the snow flies."

Laurie returned from the kitchen and handed me a cup of coffee. "Dad wants to know if he can have an advance in wages to pay for it." Her attempt either to nudge her father to make his point or to save the carpet in front of his chair.

"Now that the leaves are off the birch trees, we can increase production to make payments."

"Doesn't the county offer to pay and then place an easement on the property?"

"There's a government fund to cover half, but I got to come up with the rest."

"How much?" I glanced at Laurie but got no help with my decision. Richard had recently repaid what he borrowed to cover his real estate taxes, and I anticipated he'd need help with fuel oil this winter.

"Five hundred dollars. There's a local contractor who's doing a bunch of them, and we got sort of a group price."

"Well, you're going to have to get it done sooner or later, so we better take advantage of that federal money. Hire the contractor and send Laurie the bill." I purposely drew her into the decision. *They are your family, after all*, my response to her *I warned you about them*. My flippant attitude about family involvement might have been a premonition of a crisis that pulled her family together and then alienated members worse than before.

Chapter Three

Shortly after the start of the 1998-99 school year, a fellow teacher stopped me in the hall and said, "Laurie's parents have been in a car accident." No details other than his student, Richard's grandson, received the information via his cell phone. I wouldn't expect his family to inform me and not Laurie, but I double checked to see if she had heard. She hadn't. Her office about ten blocks out, a taxi or bus would have gotten her to Regents Hospital faster than waiting for me. She walked—ran the distance.

When I arrived, the nurse allowed me to join my wife staring through a window into the emergency receiving area. Laurie grabbed my arm but didn't take her eyes off the team of gowned medical staff attempting to revive her mother.

"We lost her!" No sound, but lip movement and facial expression penetrated the double-plated glass.

Laurie's fist clamped tighter, neither of us spoke. A flurry of activity and a few expressions of success, or hope, permeated our hearts, as lips formed, "She's back." We had witnessed her death and revival. I could hardly wait to ask Norma about her experience in the afterlife. As it turned out, she didn't recall anything from moments before the accident to waking in the recovery room.

Richard's injuries were not life threatening, broken ribs and a concussion, but he suffered permanent physical and emotional consequences. Concerned about his mental state, the doctors withheld information about his wife's injuries and kept them separated for a couple of days. It drove him crazy.

His most serious repercussion plagued him the rest of his life; he had been driving—it appeared to have been his fault. Ultimately, a law suit filed against the driver, Norma's husband, awarded to the passenger, Norma Leslie, a settlement that affected Richard's already low self esteem and created more dysfunction than usual within the family.

I visited Richard and Norma in the hospital, but Laurie slept on a reclining chair alongside her mother's bed most nights during her months-long confinement. Laurie's reward: a sense of mother-daughter bonding for the first time in her life. Years later, after Norma succumbed to dementia, she inquired why Laurie never came to see her in the hospital. Resentment, we concluded, caused certain family members to manipulate her mother's memory, a rift within the family that would never heal.

Released from the hospital but unable to live on their own, Richard often lamented, "I lost my country dream home," a stinging jab directed at the daughter who negotiated the sale of his property.

Laurie defended her actions. "Dad, you and Mother couldn't survive out in the country. She's on oxygen and you don't have a driver's license."

"I asked the doctor if I could still drive, and she said, 'Not if I have to be on the same road with you.'" Typical Richard, complaining about yet exaggerating his infirmities.

Laurie reminded her father of his new fiscal responsibility. "Money from the sale has to last you and Mother the rest of your lives." She invested her parents' money in a ladder of CD's, later adding the insurance settlement, that extended ten years with built-in penalties for early withdrawal.

A few years later when she gained total control of his finances, four of the CD's had been cashed ahead of their maturity date.

While Richard looked to Laurie for support, Norma sought refuge from a different faction of the family; workable for the time being, but the division bound to accelerate.

Laurie developed a chronic stomach disorder that forced her from her job, and I decided to take an early retirement from teaching. We moved to Las Vegas where my birch product production in Minnesota continued to function without the Leslie family input.

Richard brought Norma to visit us in Las Vegas twice before her dementia set in; before the festering between factions of the family ruptured like a boil. Laurie was denied entry into her sister's house where Norman and Richard lived, and all phone messages were ignored.

Norma passed away July 2, 2003, but Laurie had already grieved the loss of her mother a year earlier. We chose not to cause a family disruption by attending her funeral. Richard's forced separation from us continued.

During one of our business trips back to Minnesota, Laurie's sister, Mary Ann, who had avoided taking sides throughout the ordeal, leaked information about Richard convalescing from pneumonia at a nursing home. After hours, Laurie and I made a surprise visit. Like King Lear realizing he made a bad daughter choice, Richard cried at the reunion.

"You could at least have called us." I threw a wet towel on the happy occasion.

"I would have been kicked out with no place to live. Norma and I could stay, but I had to obey house rules. Would have been forced out without my wife." Richard sobbed.

A fear all too real; due to our interference, when his lungs cleared up, he was no longer allowed back into his home.

Laurie and MaryAnn debated where to move their father. I took a firm stand against Richard moving to Las Vegas. Mary Ann's husband, Leroy, offered Richard a room in their house at Big Lake, Minnesota, a small town eighty miles from St. Paul. With each of them working full time, their empty house throughout the day left Richard feeling isolated from family and friends.

Laurie invited her dad to spend a week with us in Las Vegas. We took him to visit his sister in Kingman, Arizona, a hundred miles south of Vegas, the entire distance on the way back filled with silence. We had barely left Margaret's yard when Richard announced, "I made up my mind to spend winters in Las Vegas and summers at MaryAnn's."

"I suppose we could find an assisted living arrangement." I had to deflect his obvious intent.

"Oh, my daughter would never put me in a home."

Including my home, I decided immediately, and brooded all the way back to Las Vegas.

I told Laurie *no way!* and she began searching temporary housing for her father, until a major relapse hospitalized her for weeks. Richard had been granted his winter home, and New Year's day, 2005, I drove through a snow shower to pick him up at the McCarran Airport, which became one of his favorite anecdotes.

"When I came to Las Vegas, I brought Minnesota weather with me."

Near the end of our turn with Richard living in Vegas, his family decided the desert climate suited his health much better than Minnesota; he wasn't invited back.

Laurie applied for the first opening at Destinations Assisted Living, while I shuttled a few of his belongs to Vegas with each trip I made to Minnesota for birch. June, 2005, Richard rode back with Laurie and me to close his accounts and to transport his remaining possessions; mattress strapped atop the Suburban, boxes crammed in back, and electric scooter tucked under my load of birch on the trailer. Laurie, her father, his and our dogs, and me for the painful four days to cover the seventeen hundred mile stretch.

At his new apartment, Richard experienced living alone for the first time in his life. He had shared kitchen duties with Norma when their kids were growing up, and he took over complete responsibility for meals when they moved to Wisconsin. But he stymied when preparing meals just for himself.

"Buffets are so cheap." He peered across the kitchen table at his checkbook, while Laurie marked off the cancelled checks. "It would cost more for me to eat at home."

"Four hefty cash withdrawals this month certainly wasn't just for those cheap casino brunches."

"I gamble a little bit. It gets too boring just sitting around here. Most of the time I just go to study the people."

Waiting for the shuttle after running out of money. Not bothering to sit because Laurie said we would stay just a minute or two, I assessed his situation. Basket of dirty clothes, calendar marked for doctor appointments, and a shopping list, all needing our assistance while the casinos drain his savings.

Then, another crisis, one to change his life and ours for the next eight years. While walking his dog within the secured area, a man approached and introduced himself as the son of a neighbor.

The father, according to the son, was deathly ill and needed to have documents witnessed at a local bank. Richard and his dog, Salomon, got into the car and didn't return until $1800 dollars had been withdrawn from Richard's account at Wells Fargo with a promise—threat—of a return visit the next day. To repay the debt. The guy came back, but only to demand more money.

When Laure and her father did routine checkbook maintenance, she demanded, "What in the world was this chunk of cash for?"

Richard shifted in his chair. "Do you think I might have taken the money and can't remember doing it?"

"Well, where's the cash?" She glared. "Did you gamble it away?"

"No. I always use the ATM, never more than three hundred dollars at a time." He stood and reached across the table and pointed. "See those withdrawals."

Laurie admitted she had noticed them.

"The guy's father…he's my neighbor…was dying and needed a document witnessed…I got into his son's car with Salomon." Between gasps, he said, "I know I shouldn't have done it, but it was for my neighbor."

The neighbor turned out to be someone in good health who had no documents that needed signing and who had no knowledge of a supposed son. As Richard's story unfolded, we realized the money was lost, and so was a good deal of Richard's dignity. Police investigations kept his painful memory fresh until a year later when summoned to court to identify a man who'd been accused of preying on vulnerable senior citizens. Despite pressure to add another crime to an already long list, Richard admitted he couldn't positively identify the accused. I felt proud of his integrity, Laurie felt he responded out of fear.

Immediately following the incident, Richard certainly felt intimidated. "I can't stay there. I know he will come to get me. Told me not to tell anyone…that he would…." Richard whispered, "He came back." He glanced from Laurie to me. "I didn't let him in, but he said he'd be back again." Richard closed his eyes. "I can't live there any more," his pronouncement through tears, but a firm assertion none-the-less.

"You can move in with us." My comment surprised all three of us. I saw no other choice. "And you can pay us just half of what it costs to live at Destinations." My decision was neither impulsive nor selfless. His needs had consumed all of Laurie's energy, much of my time, and many miles driven for his medical needs, entertainment, and church activities. He had befriended a female resident whom he dated, double dated, since both needed transportation. We already lived together yet five miles apart.

Laurie added to the equation. "I want complete charge of your finances so this sort of thing doesn't happen again."

The deal had been negotiated with no protest, only expressions of relief, mine as well as Richard's. Laurie smiled.

Chapter Four

The newsletter from the 503rd Combat reunion featuring the review of their recent convention lay face up on the kitchen table alongside the opened Variety Section of the *Las Vegas Review Journal.* Jointly completing crossword puzzles had become one example of cooperative spirit that developed between Richard and me since he moved in with us. He would be quite sure that I would check on his progress with the morning's puzzle.

The pride of a few octogenarians short of a platoon billowed and blossomed like parachutes that dropped them onto Japanese-held islands in the South Pacific sixty-five years ago. As the mythical bird that rose from its own ashes, the former paratroopers gathered in Phoenix, Arizona, to resurrect the 503rd Airborne Combat Regiment from the dusty pages of history.

As my father-in-law, Richard Leslie, registered at the hotel, Laurie and I gazed at the wall-to-ceiling poster in the lobby; *General Jones and His 3000 Thieves Have Landed.* Her father's stories about the antics of his regiment had been confirmed, and I eagerly awaited meeting his war buddies.

Although accounts of battles were rehashed, most conversations centered around the bonding of the men, their wives and families, and, of course, honoring fellow members who had mustered out since their last meeting.

A videographer circled among the groups to record eye witness accounts of various battles for a website. Official photos from both governments and candid snapshots from American and Japanese cameras supplemented the regiment's history.

One member from the group had removed the film from cameras of fallen enemy and sent them home for souvenirs. The dozen or so Japanese survivors of Corregidor, with whom the group had recently established contact, might also be interested in the website.

The five day conference culminated with a business meeting followed by a banquet. Rather than merge their association with the 101st Airborne's, the members endorsed the last-man-standing rule for the retirement of their flag.

In the course of five short days, Laurie and I gained insights into the horror of war, its affect on the men who experienced combat, and the human bonding that resulted. We have a deeper understanding of, and respect for, the torment that plagued her father most of his life. Our greatest generation must not be forgotten.

Roger Storkamp
September 2009

"That's a nice account of the convention that you wrote," came his voice from in front of the silent TV.

"Thanks." I sat on the rocker alongside his electric lift chair, grabbed the remote, and unmuted the John Wayne Western he'd been watching. He slipped off his headphones, his concession to peace and quiet in our house, and together we watched and guffawed as the bad guys died from gunshot without complaint.

"Getting killed doesn't happen that quick. There should be a lot of squirming and screaming."

"Speaking of killing and dying, I read what you wrote about your war experiences. It's a pretty good start." As I anticipated, he began with the option he faced as a teenager, jail or the Army.

"I can't write like you can. My hand doesn't cooperate with my brain. Ever since the accident…"

He either caught my grimace or realized that his accident a dozen years back had become a scapegoat for his overall failing health. Two minor strokes had affected his equilibrium and, after a number of falls, Laurie insisted he use a walker. The VA had recently sent a wheel chair which he had yet to use.

"I can't spell, and what I write doesn't make sense."

"That's because you're a reader, not a writer." I avoided the possibility of him dying without getting his experiences down on paper. After the convention, he did a one-hundred-and-eighty degree concession about eye witness accounts of the battles. The 503rd Regiment was no longer a secret or covert operation. "My offer still holds. If you dictate what you remember, I'll edit and type it."

"Just the war years and no publishing until after I'm gone."

We consummated our agreement as John Wayne mowed down a passel of Indians.

With the input from three more annual conventions of the 503rd to refresh his memory, numerous interview-like discussions between us, and many drafts followed by *that's not quite the way it was*, we created the first person narrative of his war experiences.

Our six years under the same roof, Richard opened his entire life to me, not just the war experiences. When Margaret moved to Las Vegas after Bob died, we'd meet and discuss family matters that would trigger Richard's memory of interesting family interplay, enough for a complete biography. Perhaps his most significant introspection, as with most people, occurred during his final years on earth. For instance, Richard reinstated the daughter he had previously disinherited.

An earlier assertion, "No other woman could ever replace Norma," faded to, "Do you think Dorothy would accept a ring? She's younger...."

Twenty years younger, and she took herself out of the picture when, in my opinion, the relationship became too intimate. One Sunday on our way to church, I knocked on her door—steps to her second floor apartment too difficult for Richard to negotiate—but no response. She had moved to New York without advance notice nor any good bye to Richard.

As it turned out, she hadn't run from an entangled relationship, but an attempt to rebuild one with her estranged son back East. The effort unsuccessful, she returned to Las Vegas four years later humbled and embarrassed, but Richard's interest had cooled.

"I could never trust that she would be there for me." A different revelation probably contributed to his reluctance to reestablish any permanent relationship.

"I'm eighty-five years old and no one in my family ever lived beyond age eighty-seven."

Laurie accepted her father's desire to remain single, but denied his premonition of dying within two years. However, she invited Dorothy into our intimate circle for social events; movies, dining in or out, etc. Despite embedded feelings of rejection, Richard enjoyed Dorothy's companionship, always reminding us the she was basically *your* friend. Unfortunately, due to a perception of them being a couple, or the opposite, just being tolerated, Dorothy skipped town again without ever having to leave Las Vegas. She closed her door to us.

"At least they aren't laughing at me," Dorothy's explained when I encounter her after church one Sunday.

Rather than a single close relationship, Richard participated in two closely knitted groups; his poker pals of mixed genders and a veteran's support group, each meeting once a week. He and I attended an Alcoholic Anonymous meeting once, but that need in our lives had long past.

My relationship with Richard grew from functional—I delivered him places as part of our rental agreement—to one of genuine friendship. Even his annoying quirks became quite palpable.

When the pain specialist asked his pain level on a range from one to ten, Richard would respond , "Eleven or twelve." He had become a hypochondriac, and I had to keep reminding myself that excessive doctor visits were included in our financial arrangement. I quit my frequent business trips to Minnesota, partly to accommodate Richard's medical needs and partly because Laurie had developed breast cancer, but mostly because it had become too difficult for me. I was about to embark on my seventh decade.

His final concern, "I'm going to be too much of a burden for you and Laurie to handle," said as I diapered and bathed him.

"You're going to leave this house in a wooden box," brought a smile and I hoped some relief from his fears. I never doubted I could take care of the man I had learned to love and respect.

Enter Richard's final phase of needing care, our relationship became as intimate as father-son. Months before he died, I escorted him back to Minnesota for a granddaughter's wedding, and weeks before he died, a son and a daughter along with their families came to visit. He treated us to a final dinner at his favorite casino where we openly toasted his life with a glass of wine. He and I had broken our combined half-century of sobriety a few times prior, but this was meant to be a public statement.

Attending Richard on his deathbed, I realized what I'd stubbornly resisted for nearly a quarter century, he had become a stand-in for my long-deceased father, and possibly an imaginary older brother whom I respected and resented in equal quantities.

With Hospice as a back up, we placed his bed in the family room where Laurie and I took turns sitting with him, she calling me if he had a bowel movement during her watch. The night before he died, she had to wake me twice, and after the last diapering, I took an early turn at his bedside. About midnight his breathing became rattled. I called Laurie and we held his hands while his breathing slowed and then stopped. We alerted hospice, as instructed, and a representative arrived so quickly we assumed she'd been circling like a buzzard over carrion.

"Should I pull out his catheter and empty the bag?"

"Just leave everything as is. They'll come for the body shortly." She gathered all his medicine including the pump attached to the the patch on his arm. "Is this everything?"

Laurie retrieved an armful of bottles from his bathroom, and the hospice lady selected everything narcotic, emptied contents in a fresh diaper, and drenched the concoction under the faucet.

"Where do you store Richard's messed diapers?"

I opened the door to our patio, lifted the lid on the container, and stood back.

She dropped the bundle inside and chuckled. "No one will try to salvage this to sell on the streets."

I replaced the lid, grateful Richard's ordeal hadn't occurred during the hot summer months.

The body gatherers arrived and Richard left our/his home in a body bag, not a wooden box as promised.

Easter Sunday, 1990, Richard Leslie breezed into my life at his home in St. Paul, Minnesota; I whispered my final *goodbye* as he exhaled his last shallow breath at our home in Las Vegas, Nevada, on Good Friday, 2013, at 3 AM.

Part Four

Introduction

"Sir, I present you Fortress Corregidor."
Col. Jones to General McArthur, March 2, 1945

Friends and family have been pestering me for years to write about my war experiences, but I resisted. Parts are easy to think about, but some are very hard. With the help of my son-in-law, Roger Storkamp, to make sense of my chicken scratching and my ramblings, I am ready to give an honest account of my actions as a paratrooper in the South Pacific during the war with Japan.

I was inducted into the Army at Fort Snelling, Minnesota, December 11, 1943 and mustered out twenty-five months later. Those two plus years have defined the remaining years of my life.

I request this memoir not be made available to the public until after I'm gone.

Richard Leslie 9/19/1925 – 3/29/2013

Author's notes

Living with Richard the last eight years of his life, his war experiences have practically become mine, to the extent that his inner voice came naturally to me. A reader might question my literary style representing the voice of a man who earned a high school equivalency in his fifties.

He might not have been a skilled writer, but he read extensively all his adult life. His views, often opinionated, were supported by keen observation, interest in history and current affairs, and a logical mind. Even in his eighties, he remained sharp.

Throughout his last year, as his short-term memory continued to fail, details of his war experiences almost seven decades earlier became more precise. From a roster of his 503rd Regiment, he recalled the names of his squad and those officers he served under.

From an atlas, he traced the movements of his "d" battery, and described his experiences in each combat zone. After taking notes during each of our sessions, I created a narrative for him to read and make changes.

The primary focus of any recalled memory is sometimes interrupted by random past or present events that pop up, often breaking the train of thought. In a novel, this constant foreshadowing and flashbacking interrupts the flow of the plot, but in a memoir, it reflects how the human mind works.

During our conversations, train-of-thought interruptions produced some of the more interesting details of combat life and offered a window into Richard's character. Such triggered memories become especially significant when the individual has been trained to kill people.

I included historical details that Richard could not have known at the time and probably information he hadn't concerned himself with since then. I felt it gave his part in the conflict some perspective. Some details, especially in dialogue, have been created; I took poetic license to enhance Richard's story. The facts stand for themselves.

***

President Truman's letter to Richard stated; *You have done enough for your country. It is time for your country to take care of you.*

He should have added ...*because your toughest battles lay ahead.*

Divisions of Location
Rather Than Chapters

Fort Snelling, Minnesota

A catch-22, I had to join the Army to avoid going to jail, but the military would not accept me with a criminal record. It took six months to get my record cleared, but I no longer had to lie about my age or get Mother's permission since I turned eighteen that September. I doubt she would have consented to sending her second son into war. The district judge gave me an early birthday present, but I didn't get to open it until three months after my birthday.

After receiving my army uniforms, a sergeant assigned my barrack and ordered to change into olive drabs before reporting back outside. After an officer checked us recent inductees, he gave the group the rest of the day off. I could have requested a day pass at the head office to go back into town until 2200 hours, but I didn't feel homesick. I had already spent two summers isolated on a Montana ranch herding sheep. I concerned myself with learning the military jargon.

After a week of boredom reading the Army Manual and memorizing the ten commandments of military behavior, I requested a day pass (0800-1600 hours) and caught a bus to my home in St. Paul. When my mother saw me in uniform, she hugged me tight.

She sobbed, "My son. My son. They took Edward and now you too."

I spent the afternoon with friends including Patsy with whom I still keep in touch. My next pass didn't happen until after basic training.

I was assigned the job of night clerk, taking calls, checking that all personal were back from leave by 2200 hours, and waking the men who were assigned to KP duty at 0400 hours. Into my fourth week at Fort Snelling, I earned a night free of duty, a chance to catch up on some sleep.

At 0230 the sergeant of our barracks yelled, "Everyone up! Pack your bags. We're pulling out."

I headed to Fort Sill, Oklahoma, for thirteen weeks of basic training.

Fort Sill, Oklahoma

Fort Sill, Oklahoma, the armpit of the world. The drill sergeant explained what would be happening—drilling, marching, and combat exercises. Our first day we were rousted from our sleep at 0400 hours by "Reveille" and a sergeant yelling orders for roll call by 0500 in front of the barracks. Those who thought an hour allowed enough time for a few more winks found themselves on the floor, their mattresses on top of them. Standing at attention in chilly Oklahoma air, we were rebuked for our clumsy attempt to form ranks, yelled at for not sounding off proper when called, and finally released for breakfast at the mess hall. By 0600 our basic training had begun.

Field exercises turned out to be the worst experience yet. (Except for paratroop training and actual combat when I learned to appreciate rather than hate my drill sergeant.) I teamed up with Frank, another St. Paul fellow, and through hard training we became soldiers who could work as a team. However, Frank and I got separated, never to meet up again throughout the entire war, one reason I hesitated to enter into relationships.

At gunnery school I learned how to fire a carbine, how to man a 50 caliber machine gun, and how to maneuver a 105 Howitzer. I only got into serious trouble once in the line of duty and faced a court martial.

"Guilty." The verdict felt like the sting of an angry wasp. My mind reeled at the officers' decision. I had just been doing my duty. Back in Ramsey County Court, the judge's guilty verdict came with an option. I could enlist in the army. These military judges did not offer any alternative.

For the first time, I questioned the wisdom of choosing the military over jail. Later when confronted by bonsai attacks, I wished to be back in a Minnesota prison. My military offense could land me in the stockade, and who knew what else.

My defending officer whispered, "This is merely a formality to protect you from a civil suit. Accept the decision and be prepared to pay a fine of a carton of cigarettes."

I was only doing my duty. The car ran through my post ignoring my demands to halt. I raised my rifle and shot as I had been instructed. And shot and shot and shot, like the frightened teenaged kid that I still was. I immediately called the officer of the day, a captain if I remember, and reported the incident. He relieved me of duty and restricted me to barracks. When he informed me that I had killed a German POW who attempted to escape, I felt a rush of relief, not having shot some silly kid out on a joy ride. I made my first enemy kill before I left stateside, nothing to brag about.

The judge asked, "What part of the car were you aiming at, Soldier?"

"At the tires, Sir," seemed like the proper response for something I couldn't fully recall.

"Lieutenant, assign this solder to the rifle range indefinitely if necessary," which he did, and it gave me another experience worthy of mention in this memoir.

"Fire a single round," the gunnery officer commanded.

Rrrip, all five rounds emptied the clip.

"Just a single shot, Soldier!"

I loaded a fresh clip and *rrrrip*.

"Give me that weapon!"

223

I objected but decided not to pursue what I had learned from the Army Manual as my right. Nobody can take a soldier's weapon from him, a lesson learned by a second lieutenant who confiscated my shotgun during combat. (More about that later)

The gunnery officer loaded a clip and experienced the same automatic rapid fire.

"Give this guy a different rifle," he directed his junior.

I took careful aim, fired, and received a waving white flag. A total miss! Five more attempts and not a single shot hit the target. Upon further inspection, the target beyond that I was supposed to aim for had five direct hits. My first step on the way to become a sharpshooter with a sniper job assignment in combat.

After thirteen weeks of training, I got my wish to leave Fort Sill with a seven-day pass. Within a few days back at St. Paul, I began to feel bored and could hardly wait to return to my new life.

Fort Campbell, Kentucky

My next assignment, extensive training in artillery at Fort Campbell, Kentucky. I rode an M-7 Half Track, basically a tank without the turret. I manned the 1.05 Howitzer and a .50 caliber machine gun. I didn't care for the M-7 assignment, and I soon found a way out of it.

We attended a lecture on a new type of warfare. The officers who spoke wore fancy jerseys and tucked-in trousers blousing over shiny boots. Paratroopers. I decided to join when they mentioned an extra fifty-dollar monthly increase for jump pay doubled when in combat. I could hardly wait. I had escaped Fort Campbell, latched on to a new adventure, and got rich all at one time. I would soon learn the price required of me, often times with my life on the line.

Fort Banning, Georgia

Just a few days after signing on to the paratroops, I wound up at Fort Banning, Georgia, to train and live in a *frying pan* for eight weeks. All physical exercises to this point were a breeze compared to what I encountered during paratroop training.

From the very beginning our drill instructor warned, "You will never walk from your barracks to anywhere on base."

Will we be given rides? I wondered, but not for long.

"You will *run* wherever you go. And if I catch you walking..." He didn't need to state the consequences. We ran from our barrack to the mess hall after a full mile detour, we ran from one place to another within the base, and we ran a seven-mile stretch around the airport once a week. The one time I stopped running, I was given a second chance because I suffered from heat stroke. I would do anything to escape Fort Banning short of going AWOL, something I often did overseas, each time leaving an accented line on my sleeve where the insignia of rank had been ripped off. Once for punishment, I had to dig a six foot grave to bury an officer's cigarette. I didn't mind losing rank, but I couldn't see wasting a perfectly good cigarette. Besides, every time I went into combat, a rating of at least *private first class* was required.

We were taught survival skills, how to pack a chute, and Martial Arts. We were treated like scum bags, and the sergeant in charge chose me for his personal punching bag. He probably selected me because of my size.

My 133 pounds when I enlisted—the recruiting officer had to press the scale with his foot to register two additional pounds to meet the minimum requirement—probably fell below 130 by this time.

The sergeant would scan the group and yell, "Leslie! Up front pronto."

I expected to be beaten up, but not as a target for the art of killing with bare hands. I didn't die, but I bled and bruised and hurt after each session. The more I hated the bastard, the harder he came at me.

I vowed to perfect the skill and claim him as my first hand-to-hand kill. When I felt sure of my ability, I volunteered to be his victim, knowing that one of us wouldn't walk away from the fight alive. He must have had the same inkling.

He said, "Not this time, Leslie."

I answered, "It's either here or off base. One way or the other you're a dead man."

He said, "Save your anger for the enemy."

"You are my enemy."

"I may be the best friend you ever had, Leslie. As for an altercation with me off base, it ain't gonna happen. We won't ever see each other again. You're shipping out tomorrow."

He was right on all three accounts; no face off, no back alley fight, and I did thank him after my first face-to-face encounter with a Japanese soldier probably my own age. I still hated my Martial Arts instructor out of principle.

Of the fourteen hundred who started paratroop training, only four hundred and fifty of us earned our wings. Many couldn't handle the intensive physical workout, some lacked courage to jump, and a few disappeared from our ranks the day before graduation. I worried that I might be one of few who got weeded out on the last day, probably because of attitude problems. Little did I know at the time that Col. Jones looked for soldiers with aggressive attitudes.

Southern hospitality

I have one pleasant and somewhat humorous memory of an incident that occurred at the home of a southern aristocrat. As part of a good will gesture, a notable family invited small groups of privates to their home for a formal dinner. My name came up as one of their guests, and we were instructed how to behave as a representative of American Paratroopers. We were seated at a large table along with the head of the household and his family, one place unoccupied.

The man said, "Mother will be down shortly, and we can start."

The adults sat quietly, but I heard some whispered giggles between the kids.

Soon a withered but perky old lady straight out of a *Gone with the Wind* movie set sashayed through the door. She growled, "Who allowed these damn Yankees to sit at our table?"

The man stood and we followed. "Now, Mama. We are no longer fighting the Civil War. Please join us and show some appreciation for these gallant soldiers who are on our side in this war."

The man seated his Mother and we followed, but she continued to glare. We sat and the servers brought our food. To this day, I'm not sure if she really hated Yankees or just put on a show for us. If she really felt that way toward us, she wouldn't have come down from her room. The Civil war had been over for eighty years, too long ago for her to remember, but she obviously lived through some of the horrible reconstruction.

An Unscheduled jump

Shortly, before graduation, I got involved in a situation that could have ended in a second court-martial, or equally likely, it proved I had courage and could think on my feet. Actually, think *off* my feet, as I made a successful non-scheduled jump under unfavorable circumstances.

I had earned a three-day pass, enough time to catch military flights to St. Paul and back. I hopped on a Jeep heading to the military airport where I asked Air Traffic Control about a flight to Minnesota.

The guy pointed to a bomber warming up on the field. "That plane's headed there. Go see what the pilot says."

To me it sounded like permission, so I grabbed a chute and high tailed out to the field.

"Can I bum a ride to Minnesota?" I'm sure I said *Minnesota,* but I would debate that detail in my mind after I landed.

"Climb aboard and take the jump seat behind the copilot."

When the roar of takeoff settled down, I asked how long the flight would take. That time I definitely mentioned *Minnesota.*

"We're heading to Canada."

"Hey, I was told..."

"Well you was told wrong. Chicago maybe, but we're not approved to stop there."

From Chicago I could take a train to St. Paul, but I would have to catch a flight back almost immediately, or be AWOL.

He chuckled. "Get in back and I'll see what I can do."

I crawled into the bomb bay and fretted until I felt the plane start its descent. Obviously, the pilot had concocted an engine problem and got permission to land. Suddenly the floor opened up, and I dropped thirty-two-feet-per-second squared, in other words, a damn fast acceleration toward the ground. On impulse, I yanked the ripcord; in training these were attached to a static line that automatically released the chute as we left the plane to insure we'd land close together. Below loomed an airport attached to a city attached to a lake. The pilot had said his flight plan crossed Chicago, and I foolishly thought the plane would land with me still aboard. I managed to manipulate my descent and landed on the grassy area beyond the runway.

You'd think World War III had started by all the lights and sirens. I didn't get to St. Paul, and I nearly took up residence in the stockade. Apparently, the pilot had requested permission from flight control to do a flyover to check his instruments, and responded on his radio as surprised as I had been when a chute blossomed.

"Must have been a stowaway," he radioed to the tower and continued on his merry way to Canada.

I had no choice but to support his story and take the consequences. After a couple of days of interrogation, I boarded a train at my expense and returned to base a week late.

My sergeant smirked and said, "Captain wants to see you."

I saluted and stood at attention, prepared to get my ass reamed.

"What kind of stunt were you pulling?"

"Just trying to catch a flight to Minnesota, Sir. I must have gotten on the wrong plane."

"In cahoots with the pilot, no doubt. But he's off the hook and you're stuck with me."

"Yes, Sir."

"Go back to your barracks, and we'll see what effect this little incident has on earning your wings."

"Yes, Sir. Thank you, Sir."

I graduated, so the stowaway incident had no apparent consequences, maybe it even impressed the officer in charge. As part of the ceremony, we performed a *Pass and Review* and saluted a slew of officers standing on a platform. Three of them gave speeches, while we stood at attention in the hot sun.

The 950 candidates who failed to complete the program either went back to finish artillery training or directly to either Europe or Asia. Who knew what was in store for us?

Paratroop training ended as abruptly as it began, the privilege of advance notice about what to expect is not a military concept. I didn't feel any different after three training experiences: basic, artillery, and parachute. I was in excellent shape with skills that would make me dangerous back home on the streets. Unfortunately, that didn't change when the war ended. Much more about that later.

I earned a fifteen-day furlough, but I cut my visit home short because of anxiety either over my next assignment or just plain boredom. I had become an entirely different person, and my old friendships didn't appeal to me. As a warrior, and I needed to be back with my own kind before the war ended without me.

No such luck. I would face a continuous eighteen months in a combat zone until Japan surrendered.

Fort Bragg, North Carolina

I reported to Fort Bragg ahead of my orders, so they had to make special arrangements to accommodate me. I felt like an unwanted guest given a bed but no instructions about what to do. The place should have been called Camp Wait-and-See, because I could find no useful purpose other than exhibition jumps. The weather was pleasant compared to middle-summer in Georgia, and my duties there were minimal. However, I had become a mechanical soldier wound tight with no release in sight. I dreaded what I had been told to expect, but the tension I felt needed the release of combat, or so I thought.

Exhibition jumps

Our number of exhibition jumps far exceeded the required minimum of one a month to earn the extra fifty dollars, one hundred include training jumps without any failed chutes or even a minor injury. I felt invincible. One paratrooper experienced two failed chutes, possibly not a record except for the fact that he survived both. Each time he rode spread eagle atop another chute nearly getting both men killed. It earned him an offer for an honorable discharge, which he accepted. Whoever said the military wasn't superstitious?

We did a jump at Washington D.C. to impress congress with the military's capability to drop soldiers directly into combat. The concept of landing behind enemy lines had been tested against the German/Italian forces in Italy with mixed results. I learned later that just the presence of a paratroop regiment puts pressure on the enemy, because an attack from the air cannot be predicted. To keep the airborne budget fat, congress needed to be impressed.

For a little R&R we got to stay at a hotel in New York City overnight. Too much too soon for some of the rural guys, but I felt comfortable. Except for the immense height of its buildings—their tallest three times that of the Minneapolis Foshay Tower—most city blocks felt just like the Twin Cities.

Four of us stood gawking when a cab driver pulled over. "What are you guys looking for?"

I answered, "We got the day off to check out the city, but we don't know where to start."

"Hop in. I know just the place for you."

I expected a flop hotel with an hourly rate, but he took us to Coney Island and dropped us off at the end of the Boardwalk, two-and-a-half miles of wooden planking. We covered its entire length. A barker called us to the Double Ring Wonder Wheel for a free ride because we were in uniform.

A bit further down the Boardwalk, we chuckled watching the mostly young boys getting hitched to a harness, hoisted 262 feet to a sort of Eiffel Tower structure with a circle of arms extending from the top, and floated back to the ground under a parachute canopy fixed open. We stood, pant legs bloused in our boots, but no one recognized us a real Paratroopers.

We accepted a free ride on the Cyclone, only because one of my buddies remembered reading about it being world famous. The two minute ride promised a sensational belly tickle, but none of us would admit it did anything of the sort.

Our greatest sport was watching people fight their way through the mob, especially while bellying up to Feltman's Famous Frankfurter Stand. We joined the crowd, got our 'dog' and followed the Board Walk back to our awaiting cab driver.

Back at the hotel I asked, "How much do we owe."

He said, "Not a single dime. What you boys are doing is payment enough." I experienced a lot of favorable attitudes toward men in uniform, but somewhat less after the war.

On returning to camp, we immediately took off for Texas to make a jump at Fort Berkley. That time things went bad. Cars had parked in the landing area and some of the Paratroopers got injured.

New Orleans race riot

In the fall of '43, about 150 of us were *volunteered* and sent to New Orleans to quell a race riot with orders to break up the mob at any cost. I manned the .50 caliber mounted on a halftrack. Our lieutenant hollered through a bull horn for the crowd to disperse. A tall Negro in front of the crowd who had done most of the yelling threw what looked like a rock. It barely missed the lieutenant's helmet.

My officer yelled, "Fire."

I hesitated, not sure if he really meant it, and hoped he would rescind his order.

Instead, he bellowed, "That's an order, Soldier."

I fired one shot and the man flew backward. The bullet pierced his chest and possibly hit others tightly formed behind him. The crowd scattered and we returned to camp. Word never got back to me about the incident, but I never saw that lieutenant again.

Alaska Jump

The Naval Arctic Research Laboratory in Point Barrow, Alaska, was vulnerable to Japanese invasion, and the quickest possible response would be to send paratroopers. A negro regiment had completed the Alcan Highway, but only as far as Fairbanks. However, no one knew if jumping in the cold climate was practical, or even possible.

Two platoons of us jump school graduates stationed at Fort Bragg flew to northern Alaska and performed an exploratory jump in simulated winter conditions. Our stick of seven Paratroopers hooked onto ripcords to the static line, awaited orders from the jump officer, and tumbled out the door into minus seventy degrees at an extreme jump altitude of 7500 feet, not factoring the wind factor on the way down. Every inch of skin needed protection or it would instantly freeze. We didn't have modern thermal insulation so we relied on many layers of clothes. If we had paid attention to the natives, we could have borrowed their outerwear. We didn't freeze to death, but we landed in no condition to fight or even operate our rifles. The firing mechanisms on our weapons became stiff and unresponsive.

They did some experimenting with different lubricants, and we made a second jump. Upon landing, we pulled off our bulky mittens and released our chutes. The cold metal stung our bare hands and our rifles still refused to function. Trucked back to the barracks, we awaited the next cold weather experiment. Whatever was decided didn't involve my *stick* of seven Paratroopers from the first two runs. We flew back to our staging area at Fort Bragg and endless close order drills. And, more exhibition jumps just to prove a point, I assumed.

Train ride west

Not too long after we got back from Alaska, we received orders to pack our things; we would be moving to an unspecified location. We boarded a train with the windows blacked out and were given orders not to lift the shades or even peer out the windows. Sensing no direct sunrise or sunset, so figured we were heading either east or west. East would have been the Atlantic Ocean from Georgia.

After two days, we got side tracked by an oncoming train, and our officers allowed us to get off and exercise. From a small nearby town, a few people came to gawk.

A wide-eyed girl about twelve years old approached me and asked, "Where are you going?" She pretty well guessed that we were military, probably not the first troop train to pass this way.

I said, "I can't tell you because it's a secret." Truthfully, I had no idea where we were heading, other than west. Probably to the Far East mostly controlled by Japan, but we headed west to get there.

Our officers ordered us to re-board the train, but I still had her full attention.

I handed her my wings insignia and said, "Take care of this for me."

Her eyes lit up and she reached out her hand. Against all orders and probably common sense, I placed the patch in her palm and closed small fingers around it. As I boarded the car, I glanced back. One hand waved, the other clutched her little gift.

I wonder if she still has it and how many times she told the story about the soldier who gave her his Airborne emblem.

Fort Ord, California

We continued on to California, to be attached to Fort Ord, near Marina. Like Fort Bragg, it turned out to be another holding station awaiting orders. It was my sixth fort assignment starting at St. Paul. Ord was an old fort established in 1917 and remained active until September of 1994. When my outfit was there, the 7th Light Infantry (Cavalry) Division, 6th Army claimed it as home base. I didn't know at the time that the 503rd Regiment was part of the 6th Army, nor did I know that the 503rd would be my Paratroop assignment. Most of the regiment had departed for Australia a year earlier, where I would join them shortly.

Our group wore no insignia, and our officers gave strict orders not to tell anyone that we were paratroopers. After a few days of boredom, our captain gave permission to visit the PX. A few of us took advantage of the offer but got into trouble. Soldiers from the 7th Infantry objected to our wearing our pant legs bloused. Only Airborne can display this custom, and we wore no insignias designating Paratroopers.

Kilroy, a fellow I hung around with off and on, faced the soldier with the loudest mouth and said, "If you don't like it, you pull the blousing out of my boots."

Like a damn fool, the soldier stooped over and started to tug on Kilroy's pant leg. Kilroy's knee connected with the guy's chin, and the fight erupted. Geronimo, an oversized Indian who turned out to be my protector in and out of combat, bear-hugged the soldier as he squirmed and yelled for help. We caused extensive damage to the PX.

The fort commander wanted to court marshal seven of us, until he learned that the soldiers in his command started the fight.

He realized we were heading toward the combat zone where the fighting skills we had demonstrated were an asset. I felt our officers were secretly proud of us. We became more cautious, but we kept our pant legs bloused, except at the PX.

The incident developed a kinship between our group of seven: Geronimo—I don't think I ever knew his real name—Kiltau, we called *Kilroy*, Jenkins, Heidt, Reed, Jennings, and Richard—thanks to my mother's insistence, I never allowed a nickname like *Rich* or *Rick*.

Heidt grew up in Riverside, a city close by, and he invited us to dinner with his family. We each requested a pass and rode a bus to his family's home. We ate a nice meal and visited with his parents and siblings. Waiting for our ride back to base, we stepped into a local bar. After a few drinks—no one questioned an under-age soldier's legal right to alcohol back then—we decided to bond in a very special way.

I hesitated at first because growing up on the streets of St. Paul I learned not to trust anyone. As a nine-year-old kid, I fought to protect my shoeshine spot on Seventh Avenue. It provided partial income for my mother and our family. I also fought a few battles, some with older kids, for my magazine sales route.

When Geronimo insisted that back-up in combat would be a good idea, I reflected on the time my older sisters got even with some mean kids down the street from us who beat me up. I got the bullies' attention and ran, leading them into a trap set up ahead of time. My sisters taught them a lesson not to mess with the Leslie family. I never admitted that *sisters* convinced me to join our brotherhood.

I approached the bartender with our plan, an initiative that set me apart from the others as an unofficial spokesman.

"Do you have seven bottles of champagne that we can buy at a reasonable price." He more so than the other bartender showed a sympathetic eye, probably had his own kid in the service.

"What have you got in mind? You can't take them back to base."

"Me and my buddies want to each pay for a bottle, but not claim it until after the war."

"I could work out something like that. But what if...?" He stopped in mid sentence.

I finished his words. "If any one of us doesn't make it through the war, the survivors will come back to break their buddy's bottle and toast his honor by drinking the rest."

He selected a bottle from the back bar and reached into a drawer to count out seven chits with the bar's name etched on them. "I would give you seven of this brand for free, but I think you should have some investment in them." He shifted his glance to the six guys clustered tightly around me. "How much can you afford to pay?"

"How much do they cost?" I asked.

"That's between me and the," he glanced around. "Between me and the lamp post."

We huddled and collected $12.37 between us. I held out the money and asked, "Would this cover it?"

He nodded and reached with his free hand, then uncorked a bottle and split it between eight glasses. Each of us ready with a glass in hand, he hoisted his and said, "A toast to confirm your compact." He took a swig and we followed his lead. "I expect to get all seven of my chits back, and with a little luck, each of you will present his own so we won't have to break any bottles."

We each pocketed a chit, thanked the barman, and caught the bus back to base.

I experienced my first-ever hangover at Fort Ord. One evening a few of us guys were just hanging around looking for trouble, and we ended up in a local bar specializing in wines from the Napa Valley, famous for its vineyards. We weren't interested back then, but we proceeded to drink the place dry. That night on base, I slept with my head swirling, and a thick tongue stuck to the roof of my mouth in the morning. I drank about a gallon of water to free my tongue and wash down the taste, a big mistake. An officer approached me at the mess tent during breakfast.

"Leslie, you were drinking wine last night."

I saluted cautiously and replied, "Yes, sir."

"And you drank about as much water this morning."

"Yes Sir."

"Have a hearty breakfast, and hope to keep it down."

"Yes, Sir." I had yet to meet an officer as understanding as this fellow. He broke eye contact, and I glanced toward the chow line nearly gagging.

"Is that all, Sir?"

"For now, Leslie." He made no effort to hold back a grin. "But meet me at the obstacle course at 0800 hours."

"Yes, Sir."

He had my name, and I felt sure he wouldn't forget. It would be too much fun watching me sweat through two rounds in one of the meanest obstacle courses yet, considering my wicked hangover and an empty stomach. The hearty breakfast he suggested didn't stay with me.

USS AMERICA

About mid January, 1944, a few hundred of us trained in artillery boarded the USS AMERICA, the fastest ship afloat at the time, to join the recently formed 503rd Parachute Regiment in Australia. Evasive maneuvers like zigzagging weren't needed, because no submarine could ever catch us. We crossed in nineteen days, excluding time at Pearl Harbor for engine repairs, probably the result of pushing too hard. We weren't allowed off ship during our stopover, but seeing the destruction caused by the Japs two years earlier added motivation for revenge and incentive to get into the action.

Three battalions of infantry sailed six months earlier, taking a leisurely forty-two days with a brief stop in Panama City to pick up a battalion commander, Lt. Col. George M. Jones. The 503rd had been shorted its artillery battery. We were its missing component, scheduled to rendezvous with our regiment presently on R&R near Sidney following its first combat engagement in Markham Valley, New Guinea.

My daughter found a picture of the USS America on the internet and confirmed the facts about the crossing. It had sailed three times between California and Australia, the first transported the three battalions of infantry, the second (my turn) transported the 462nd Artillery Battalion consisting of four batteries: A, B, C, and D (my battery.) It's third crossing with supplies and replacements.

A copy of the boarding pass, like the one issued to me in 1944, listed the berth shared by 4-6 men on bunks, mess schedules and location, latrine location, seawater shower location (only drinking water was fresh) and the exit route to *abandon ship*. Modern cruise ships mark routes to the *lifeboats*, but Merchant Marine ships used the harsher language. I remember my assigned area deep and sweltering below deck.

During a two-day stopover at Guadalcanal to deliver supplies, we disembarked. The Marines had retaken the island back from the Japanese, but a contingent enemy force resisted surrender.

When I asked a Marine if any Japs remained on the island, he answered, "Just a few that we use for target practice when we get bored." My first taste of fanatic Japanese soldiers who would prefer death to the humility and shame of surrendering. These holdouts were part of the force that took the island from the Marines soon after Pearl Harbor, and as a result they treated the few marine POWs as dishonorable and deserving atrocities. We learned to avoid surrendering, and we anticipated orders to take no prisoners. Like submariners, paratroopers don't have facilities to accommodate the extra human baggage.

The Marines treated us to a cookout with hot dogs and beer. Those guys were okay, but I still believe Marines to be glory hounds. Little did I realize at the time what our futures had in store for us. From Guadalcanal they would island hop to Iwo Jima, Tarawa, and Okinawa at tremendous loss of life. Their goal was to acquire a base close enough to Japan's mainland for our B29 heavy bombers to reach.

Our destination would be the Philippine Islands to fulfill the now famous vow MacArthur made as he slipped out of Manila Bay under cover of night. From the deck of a PT boat about to depart Manila in disgrace, he shouted into the night, "I shall return!"

He didn't mention the tens of thousands of civilians that would die, not counting a few thousand American, Australian, and Philippine soldiers. The Sixth Army would work its way through New Guinea and up the Philippine chain of islands to Corregidor, the gateway to Manila. Fortunately, neither those Marines nor we Paratroopers knew what lay ahead.

Back aboard the USS AMERICA, the final leg of our deployment tested our patience for boredom. You can only play cards 12-14 hours a day for so long. At the equator, the heat became stifling below deck where we were confined at night. A few of us crept topside and were immediately confronted by a Marine Military Police Officer. A few dozen of them were aboard to maintain peace between soldiers and Merchant Marines.

"Hey, you guys gotta stay below."

"Come on. It's hot down there. We won't cause any trouble."

"Sorry, Captain's orders."

We weren't about to tangle with the captain again, like we did soon after leaving California. Back then, a junior officer handed some of us mops and told us to swab the deck. We snubbed the guy, reminding him we were Army, not Merchant Marine. The issue went all the way to the captain, and we were reminded that he rules his ship. He made his point, but we weren't asked to swab the deck again.

A couple of us guys stole a ham from the ship's stores and used it for shark bait. Some fins had been sighted gliding through the water, and we set out to catch us a shark. Success, followed by disappointment. After a long tug of war, the fish gave in, but we couldn't pull it over the guardrail. A couple of ship's officers offered the use of the deck crane. Nice guys! Once on board, they commandeered our prize trophy. No fried shark liver that day. However, the ship's meals were sort of okay, the only break in an otherwise boring day.

After what seemed like endless days aboard ship, our small cluster of seven alternated between pushing the limits of authority on deck and retreating below deck to smoke cigarettes and play cards. I seldom smoked but learned very quickly that cigarettes replaced money when bartering for life's little pleasures.

Throughout my preparation for combat, I'd avoided developing this kind of close relationships, partly because I couldn't trust that the guy next to me would survive jump school, partly because we'd been warned of the emotional hazards from losing a close buddy, and partly because of my background. My mother had taught me to fight my own battles.

"If you come home bloodied and complain, I'll whip you some more. You have to stand your own out on the street, because you don't have a father to protect you."

I credit her with my surviving jump school when over half dropped out, and she continued to be a strong influence when my courage was tested in battle.

One sweltering morning in early February, word spread that our destination would be sighted sometime that day. When we caught a glimpse of land, someone yelled, "Australia!"

Australia

The word spread quickly among the men crowded on deck. I felt relief after feeling our ship tousled for so many days bucking the waves of the Pacific, yet some apprehension realizing the purpose for which we prepared so rigorously. We were one-step closer to combat after countless lectures of what it would be like. I must not have been the only paratrooper contemplating our future because a silence spread throughout the crowd as we approached the harbor, the clamor burst forth when orders came to disembark.

Numerous trucks shuttled us yet-to-be-assigned paratroopers to a tented area named Camp Cable a few miles from town that would be our temporary home for days, weeks, or months, we had no idea. Led by Kilroy, five of my buddies scrambled onto a truck bed; the Native American we called Geronimo saved my butt by yanking me aboard after the truck had already filled and was rolling away.

Our transport pulled alongside a row of tents and the driver yelled, "Get your asses off. I gotta get another load of you jokers."

We wandered aimlessly down a dusty path, when an officer stepped out of a tent and said, "Seven empty cots in here."

As we saluted, I glimpsed his name tag, *Lt. Serangeles,* and made a mental note that there was an *angel* in that name, and perhaps there was one in his person. He ultimately became that angel our first night on Negros Island when he stepped on a land mine.

Kilroy, who demanded to be first at everything, ducked inside the tent yelling, "Come on guys. We got one." Geronimo grabbed my arm and pulled me in, Jenkins, Heidt, Reed, and Jennings followed. By chance, we had established the fourth squad needed to fill the tent's quota, a bit of fate that bonded our friendship until the Atomic bomb ended the war, and a much smaller bomb decimated our relationship.

Twenty-one men in various states of undress sitting or lying on cots eyed us suspiciously, as if exclaiming *create your own space and leave mine alone*. What I had misread was the vacant stare of combat veterans caught between battles, of which we would soon join ranks.

A voice from a few cots away, "What's your outfit?"

"Artillery!" I sounded off as if under inspection, but caught myself before mistakenly adding, "Sir," to the sergeant.

The group stirred as voices mumbled, "About time," and "Screw the Aussies."

Soon the full story emerged. The 503rd had been constructed piecemeal and sent into battle without its full contingency. Their temporary artillery battery consisted of volunteers from the Australian Military who had never jumped. After a crash course, they bundled their weapons and followed three battalions out of the plane onto an airfield in New Guinea with the seventeen hundred infantry of the 503rd. The statistics of the jump were unremarkable, three killed and thirty-three injured on the jump; eight killed and twelve wounded in combat. One of the squads in our tent had lost a man on the jump, probably why they were despondent when we entered. Also, their eight weeks of R&R in Australia neared its end.

As an interesting side note, the 503rd commander, General Kinsler, jokingly referred to as *The Eggshell General* because he had aides tape his ankles before every jump, committed suicide after a victory celebration with his officers at a cocktail party. He left no note, but his body was found in a gravel pit with a bullet wound to the head. They didn't say whether his ankles were taped or not. Lt. Colonel George M. Jones had advanced from battalion to regiment commander. Shortly after we arrived, he'd been promoted to full colonel, which could have indicated how serious the action ahead of us would be.

Whatever the reason for our tent mates' despondency, the ice had been broken and we became comrades-in-arms. We absorbed their combat experiences and soon felt we had actually been there, and their lost brother had been ours as well. We were a seven-man squad of raw recruits, none of us having seen prior action. No combat-experienced soldier wanted a green replacement in his squad, and they would be leery of an entirely green squad as their artillery backup, which we were. That concept hit me hard later on Negros Island when a greenie joined our squad when under fire. His bobbing head became an easy target. Not only did he take a bullet, but he could have gotten all of us killed. Jap snipers as well as many of their foot soldiers were sharp-shooters. Other than that guy, I never lost any member of my squad.

Fortunately, the men in our tent were willing to talk about their experience under fire, and we became eager learners. Others were not so lucky to find a tent with combat veterans. Four squads of well-trained but inexperienced paratroopers in a single tent could only share their ignorance and had to learn the hard way, often at the loss of one or two within the squad.

Unfortunately, with 2700 men landing at Noemfoor, we never met up with any of our tent mates again. However, their advice and some harrowing experiences of our own developed us into seasoned combat veterans.

In the meantime, we became familiar with Australian culture. Me and my friends each got a pass to explore the city of Sidney, and I broke from their ranks to test whether Australia had a legal drinking age. At a local bar, they called it a pub, I asked for a beer.

The female bartender said, "What's that, Mate?" Her accent was thick, and I thought that maybe she was making fun of me.

243

I puffed up my one-hundred-and-thirty-five-pound-nineteen-year-old body and repeated, "I want to buy a beer."

"Beer? Ain't got nuthin' like that here, Mate." She returned her attention to wiping the bar, but I detected a slight grin cross her face.

An Australian from down the bar edged closer and I braced myself for trouble. My buddies had opted to buy trinkets at the market rather than beer. The Australian and I were the only customers.

He put his arm around my neck and said to the barmaid, "I think me mate here wants a pint o' ale." They both laughed, and I relaxed the fist I had been preparing.

We spent the afternoon and part of the evening comparing Sidney and St. Paul, arguing who had the better opera. I got a sense of the Australian culture as well as their rugged and determined individualism, and later I got to see their *guts and glory* on the battle field. They didn't even wear protective helmets, just the wide brimmed hats flattened in front.

Lt. Serangeles kept a low profile our first couple of weeks at Camp Cable; after all, the entire regiment was on R&R. Col. Jones wasn't so compliant. He ordered the troops to drill and fight mock battles almost every day. We didn't do any practice jumps, but we simulated ground action after a make-believe jump where we had to locate land marks and assemble our fifty-caliber in position ready for combat. Our last simulation had such details that we suspected it might be for real, and possibly it was. Part of the effect paratroopers have on the enemy is their ability to change objectives on a moment's notice. There were situations where we stood jump-ready on the field, and once already in flight, only to have the mission canceled. Noemfoor proved to be one of those in-flight cancelled jumps.

Col. George M. Jones assembled the entire regiment in an open field and spoke to us, some of what he said I still recall.

My style of leadership is to put out as few orders as possible, and each will be acknowledged by roll call down to the individual private within each squad. Any officer not carrying out an order will receive a court martial for disobedience. In the course of combat, I will be sending men into harm's way. Be assured I will never send my men into a situation that I myself would not follow.

Col. Jones, a graduate of West Point, proved to be an officer of his word. He sent at least one of his officers, Lt. Smith, to the stockade for insubordination, and he made each jump with his men, actually breaking his leg on Corregidor. He also mentioned we'd be boarding a ship the following morning, but our squad hadn't yet received orders. We returned to our tent with no sign of the other squads. Lt. Serangeles approached out of breath barely acknowledging our salute.

"Get your combat gear and report to the parade ground."

Either we didn't respond quick enough or our lieutenant still felt the element of surprise. He yelled, "Now!" Assessing our continued confusion, he added, "No chutes. We won't be jumping."

New Guinea: Kamiri Air Field, July 1944

My *first combat jump* became my *first cancelled combat jump*. The 503rd was scheduled for its second jump on the main island of New Guinea, their previous one at Markham Valley before I joined the regiment. All the hype and prep for my 2d Battery jump with its heavy weaponry fizzled after Col. Jones with 1a and 3a Battalions landed hard on a coral field cluttered with earth moving equipment. Col. Jones cancelled the drop, not only because of injuries on the jump, but there was no strategic need. The Japanese had abandoned the Kamiri Airfield that they built two years earlier. I'm sure some heads rolled for that command snafu in intelligence. However, General MacArthur's reputation and authority were untouchable at that time.

After what seemed like a long truck ride, our convoy stopped at the harbor, and we boarded a Dutch liner, the *Van Der Linj,* which became our effective home for the next week mostly moored in Oro Bay, New Guinea. Apparently, Command wasn't sure exactly where we should be utilized. Or perhaps just to keep the enemy off balance. Finally, we sailed to Hollandia, a town on the northern coast of New Guinea.

We climbed down rope ladders to assault boats waiting to take us ashore. Battery D traded a hard landing for a water-slogged wading ashore, but uncontested by Japanese troops. Then we spent two bloody months flushing a few thousand of them out of their caves and jungle hideouts.

On Papua, New Guinea, we established Base Camp Sudest in the hottest most inhospitable piece of geography on that side of our planet. Even the fields of waving grass turned out to be ten foot high razor blades—kunai grass.

Charging through it meant lacerations across our entire bodies. To create a path, one soldier would fall forward while the man behind would walk over him and flop down for the first guy to advance one body length at a time.

I had been following a trail through the grass, when I heard voices that didn't sound Japanese. I approached cautiously, not exposing my presence until I figured out who they might be. A squad of Australians had settled down for an afternoon cup of tea, my mother's usual drink and one of my favorite drinks as well. I accepted the cup handed to me, as if I had been invited and they were waiting for me. I still have a soft spot in my heart for the Australian soldier, and they certainly appreciated Americans for helping them defend their country against the Japanese early in the war.

Moving further inland, we came upon numerous native villages and vast fields of yams. Having completed our mission, we moved into a large valley, probably one of the most beautiful spots on Earth. Here we dug foxholes and set up a perimeter with the yam field to our front and a native village to our rear. Young boys enjoyed spending their time with us, showing how to cover our foxholes with woven banana leaves to protect us from the constant rain.

Our engineers created showers out of fuel barrels filled with hot water up on stands and valves that would spray naked soldiers, eager to have bare breasted native women rub our bodies with ointment.

Rumor had it that Gen. MacArthur intended to build a mansion for his personal use in this valley.

Contact with the Japanese grew less and less. We enjoyed complete freedom around the village and the jungles of the area. Having become friendly with the natives, they introduced us to their most popular alcoholic beverage.

Tuba was the fermented juice from a coconut palm tree. Their technique to extract it was to climb the tree, cut a spout, and hang a jug to catch the sap. After several weeks they'd remove the jug, strain its contents, and drink the fermented liquid. The taste reminded me of rotten fruit, but I must admit it had a kick.

As with all good things, our stay ended and we were assigned another mission.

Nocmfoor Island, New Guinea

In July we boarded C-47's at Kamiri Strip with full combat gear: boots with serrated blades protruding from the toes and spikes on the heels and knives sheaved each side; attached to our uniforms an array of grenades, ammo, medical kit with morphine, additional knives, C-rations, water, a shovel, and, of course, two parachutes totaling about ninety pounds. Everyone needed a boost from the guy behind, the last man pulled into the fuselage.

But we didn't jump. The plane landed at our objective, Cyclops Field, Noemfoor Island, recently taken but still under constant threat. During our patrolling action we killed 56 of the enemy, one of those kills embedded in my memory and recurs in nightmares.

Patrolling an area of outlying airport hangers, I rounded a corner and came face-to-face with a Japanese soldier probably my age. In another world, we would have excused ourselves and continued our business, but this was war. I reacted and he didn't. Grabbing the handiest knife from its sheaf, I thrust it under his rib cage. His feet came off the ground, and his wide-open eyes stared down at me until I released the knife. He crumbled to the ground.

You killed me!

Sometimes in my nightmares, he actually mouths what his silent stare yelled at me that morning.

My squad fanned out but we sighted no more enemy. I remember wiping the blood from the blade onto his uniform and sheaving the knife, but I can't reconstruct my pulling the blade from his body.

Maybe one of my squad took care of that grisly business, probably Geronimo, who would have handed it back to me, a bloody trophy.

I can still hear his low gravely voice. "Gotta take care of the little guy."

Since my job was to man the .50 caliber machine gun, I assumed the leadership role when operating from fixed positions, some of those times earning field sergeant rating when one wasn't available to our squad. Geronimo positioned himself protectively over my back while I sat legs straddling the weapon, often to my annoyance. He would just smile. *Gotta take care of the little guy.*

Col. Jones' 503rd Regiment had been assigned the southern half of Noemfoor Island overgrown with dense jungle and punctuated with high peaks. The enemy escaped from the northern flat and dry half the island and hid in our sector from early July until the end of August.

We chased Col. Shimizu and his 219th Infantry around the island, slowly decimating his regiment, while the SeaBee's restored the two airstrips. We had his back against the ocean, but like our General MacArthur in 1941, he abandoned his troops and slipped away across the bay.

The 503rd lost 38 paratroopers with 72 wounded. Actually, 73 wounded, but I felt too embarrassed to apply for a purple heart. We had a group of stragglers on the run, and I jumped over what should have been an abandoned foxhole. I caught a bayonet in the groin, and the Jap got a slug from Geronimo's carbine for his efforts.

The wound burned like hell. I limped to a field hospital and learned that I would still be able to have children. (Six, as a matter of fact, but I raised eight.)

When a junior officer in a clean uniform and a clipboard quizzed me, the men with limbs and organs protruding from their bodies came to mind. I refused a Purple Heart.

While recuperating, I won a lottery to have a date with a Woman's Army Corp who had recently arrived. Not a beauty queen, but she was female, and after months without seeing a white woman, just being in her presence was a pleasure. I considered a trick the 503rd had perfected, commandeering equipment through the midnight supply line, our biggest catch, a 50-volt portable generator from an engineer unit that left it unguarded.

This time I used my month's supply of cigarettes and beer to get the sergeant at the motor pool to make an urgent run to the latrine, so urgent he forgot to put someone in charge of the Jeeps. The WAC and I waved as we left his dumbfounded grease monkeys in the dust.

I took her to an area where I had been recently wounded, still off limits except for scheduled patrols. I avoided telling her about my injuries, for obvious reasons, but an opportunity to test my recovery never happened. Parking on a somewhat dry grassy spot, I fluffed an army blanket in the breeze allowing it to settle. A Jap leapt out from behind the brush! I had my 45 out of the holster and leveled when the guy fell dead. My lady friend beat me to the draw. We spent the rest of the day talking about combat experiences and returned at nightfall to report the dead body. I lost a stripe for that escapade, but I didn't care. We had a good time, and I was the envy of the platoon.

I returned to my unit, their attitude, *all in a day's work*, about the injury not the date with a woman. That earned their envy.

Leyte, my semi private jump

Crunched between paratroopers I didn't know, some of whose names on their uniforms I might have read but quickly forgot, our C-47 lifted followed by a second C-47, not the hundreds for a major assault.

Lt. Serangeles had approached my squad earlier that morning as we returned from the mess tent. "Leslie."

"Yes sir?"

"Report to the equipment tent immediately for combat gear and a chute. You're going on a mission."

Kilroy yelled, "Hey, you can't take him without us," after the officer was safely out of hearing range.

Geronimo said, "I'm going with you." He glanced around and realized how improbable that would be. "I'm gonna volunteer. Our gunner needs protection."

Kilroy eyed me suspiciously. "You didn't volunteer for anything, did you?"

After two cancelled jumps I had joked, "I'm gonna stow-a-way on some reconnaissance flight and jump on my own." When their laughter quieted, I added, "I did it before in Chicago." I had told them about my unscheduled jump on O'Hare airfield, and ever since they considered my behavior erratic. That was before my transformation that happened on the island of Negros after Corregidor. By then I had slipped over the edge emotionally.

250

I told Geronimo, "Do what you want, but I gotta follow orders."

As the C-47 shuddered and roared us airborne, I studied the faces of men across from our string for any sign of confidence or fear; they had been briefed on the mission, and I was added at the last minute to offer additional cover.

My sharpshooter rating got me involved more often than I wanted. I learned our goal was to secure a sugar factory on Leyte, as with most missions, the reasons were not our concern. Other than a construction battalion repairing an airfield a few miles away, we had no escape route established.

All thirty-four of us landed on soggy ground without injury, our objective a few hundred yards off in the distance. We fanned out, an officer with about half the platoon to the left and the sergeant's group to the right. I and two other guys were to head straight on and establish positions from which we could cover three sides.

Our mission, to take control of the mill, not to destroy it. I spotted a grassy knoll about 100 yards out that I could reach by time those flanking the target attained their goal if I ran fast, a bad idea on such irregular terrain. I tumbled into a ravine camouflaged by tall kunai grass; my first concern was lacerations on my face and arms. My second concern, had I survived and was I still in one piece after the blast?

My ears rang and my eyes stung from the wave of dust and debris zooming over my head. I parted the now matted kunai grass with my rifle and peered at what had been thirty Paratroopers approaching a sugar mill from two sides. I had seen men shot and a few blown apart by hand grenades, but this blast leveled a building, an acre of vegetation, and decimated a platoon.

I ran to assist the injured but found none, only a few bodies that were still complete. Two others of my team had avoided the blast, probably due to circumstances similar to mine. Visibly shaken yet able to walk, we reconnoitered and decided to follow a trail to any native village and get help. If a stray Jap patrol had stumbled on us, we would have been dead meat.

I envisioned a Jap interrogation. "What was the purpose of your mission?"

Our only information: "What used to be a sugar mill."

"Why did you want it destroyed?"

"We didn't. Our orders were to protect it."

"You failed miserably."

A couple of miles down the trail we came across a small settlement, the natives friendly and cooperative. They took us to their local airport, a cleared spongy bog that could only support light fabric-covered airplanes. It had been uprooted by the heavy equipment of our engineers attempting to prepare it for C-47's. Their mission remained as unsuccessful as ours without the body count. We caught a ride on one of their supply boats back to base.

The officer in charge accepted our report with a casual attitude. "In war that happens sometimes. Return to your units. We're about to issue orders for another mission, a full regimental jump from Leyte."

I could have told them that wouldn't happen from the airport I'd just seen, but High Command had already made the change. Local Command didn't know ahead of time, but flat bottomed boats would deliver the 503rd onto the Noemfoor beaches of New Guinea.

By August 31, 1944, The Sixth Army declared the operation completed with 38 killed, 72 wounded, and 400 ineffectives due to various jungle diseases. As always, the 503rd remained to clean up the mess, which included killing a few stragglers and locating supply depots abandoned by retreating Japanese or left over from various branches of the Sixth Army.

I began looting and stashing, and when convenient, selling food, liquor, and cigarettes to eager natives, an operation a buddy and I perfected later on Negros Island, our last combat zone.

During that operation, one of our own, Ray E. Eubanks, earned a Congressional Medal of Honor. He had the good fortune to have an officer observe an action that most of us performed on a regular basis, but he had the bad fortune of getting killed in the process. From my point of view, his reward was not having to worry about staying alive. Over the years, I've discussed combat experiences with fellow combatants as well as mental health workers, and we concluded the life-long fallout from constant fear in battle is never feeling entirely safe. I still have a minor panic attack with every sudden and loud noise.

Mindoro, December 1944

Early December we got orders to collect our full combat gear and ride 6x6 Army trucks to Kamiri airstrip that we took from the enemy. There we boarded C-47s, seven or eight of us aligned along each side of the fuselage in jump-ready positions, when word came through our officer in charge that we would be landing rather than jumping. I experienced a mixed reaction, my emotions slammed from an intense high to disappointment mixed with relief. We disembarked with orders to remove only our chutes. In full combat gear, we marched to the nearby harbor and boarded flat-bottomed boats, 30-40 men on each.

We made our beachhead on Mindoro Island but found the area deserted of natives and all but a few Japs who were left behind as rear guard to the retreating enemy. We found pamphlets dropped in advance of our scheduled jump. Perhaps the message brought about the Japanese retreat that got our jump cancelled at the last minute.

When our interpreters summarized what had been written in Japanese, we had a hearty laugh.

> *We are the 503rd Paratroop Regiment, trained killers never to give quarter to an enemy. These are savage men, each having to kill a member of their own family to qualify. Your only hope is to run fast.*

I doubt this threat had an effect on the Japanese leadership since they didn't value the life of a foot soldier. Their retreat inland was a strategic decision, probably a foolish one or one based on false information.

One well-coordinated bonzai attack could have pushed us back into the sea. Instead, they conducted a war of attrition. We would advance a couple hundred feet, lose a few men, and hunker down. We of Dog Battery had to lug eight .50 caliber and thirteen .30 caliber machine guns, twelve BAR's, and, of course, each of us had our regular carbine.

From December 15 to our jump on Corregidor two months later, I spent nearly half that time with a lost patrol, long enough for my mother to receive a MIA telegram. A squad of twenty paratroopers conducted what should have been a routine two-three day patrol into the jungle, but our lieutenant lost his compass.

Our search for the enemy became a struggle for survival. *Eat what the monkeys eat*, the survival manual had instructed, so we survived on fruit and insect larvae for protein. After a week of rain, bugs, and stinking jungle, we intercepted what looked like a few Japanese stragglers.

Our lieutenant—I never said he was smart—approached waiving a white flag. Soon he motioned for us to lower our rifles and join him at a parley with a squad of Japanese soldiers, one of them English speaking. They too were lost. We boiled some precious coffee grounds and tea leaves to share. They contributed some caked rice to our little party.

Before we separated, their officer said, "It's too bad, but the next time we meet, we must try to kill each other."

I don't know what happened to them, but we finally came upon a small but friendly village who appreciated the American invasion to rid the island of the Japanese. They insisted we feast before returning us to our regiment. Stew never tasted so good, until we discovered it was dog meat.

When Captain Daugherty told me he had sent my mother a message declaring us MIA, I lost my cool.

His response, "Missing in action means missing in action. You weren't around for nearly a month, and I reported your absence as was required."

I demanded that he send a retraction and an apology.

"Now that you're safe and sound, *you* can write her to explain the situation. Coming from you will remove all doubt that you are still alive and back where you're supposed to be."

We had more discussion that resulted in the loss of my second stripe, again.

I gritted my teeth and wrote the letter including some not-so-subtle accusations about my superior officer. My mother could have had a heart attack assuming the death of her second son, Edward, already killed at Monte Casino during the Italian campaign.

Her letter of response didn't reach me until after Corregidor, and it set me on a course of action that drove my behavior until the end of the war. Earlier, she had requested my release from the military as her only remaining son, but that response was short and to the point. I summarize below.

> We regret the loss of your oldest son, but the release of a surviving son does not apply to paratroopers. Their rigorous training makes them indispensible. That was made clear when your second son volunteered for the Airborne.

Indispensible, hell! We were just a statistic for the generals to mull over before sending a predictable number of us to the happy hunting ground.

An assassination order

Why me? A question that plagued me with each operation, especially on Mindoro. A squad of 20 was selected for a special assassination mission, my role to be the sniper. The task didn't seem shocking at the time since killing was our business. The enemy wasn't human, just targets as they considered us. The only difference is that they seemed to willingly present themselves to get shot, where as we tried to avoid getting killed. They would die for their emperor, Hirohito, where I would just as soon kill our five star general, Douglas McArthur. At Corregidor I had the opportunity, but resisted.

This mission was neither the killing of Hirohito or MacArthur, but an important Japanese General, who if I had missed might have turned some of our successes into failures. I was told his name—which I have since forgotten—the hut of his favorite native mistress, and a routine he foolishly followed.

Our transportation to the site created our biggest obstacle, to my notion. We were sealed in a watertight container and sunk to the bottom of the ocean, or so it seemed. A submarine! In addition to an annoying pinging that drove me crazy, I had no concept of time, one day or a couple of days, I had no way of knowing. The smells of body odor, diesel oil, and a head that was in continuous use still bothered me because we hadn't yet experienced the decaying of hundreds of bodies on Corregidor. I enjoyed playing poker with the crew, even though I lost a hundred dollars. How I managed to carry around hundred dollar bills will be explained when I write about the last six months of the war on Negros Island.

We set up the 50 caliber a few hundred yards from the hut where the general usually slept. Patience is as important to a sniper as is precision. My team covered the operation and continued to check wind velocity, as I kept my eye attached to the scope. When the door opened, my anxiety soared. Would he or perhaps his native girlfriend appear? Had I compensated for the most recent wind velocity report? Would this turn out to be a suicide mission, especially if I missed and he sends out a search party? I pulled the trigger and waited. One second, two. He must have seen the flash because he glanced my way before he grabbed his chest and toppled to the ground.

I dropped a grenade onto the firing mechanism to permanently destroy the gun, and we ran like hell, but not directly to the coast. Our sub would appear at 1900 hours for only five minutes. With time to kill, we took a diversionary course and rendezvoused moments before the sub surfaced. The ride back felt less scary than a swarm of Japs eager to extract revenge for the loss of their general. I didn't feel much like playing poker for awhile, until I decided to win my hundred dollars back. I didn't.

Corregidor Island (Major Battle) February 16, 1945 to March 13, 1945

I had revisited the Battle of Corregidor many times over the years, often in my sleep, but now I concentrate to recall minute details for this memoir. I expected to die on the jump or during the ensuing battle, but the reality is I survived an additional 68 years. I couldn't imagine it back then, and I am still amazed and thankful.

A ranking officer from headquarters assembled our Platoon and briefed the details of Col. Jones' decision to make the Corregidor Island jump onto Topside, a small golf course and parade ground surrounded by steep cliffs that drop to the ocean. Extensive shelling in preparation for the attack had reduced most buildings to rubble, and the landing site extended a mere 1500 feet, the normal drift rate for a stick of seven or eight Paratroopers. With the plane flying at 120 miles an hour and allowing five-to-six seconds to exit the plane, some Paratroopers might miss the zone and slam against the cliffs or land in the water.

The hundred or so of us packed into the tent that day understood these statistics, and we reacted in unison. The odds were against us, but the fact that Jones developed the strategy made it possible although extremely dangerous. We planned to make the jump at 600 feet. Conditions on D-day were such that we exited the plane at almost half that altitude.

We listened in awe of our commander when we heard Col. Jones had stood up to General McArthur who had planned for us to jump on level ground near the ocean.

Supposedly, Jones said, "Sir, we will execute your order to jump, but not where you propose. We would be nearly decimated by enemy fire before we hit the ground, and those of us who survived would experience cross fire from our own troops making the beachhead." He jabbed his finger on the small area at the top of the mountain. "We will land here and take the high ground."

When a staff member assured the general that a jump there would be impossible, Jones replied, "That's what the enemy thinks. I have personally flown over the island. I know my men can make that topside jump."

His words, *my men can make that topside jump,* brought a cheer from every Paratrooper. Col. Jones was our hero, and if he said we can do it, we would die trying if necessary. He had a way of inspiring his men. For example, he sent for a Lt. Smith who had been doing time in the stockade for various infractions, including insubordination.

According to various accounts, Jones brushed off Smith's mandatory salute and remained seated behind his desk. "Lieutenant, we don't like each other very much."

Smith replied, "No, Sir, we don't."

"Well, I have a mission for you that will not only redeem your reputation, but if you carry out your orders I will personally pin a medal on you."

Smith glared defiantly. "You took away my jump status."

"You and your squad will be shuttling supplies from the South Harbor on Corregidor to the Paratroopers on topside."

"I have no squad."

Jones returned his attention to the papers in front of him. "You will hand pick your men."

"Who will want to serve under a disgraced officer?"

"Your mates at the stockade. You can offer to have their records purged and, if successful, will also earn medals." Lt. Smith stood, grabbed his orders from Col. Jones and headed toward the door.

"Dismissed," Col. Jones yelled after him and, supposedly, just smiled at the insubordination.

My situation wasn't much different than Lt. Smith's. I joined the army to avoid going to jail, and my attitude and behavior got me into trouble on occasion. However, I was a fighter and Col. Jones respected that.

The briefing officer filled in details of the jump including a casualty estimate of twenty five percent.

That brought a lull to the group, until someone yelled, "If Jones said we can make the jump, we will do it." We left the tent optimistic but scared.

At 0400 the next morning, February 16, 1945, twenty years old with little hope of ever seeing my 21st birthday, I clambered aboard a 6x6 truck that transported a planeload of us to the airport. Outfitted in full combat gear and chutes, my body weight nearly doubled, but Geronimo effortlessly lifted me off the ground and into the plane. Of course, he too needed a push from behind. In past battles, his enormous strength became our greatest asset when the enemy zeroed in on our position. Without taking time to disassemble the steaming hot .50 caliber machine gun, he'd wrap his field jacket around it and lug it to our next position. However, in Corregidor, we remained relatively stationery, taking bonzai attacks head on.

Sitting along each side of the aircraft, heads down as if contemplating our combat boots, we rattled down the gravel strip in the wake of the previous C-47. Once airborne, we traded a washboard runway for swaying and dipping and clinging to our benches. A free hand might pull a Lucky Strike from a vest pocket, eyes darting for a buddy with a hot coal to bum a light. A few thumbs up and the unlit cigarette dangles from a bottom lip.

Like shit from a goose, twenty eight men spewed from the rear of an airplane willing yet wondering if they made the best decision to defend their country, their honor, their quest for adventure. If killed, it's all over; if survived, a challenge accomplished; if seriously wounded.... No soldier allows his mind to consider that option.

As I time-travel the nearly seventy-year gap between then and now, I think about unintended consequences of war, a Twenty First Century concept foreign to the minds of Paratroopers who sat on either side and across from me in 1945, waiting to be dropped into the furnace of Corregidor. We anticipated collateral damage. In training, soldiers sustained injuries and in rare instances died, and in battle we had non-combat accidental injuries and death. However, the greatest collateral damage occurred with our minds after the war, developed during engagements, recurring when back in civilian life. I can attest to that.

We barely understood established rules of engagement. The enemy hadn't even acknowledged the Geneva Convention, and their behavior reflected a breech of morality in combat. We adjusted military code into our revised golden rule; *do unto the enemy as they have proven time and again to do unto us.*

With Kilroy to my left and Geronimo to my right, I felt my back covered.

A stronger memory overtakes me as I reflect on this flight into hell, a piece of cake compared to an incident that occurred 20 years after the war.

Flanked by a district attorney and a public defender, not *guts-first-Kilroy* and *got-your-back-Geronimo*, I was embroiled in a fight **with** rather than **for** my country. That confusion accounted for my silence when asked to defend myself. I allowed these two men to define who I was.

"This man is a homicidal killer. He shot up a St. Paul city block and injured two men who could have been killed."

"This is a soldier who bravely fought for his country and is suffering from a flashback to his war experiences."

"He is a killer and needs to be put away for life."

"His mind is wounded, and he needs medical attention."

A pair of eyes glares down at me. "Are you capable of killing again?" A sardonic grin. "You'd probably shoot me right now if you had a gun."

My own self-condemnation. "You damn right, you slant-eyed-son-of-a-bitch! If I had a gun I'd aim right between the two of them." He might not even have been Oriental, I don't remember, but all my hate and anger for every despicable act and atrocity committed by the enemy burst forth. Eyeballs gouged, testicles mutilated. I didn't care what they could do to me. I should have been frightened.

Seated in the C-47 heading to Corregidor, I was still capable of experiencing fear, a human emotion erased from my psyche, lost during the battle that followed. *Hope*, the antidote to *fear*, also got left on the battle field.

Today, I understand it, back then I just jumped and performed my duty to country—brainwashed through training—and my personal duty to survive out of instinct.

I glanced up at our assigned lieutenant who gripped my shoulder. "Are you ready for this, Soldier?"

"Yes sir." He broke my concentration and returned me to warrior mode.

"Just like any practice jump, right Soldier?"

"Yes, Sir."

"How many?"

"Pardon?"

"How many times have you reached the ground safely?"

"One hundred and thirty two, Sir."

"Well, this will make 133."

I nodded as he stepped down the line and leaned over Kilroy tapping his shoulder, a signal to get ready. He opened the door. We stood, checked our gear and the chute of the man in front of us. Hooked to the static line, we awaited orders to jump. A spray of bullets ripped along the floor of the fuselage between the rows of paratroopers like a zipper or an ugly burp, only our officer directly in the line of fire. He veered sideways as if to avoid the bullet with his name on it, but everything happened too fast. Blood spurted and he toppled out the door. Kilroy instinctively reacted and led our string after him. It wasn't Lieutenant Serangeles floating through space like the angel I'd predicted when I first heard his name. He would have been the first causality on Corregidor, perhaps more honorable than stepping on a land mine in Negros a couple of months later.

Had that same bullet ended my life, I would have been spared half a lifetime of living hell, but I would have missed redemption through AA meetings these last two decades of my life.

Our jump altitude turned out to be less than 200 feet, enough for the chute to blossom and yank the rate of descent from near 100 mph down to free falling from a two-story building. My immediate landing area appeared clear of obstacles, and I prepared to tumble and avoid broken ankles or legs, the most common injuries on such low-level jumps.

A gust of wind caught the silk, raised my body, and slammed me to the ground, the metal buckle from the harness hammered against the small of my back. A sharp rock or jagged tree stump would have been worse and for some it was.

I freed myself and laid still a moment to assess the damage and to will my pain to dissipate, not sure if I could even walk. As in a dream, men dangled under billowy cloud-like canopies while others struggled to free themselves from chutes that wanted to return airborne. I sighted my assigned position near our Command Post being set up at a right angle to the far end of Mile Long Barracks.

I chose a route between trees and brush for cover, past a dry swimming pool where a Paratrooper peered out over the edge. I extended my carbine, and he grabbed the barrel, pulling himself over the side. Together we hobbled to the makeshift medical unit set up in the abandoned barracks.

He accepted morphine from a very busy medic, but I refused to remain in that death trap. The sight of bodies being carted to the broken down theater, a building designed for entertainment converted into a temporary morgue, motivated me to locate my squad. Adrenalin overtook the pain in my back.

Through the leafy branches, I sighted a flash of white, and proceeded to free a paratrooper hanging from a tree branch. I wasn't the first soldier there. A Jap was using the corpse for bayonet practice, slam and slice and yank. I reached a peak of anger greater than I ever thought possible. I emptied a full clip of ammo into that Jap, reloaded and riddled his body with another round of bullets.

The guy following me said, "You can only kill him once." He pushed his spare clip into my hands. "Here! You might need this."

I rammed the clip into my weapon and zigzagged my way to Command Post where I asked an officer where to go.

His comment, "I don't even know where the hell I am," convinced me that I was on my own. Fortunately, I found my squad having sustained no serious injuries, but we'd lost our assigned lieutenant, and our Captain Doherty had holed himself up inside the Command Post where he apparently spent the entire battle.

Had he stepped out and tried to reposition us, he would have accidentally been shot by friendly fire. We commandeered one of the dozen .50 caliber machine guns dropped on Topside, and located a position in the general area assigned to us that commanded a broad view all the way down to the beach. For three days we held that position and foiled a couple of small bonzai attacks and discouraged countless sneak attacks by soon-to-be dead Japs, self sacrificed heroes to their emperor.

We felt safe with our backs to the bulk of the 503rd until we encountered snipers from inside abandoned buildings and camouflaged tunnel openings to our rear. Our landing had been lightly opposed because reserve Japanese troops hid in tunnels prepared to repel the anticipated attack from Bottom Side.

Our unorthodox choice of landing site caught General Itagaki so thoroughly off guard that he stared up at the descending paratroopers rather than take cover. He was killed immediately, and a regiment of 6,000 soldiers lost their leadership.

Snipers could fire at us from any direction, so I really appreciated Geronimo's bulk crouched behind me. The rest of the squad ran ammo, fed the gun, and kept an eye out for the enemy. snipers during the day and sneak attacks at night. Every twenty minutes the Navy fired flares over the entire island, but the enemy used the timing to their advantage. We had the first few seconds to spot movement and spray it with bullets, but when the flash died, they had the advantage before our eyes could adjust.

By late afternoon, the first wave of odor from dying flesh swept over us, and it didn't let up until we left the island 25 days later. Gathering our dead was a high priority next to assisting the wounded. Trucks brought supplies and returned wounded men and bodies if space was available. I visualized the dead and dying bouncing on those 6x6 trucks down the rough and winding road to the beach. Lt. Smith was earning a medal without ever firing a shot. I never heard how many, if any, of his squad survived. Air-dropped supplies had stopped after the first day.

Near death from thirst is a memory that never goes away. The two canteens we jumped with didn't last long, even though we conserved water. Medics had no qualms about grabbing the canteen from a soldier nearly dying of thirst to give to one dying of a bullet wound.

From our gun emplacement, the beachhead below played out like a scene from a movie.

This bird's eye view included our third string of the 503rd whose jump on Topside had been cancelled. They joined up with 34th Infantry making the beachhead. The few Paratroopers who missed the drop zone and landed in the water got picked up by PT Boats and delivered to the battalion that didn't make the jump.

Col. Jones felt we had the upper hand and didn't want to risk more jump-related injuries. I don't know which of us was luckier, but we got credit for a combat jump and they didn't. When your entire military justification is jumping into battle, it is disappointing when a scheduled jump is cancelled. We already experienced two failed attempts to jump, but after Corregidor, I prefer canceled ones. I no longer had a need to prove anything or to be a hero. However, our beachhead on Negros Island changed my mind again. More about that later.

Because I'd been trained on the 75 millimeter, I felt resentment at being assigned a weapon that anyone could operate. Not only did the bigger gun require skill, it gave the gunner some distance from the enemy. Watching even enemy soldiers get shot close up leaves an indelible mark on a person's mind. My job was to man the .50 caliber machine gun, and I assumed the lead role when operating from an established position.

Some of those times, I assumed field sergeant status when one wasn't available to our squad. Or as it happened on Negros Island, the ranking officer and sergeant were killed, and the command fell to me. My disastrous order during that incident haunts me still. Geronimo took it upon himself to lounge over my back when I squatted to fire the weapon. *Gotta take care of the little guy.*

I spotted a potential target on a hillside between our position and the beachhead, a puff of smoke coming from between trees and underbrush followed by a boom and a splash on the surf. Focusing on a spot to the left of the source of smoke, my peripheral caught a glimpse of a gun barrel extend and immediately retract. A gun and crew were camouflaged inside the mouth of a cave, and we concentrated on quieting that emplacement off and on that first day. We reported it to Central Command but no one gave it any consideration.

Lorraine and her husband, Roger, and I were watching archive newsreels of Corregidor when I yelled, "Pause the tape." She backed it up, and I recognized Geronimo's back as he crouched over me. I could verify that it was my squad by the target, the hidden gun emplacement from which the barrel would appear fire down on our troops, and disappear. I would time my shots to match his exposure, and after hours of this hide-and-seek, we got pulled from that location to cover an area exposed to bonzai attacks.

After the newsreel that night, in bed I refought the Battle for Corregidor.

If I went back to that island today, I could still direct a research team to that exact spot from my position on that ridge back in 1945. At a reunion of the 503rd years later, I learned that researchers had found that cave still harboring the barrel of a rusted cannon. I felt vindicated.

By the third day, after our reassignment and after most of the gun's damage had been done, the emplacement had been acknowledged and became a target for ships' barrages.

By our fourth day on Corregidor, confusion from the everyone-for-himself attitude subsided into a competition between officers piecing together make-shift squads to meet headquarters' ever-changing directives. Teams such as ours got broken up, Paratroopers shuffled according to perceived needs and the rank of the officers creating squads for specific missions.

I functioned better under the extreme chaos of the first three days. When Captain Doherty tried to round up his company, me, Geronimo, and Kilroy didn't report. We joined up with Leining, a crazy guy from New Jersey, and formed our own squad.

I claimed a field rank of sergeant, located an unused .50 caliber—one of a dozen that had been dropped that first day—and set up in an abandoned building whose balcony I had spotted early on. The protected location gave us ample targets of a confused enemy who scattered and made desperate attempts to die heroically. With Leining's skill at rounding up ammo, we scored enough success to be left alone for the next few days until we got absorbed back into Captain Doherty's chain of command.

Japanese soldiers don't wear steel helmets, so when we saw a bare head or one covered with a cloth cap, we shot. So did everyone else, a good reason to wear that chunk of iron no matter how tired our necks got. We had it instilled in our training to keep quiet after dark to avoid friendly fire. Any movement in the bush got a spray of bullets.

Come morning, we'd sometimes find a large rodent–like animal riddled with bullet holes. We'd gut and cook the meaty parts in someone's helmet, first making sure he hadn't used it to relieve himself throughout the night.

We would eat right within sight and smell of the decaying bodies. We were desperately hungry, even after C-rations finally got through. However, ammo and water had priority on the trucks that snaked their way along the narrow road infested with snipers who understood the importance of this single supply line.

Little did we know that the remaining Japanese forces, more than half their original 6,000, were planning a major assault on the two battalions, a couple thousand of us, that landed Topside.

Day one we had a reprieve due to a surprised enemy. Days two and three we experienced a series of unorganized attempts to retake the high ground, our perimeter held. By the fourth and fifth day after the Jap's attempt to push the 43rd Infantry's beachhead (including the third battalion of the 503rd that didn't drop on Topside) back into the sea had failed, all hell broke loose Topside.

We were perched atop a giant anthill filled with a regiment of Japanese soldiers whose tunnels at the lower level had been blasted shut. They had no place to break out but Topside. Their bonzai attacks were out of desperation, because whoever holds the high ground has the advantage. If they had tried that strategy on day one, they could have wiped us out. Unfortunately for them, they lost their leader and the chain of command had been broken. American military command passes authority all the way down to the lowest soldier when isolated from superior ranks, as I found out on Negros Island.

Despite our advantageous position, their bonzai strategy still might have overwhelmed us. The largest group to attempt success-or-suicide numbered about 200 screaming Japs tossing grenades and yielding bayoneted rifles.

They chose what looked like a gap in our defenses, but we caught them in our crossfire. Had they advanced to a point between us, we would have been firing on each other.

From my periphery, I glimpsed some movement, but before I could take evasive action, I peered into the bloodied face of a wounded Jap. With his energy nearly spent, he half lunged and half tumbled toward me. I dodged his bayonet but caught the rifle butt under my chin. I thought for sure all my teeth had broken loose. I could wiggle some of them with my tongue, thankful I still had a tongue to do the wiggling. The teeth reseated themselves, but the damage had been done. Within a year after the war, I was wearing false uppers and lowers.

Our perimeters expanded and receded in cadence with bonzai attacks usually just before daybreak after a night of individual suicide attempts designed to wear on our nerves and keep us awake. Until then, our main concern had been getting water and food and medical supplies through the gauntlet of a narrow winding road. Now ammunition became our most urgent need.

Airdrops stopped after the first day because of anti aircraft fire and limited secured areas. Too many of our men were taken out of action trying to retrieve dropped cargo, and much of it was confiscated by the enemy who placed a high value on dying for a cause as small as retrieving a few gallons of water from an open field.

The stench of decaying bodies that merely tickled our nostrils on day one had overwhelmed our sense of smell and proceeded to attack our taste buds. The two senses are connected, and when our defense against pungent odors becomes the norm, the sense of taste takes over. We could virtually taste death on Corregidor.

Sailors at bay who would catch a wave when the wind shifted had no build up of defense against the odor, and they'd get sick much like ocean waves sickened Paratroopers. Green bottle flies appeared from nowhere when the first corpse expelled bodily fluids, perhaps that of General Ithaki. Leave it to a high-ranking officer to bring a plague to the common soldier.

Flies would get in our food as we spooned it into our mouths. Why they would choose C rations over abundant decaying bodies lying around is beyond me. A screened-in mess hall was something we only dreamed about as we gnawed on hardtack and beans, often within a few yards of the enemy we had killed only minutes before. We ate out of necessity for nourishment whenever and wherever a relatively quiet moment occurred. A brave pilot in a small aircraft sprayed the entire island with a fine mist of DDT and the flies all but disappeared. Traces of that chemical are probably still in my body.

On February 25, the 34th Infantry was pulled from the island to join the assault of Manila on the mainland leaving a single battalion of the 503rd below the mountain and two battalions of us on the high ground. However, they left two M-4 Sherman tanks. One fired a round directly into the main tunnel on Monkey Point creating an explosion as if an earthquake had hit the island.

Later reports claimed the Japanese set off the explosion, so we will never know for sure. The results caused 199 American causalities, more than fifty of them fatal. One paratrooper on Topside got hit by a huge rock two thousand feet from Monkey Point and five hundred feet above it.

The blast tossed both Sherman tanks into the air like toys, one landing upside down sealing the crew inside and one lying on its side totally disabled. The commander of the second tank staggered out, pulled his .45 pistol, and placed a slug in the tank's underbelly, claiming to put it out of its misery.

The catastrophe below had a double effect on us; the chaos and demand for medical assistance deprived us of our necessary supplies, and now the Jap's only way out of the tunnels was further up the hill. If those remaining Japanese forces had overtaken us on Topside, it would have required a major assault to dislodge them, and we wouldn't be alive to help. The success of the campaign rested entirely on the 503rd, especially those of us still vulnerable but hanging on to Topside.

On February 27, the assault part of the campaign officially ended and mop-up began. My 2d Battery was awarded that honor. We no longer waited for the enemy to attack, but we pursued them beyond our perimeter. For the individual soldier, this is the most frightening and dangerous operation. We had to take turns exposing ourselves to draw fire for a desperate enemy who was forbidden to surrender. I witnessed more American casualties during mop-up than during the bonzai attacks.

In the midst of the cleanup, General McArthur decided to pay Corregidor a visit.

Col. Jones ordered us to press beyond our established perimeter to flush out any pockets of the enemy and then secure it with double the usual number of posts. We knew something big was about to happen. March 2, 1945, down on South Point a cluster of PT boats pulled up to the dock, and a group of clean khakis and visored hats disembarked and entered a convoy of Jeeps, Col. Jones at the lead.

The column snaked its way up the winding trail—past the icehouse, the hospital, Middle Side Barracks, Post Exchange, the theater that had served as a morgue—and halted on the parade ground in front of the demolished Mile Long Barracks. General MacArthur stepped down from his Jeep and stood face to face with Col. Jones.

Jones saluted and made his famous statement. "Sir, I present you Fortress Corregidor."

When my son-in-law asked, "Did you see General McArthur?" like it was an honor to witness an historical event, I gritted my teeth.

I answered truthfully, "I had him in my sites."

If an opportunist Jap chose that moment to kill one of my comrades to make himself a hero, the Jap would have been my second target. Then President Truman wouldn't have to fire him during the next war in Korea. I still blame McArthur for all the unnecessary deaths on Corregidor and Manila because he felt his honor was at stake. He took the coward's way out a few years earlier by PT boat from the South Dock on San José Beach, and at great risk to his men he returned at that location to claim victory.

However, he did acknowledge the bravery of the 503rd Regiment.

> Col. Jones, the capture of Corregidor is one of the most brilliant operations in military history. Outnumbered two to one, your command by its unfaltering courage, its invincible determination, and its professional skill overcame all obstacles and annihilated the enemy.
>
> I have cited to the order of the day all units involved, and I take great pride in awarding you as their commander the Distinguished Service Cross as a symbol of the fortitude, the devotion, and the bravery with which you have fought. I see the old flagpole still stands. Have your troops hoist the colors to its peak, and let no enemy ever haul them down.

On March 6, Lt. General Hall returned to the island and during another ceremony presented Silver Stars, Bronze Stars, and Purple Hearts to the heroic men of the 503rd. Four of these men were yet to be killed while flushing out and killing another 118 of the enemy before the 503rd was relieved of the campaign. We missed approximately twenty Japanese holdouts who marched down from Topside with a white flag half a year later. From a newspaper one of their scouts picked up during a nightly foray to find food and water, they learned that their emperor had surrendered.

By the 25th day, things got eerily quiet. Something was up. The guys who had been running ammunition and supplies didn't return. I attached a grenade to the firing mechanism of the .50 caliber in case some stray Jap might find a use for it and joined the ranks of soldiers marching down to the beach. We boarded LCI's back to Mindoro.

273

The ride on those flat-bottomed boats was rougher than the flight that brought us to this God forsaken island, and it took a lot longer.

We traded the smell of decaying bodies for an odor not quite so rank as dead bodies, live bodies that hadn't bathed for a month. As usual, the clean-shaven officers boarded separate boats.

Back on Mindoro

We landed at the harbor on Mindoro near the airstrip from which we embarked on our Corregidor drop. We marched to our base camp for some R&R; a hot water shower while sponged by native girls, a meal cooked and served in a mess tent, and 36-48 hours of sleep. We paid native boys (and girls) to guard our tent against interruptions.

I missed mail call, but the letter from my mother had been delivered to my tent waiting for when I woke up. She concluded by demanding, "Get even with the enemy," Japs or Krauts, she didn't care. "Kill as many as you can to even the score."

Then and there my mind twisted, not during the intensity of Corregidor or the jungle snipers on the upcoming Negros campaign, but right there when I read my mother's letter. She had received my account of being lost—my follow-up letter Capt. Daugherty refused to write—and I felt the full impact of her revenge. And, my responsibility to act out her revenge! *Kill the enemy, Jap or Kraut, just even the score.* I went one step farther, intending to *keep* score by taking minor trophies, a practice too macabre to follow through with. At least for very long.

My mother no longer feared for my safety already having lost both her sons in her mind. By this time I had defied death, and I no longer feared getting killed.

Years later when I rode my horse into Northfield, Minnesota, reenacting the James' Gang bank robbery, I understood what Jesse James felt having survived the Civil War.

Nothing mattered, not even his own life. He and I experienced our deaths on the battlefield—no need to fear about how it will actually happen. Unlike Jesse James, I want to be remembered for what I did for my country during the war, not for some of my actions during intense combat or as a civilian with emotional problems after the war ended.

After Corregidor, I became a loner. When not on a patrol, I'd spend nights in the tent with my regular squad but come sunup I'd disappear. When Kilroy confronted me about it, Geronimo cautioned him to give me time to settle down. He even suggested I talk to the Chaplain. That didn't work back in New Guinea when I received the letter explaining how my brother got killed in Italy. News of his death had weighed heavily on me much like my mother's demand for revenge in her recent letter. I wasn't angry back then, just unbelievably sad. I needed a quiet place to sort out my feelings.

Our base camp had amenities such as a mess tent, hospital tent, and a tent for religious services. I hadn't felt a need to pray for my brother, but I needed the seclusion of some quiet space. I sat holding the letter from my sister who got the news from Edward's wife. The military only notified a spouse or a mother if the killed soldier was not married. Edward had eloped before he shipped out, but my family accepted his bride until she shunned them after receiving the government's $10,000 death benefit.

At the time of Edward's death, I felt sympathy for the woman he loved. Sitting in the quiet tent that night, I felt no resentment of her, only sadness for the loss of an older brother. I looked up to him. When his behavior got himself into trouble like the time he took a joy ride with a *borrowed* car and wound up in jail, I repeated his mistake a few years later.

On the plus side, we planned to start a grocery business when he got back from the war. He would never come back and I doubted that I would.

A Chaplain entered the tent and asked, "What's the matter, Soldier?"

I replied, "I just learned that my brother was killed in action."

"In war, that happens." He didn't sound very sympathetic.

Without glancing up at the officer, I muttered, "I came here to sort out my thoughts."

He responded in a harsh voice. "What do you want me to do about it?"

"I want to be left the hell alone." I didn't say *get out of my face*, but my tone implied it, I'm sure.

"Be careful Soldier. I outrank you."

"That's a laugh. Everyone outranks me. Now please leave me alone. Sir."

"I could report you for that attitude."

"I don't give a damn. Get the fuck out."

He left and I didn't lose my second stripe, the rank I had regained in combat as a matter of policy. It would continue to come and go on Negros Island to the end of the war.

And now Geronimo wanted me to visit a Chaplain in the middle of a combat zone. Any Chaplain still sane after Corregidor would tell me to *buck up* and face reality. I walked away from my squad. We didn't regain our spirit of comradeship until after Japan surrendered, and that reunion turned out to be our biggest personal tragedy of the war.

I scouted around and located my Corregidor buddy, Leining, who in civilian life would have been considered a bad apple for me to hang with. His kind of friends got me in trouble back as a teenager, and some of those bad choices got me into the army. So it goes. We had done some tough time together on Corregidor, and this bonded us. His careless attitude of thumbing his nose at all rules was the kind of buddy I needed at the moment. Together me and Leining formed a black market operation that began in Mindoro and lasted throughout Negros.

Out on the streets, he would be a minor mob boss and I his first lieutenant. Years later I was offered a job as bodyguard to a real St.

Paul mobster, but I turned down the offer. My relationship with Leining probably taught me not to get involved. However, I continued to associate with the mob boss—we played cribbage together—and a few times I relied on his protection, like I had with my sisters when I was a kid with a shoe shine location. After the war someone attempted to butt in on my beer route. My association with the mob boss came to my rescue.

Our R&R on Mindoro was cut short when the 34th Army Regiment required back-up on Negros Island.

Negros Island

With less than two weeks of R&R on Mindoro, orders came to gather all our combat gear, including chutes, and report to our designated airstrip. We were scheduled to jump on Negros Island in support of the 34th Regiment who had abandoned us back on Corregidor. Little did we know that history would repeat itself on Negros.

As a contrast to our mid-air canceled jump on Mindoro, this time many of the C-47's didn't show up. Our goal had been to protect a lumberyard, probably to win over the native population by saving that part of their economy, almost like performing an exhibition jump in combat. I don't think the army planned to build us modern barracks with that lumber. However, the Japanese blew it up before retreating into the jungles and over mountains to their friendlier Oriental Providence on the east side of Negros Island.

Our batteries split between the 503rd Regiment's 2nd and 3rd battalions, and we landed on Panay Island adjacent to the Occidental (west) side of the island. From there, we sailed in flat-bottom boats directly to the harbor at Bacolod, the Occidental capital and its major city. We trucked through the city and past the bombed-out airport to a bivouac just outside of town. Part of the platoon broke away from the caravan and stopped at a friendly native village, where the locals treated us to a feast; monkey meat this time. We crossed a river and marched a few miles to establish a perimeter against a Japanese controlled part of the jungle.

There all hell broke loose. We immediately took fire and lost a couple of recruits who had joined us at Mindoro. The one assigned to my squad couldn't keep his head down, and he took a bullet the first day. It was the only time someone in my squad got killed.

The second or third day we dug in at the crest of a small hill and set up our .50 caliber. Early morning we were attacked, not a direct bonzai like on Corregidor, but under cover of the morning fog from various points. We held our ground until we heard approaching noises from behind us. Feeling surrounded we swung our rifles around, ready to fire at any movement.

A voice pierced the moist air. "Who's there?" Definitely American! Some Japs spoke English, but none could hide their accent.

We identified ourselves, and a dozen paratroopers stepped into the clearing.

"What are you guys doing up here? We gave up this hill last night and called a retreat."

"Didn't hear it." With the fog lifting, two Jap bodies became visible just a few yards in front of our foxhole.

The sergeant in command said, "Holy shit! You guys held the hill." He glanced down the hillside at scattered enemy bodies. "This gotta be worth something."

Had he been an officer, we might have qualified for some medal, but my outburst would have erased all chances of that, and my tirade might even have gotten me in trouble. We had been abandoned to face the brunt of the enemy's' charge by ourselves. I was pissed!

Our position continued to draw occasional fire, and we prepared for the Japs to stage a frontal attack. No such luck. Unlike the enemy on Corregidor, these guys dug in at established positions designed for cross fire which made them impossible to flank.

Just when we felt we got the upper hand, they'd retreat to a backup position, equally well covered. Scanning to our rear, we had a clear picture of the distance we had advanced, as the enemy must have observed us struggling to gain ground. Each new ridge became the next hard-won high ground.

By early June, we controlled an upper level, safe for our camp to relocate. Our strategy shifted between direct frontal attacks by platoons and sometimes full companies to squad-sized patrols that could pull back to camp every few days, dangerous operations but interspersed with some relief.

Our camp position was within sight of a camp of the 34th who shared the island with us, and who would later abandon us to mop up alone for a second time. From their higher elevation, camp lights at night would tease us with a luxury we hadn't experienced since we arrived. They had commandeered the former Japanese supply depot, where our scouts spotted a second unused Japanese generator. A group of us pestered Col. Jones to request it. He agreed but a general in the 34th flatly refused to give it up. Those were Jones' exact words back to us, *a general in the 34th*, capitalizing on our disdain for all authority above our colonel and our anger with the regiment that left us to the mop-up on Corregidor.

He threw up his arms and said, "There's nothing I can do," with the emphasis on "I" as if other options were available.

That night we borrowed a truck from our motor pool, drove the winding trail to their camp, and stole a generator from under their noses. Actually, we traded whatever cigarettes we had between ourselves to bribe the equipment corral sergeant to look the other way, while a dozen of us hoisted it onto the truck bed.

That night the officers of the 34th Regiment put two incidents together, our lit-up camp with their missing generator, and they drew the logical conclusion. The next morning, a Jeep-load of minor officers from the 34th parked in front of our headquarters. They returned to their commander with the following message from Col. Jones.

Possession is nine-tenths of the law. On the battlefield possession is 100 percent of the law.

We had our electricity and a life-long reputation that we developed into a slogan, *Col. Jones and his 3000 thieves.* Even today we display a wall-sized poster with that slogan printed in large letters at the lobby of whatever hotel we chose to host our reunion.

For about two months, we slogged it out with the enemy to gain some hard-earned ground. Our most dangerous but most productive operations were the patrols lasting a few days to over a week. Combat conditions were more like what we experienced when taking over Mindoro than our retaking Corregidor, but the Jap's resistance was much tougher. Japan's supply routes had been cut off by the U.S. Navy, and B29's began bombing Tokyo. Their strategy concentrated on preventing a joint Marine and Army invasion of their home land. They discovered that American soldiers liked winning and did not like dying. Thus, they accepted huge losses of their own men attempting to kill us whenever they had the opportunity. Negros and Okinawa and Manila were perfect examples of this strategy. These weren't exclusively military fortresses, but islands with large native populations.

Japan's only hope was to turn the American people against the war. That didn't work because, *in my opinion*, those not fighting were enjoying the booming economy that the war created.

Back in the States, I overheard two women lamenting the loss of their lucrative jobs manufacturing ammo. They had no concept of how many innocent lives that ammunition wiped out on Negros Island and Manila and Okinawa, only how rich they'd get if we invaded Japan. That was my opinion back then and has changed little since.

As we cleared a swath a few miles wide, camp would pull up stakes and follow up the hill. We made five such moves over the six months we remained on that island. We would occasionally free a village from Japanese occupation and reap a few rewards from the natives. When young girls wandered into our camp, we hired them as servants for a few bucks or cigarettes or chocolate bars.

Although my mother's demand for revenge simmered in my mind, survival mode kicked in. We only encountered the rear guard of a retreating Japanese regiment, but they fought with suicidal abandon trying to take as many of us with them as possible. Snipers tied themselves to their positions in the trees so their bodies would consume more American bullets. Japs would draw fire on themselves and dart into a villager's hut to trick us into taking responsibility for killing natives with our cross fire.

I was sent to assist a squad that had flushed two Japs out of the jungle who ran into what seemed like an abandoned hut, too large for a single family. We approached with caution, not wanting to kill innocent people as well as not getting ourselves shot-up. Wrong on both counts! Our lieutenant got hit and we returned fire toward the source of the sound. Sergeant now in command halted our firing and made a motion for us to surround the hut. His movement drew fire, and he took a slug in the chest before we could execute his order.

Holding the next highest rank, I yelled, "Take it out."

Pastors, counselors, and fellow veterans have told me to forgive myself, but I cannot.

When we walked to the front of what was left of the building to assess the carnage, the crucifix above the entry loomed out at me. I had no choice but to step inside to document the enemy kill. Two Japanese bodies, and quite a few others; all native women!

I reported the incident back at headquarters to an unconcerned officer. He said, "You did what you had to do."

Those ten dead women became a mere notation on a report, but it left an indelible mark on my conscience. I couldn't enter a church without these innocent souls screaming their anger at me, until decades later when my daughter in Las Vegas insisted I attend a Lutheran service with her and her husband. By coincidence, the sermon that Sunday dealt with forgiving oneself because Jesus already had done so. I'm quite sure the pastor had no idea of the load my conscience carried, but I took him at his word. After a year of Sundays, I began to take Communion.

Strange relationships developed between us and the enemy. We learned the names and ranks of a few officers from the natives who didn't collaborate with the Japs and were vengeful of those who had. One whose name and rank passed throughout our various squads had a particularly beautiful concubine in the village, two reasons why other native women didn't like her. When he got killed in a firefight, we recognized his name and rank. That night his girlfriend had a partial visitor, his head on her doorstep.

I took a nearly spent bullet directly to my forehead. It penetrated my helmet and pierced my skin, the scar visible to this day. Another purple heart rejected as laughable. The medic dabbed some anti bacterial stuff on the wound.

He handed me the metal slug. "This one had your name on it. It'll keep you safe for the rest of the war."

Further proof that I had nothing to fear! I drilled a hole through the thumb-sized metal and strung it alongside my dog tags, all lost in the blast that blew me out of the army.

Pvt. Leining, my partner in crime, convinced me that Col. Jones' definition of ownership in war applied to anything we could get our hands on. In addition to Spam and canned peaches, it included 180 proof alcohol installed in the trigger mechanism of torpedoes, which shouldn't have been stockpiled this far inland, to our notion. Diluted by half with water brought our best price from alcohol starved soldiers. We filled our footlocker with thousands of dollars, a fun but foolish enterprise because we couldn't mail cash back to the states without the censors alerting the authorities. Japanese souvenirs but not cash could be shipped after the war, a different enterprise that blew up in my squad's faces after the war ended.

Each day of combat brought on another degree of anger and lessened my fear factor an equal amount. I would drop a sniper and take a position alongside the body in case his replacement might show up. I would draw fire to expose the enemy knowing his bullet wouldn't touch me.

On one of my solitary patrols (hunts to satisfy my mother) I spotted an ambush about to take pace. Behind some bushes along a ravine, a small group of enemy soldiers hid waiting for an approaching convoy of trucks. I had no time to warn the drivers, so I attacked tossing grenades, firing my rifle, and when up close, I pulled my sawed off shotgun from its makeshift holster and splattered the group with two barrels of buckshot. The trucks roared by leaving me with a pile of dead bodies.

I reported the incident to the recently installed second lieutenant in charge of our company.

When I described the enemy kill, his eyes nearly bugged out. "A shotgun? Did you say a shotgun, Private?"

"Yes, Sir. Twelve gauge buckshot. I sawed off the barrel for easy access and a bigger spread."

"Is that the weapon?"

"Yes, Sir."

He held out his hand. "Give it to me."

With both barrels, I thought but handed it to him.

He studied it as if it might bite him. "I'll have to confiscate this, Soldier. By the Geneva Convention, it is an illegal weapon."

I reached for it. "Sir, that's my shotgun. I want it back."

"Stand down, Soldier. I will have to report any further action or discussion on this matter."

I backed off, not because I cared about his consequences, but because I considered him a dead man. One night patrol together would be his last. That opportunity never presented itself because he was transferred as far from my squad as was possible on this island. The issue went all the way to headquarters, possibly to Col. Jones' attention, according to the feedback I got through the grapevine.

"You took a man's weapon and it's not safe for you to be in command of his squad." Not sure who said it or if these were the exact words, the lieutenant's reassignment convinced me that someone up the chain of command knew me inside and out. Big deal, I no longer had my shotgun.

On a brighter note, that evening I returned to the tent shared with two squads and our officers—on Negros, lieutenants as well as sergeants bedded alongside their men—to find the remnants of both squads all shaved and smelling of government-issue disinfectant soap.

"Judy Garland and Joey Brown are performing on stage under the lights," yelled a sergeant on his way out.

I didn't relish being crammed between hundreds of similar smelling men cheering a gyrating dolly and her dog-faced boyfriend. I'd rather lie on my cot and allow the events of the day to wash over me. However, flashing lights and amplified music got my curiosity up, and I wandered to the improvised stage surrounded by paratroopers arranged according to rank, the lowly privates with the best seats. An USO show was the only place where officers lost all privileges. Often a private would be pulled onto the stage, the envy of everyone.

Barely within earshot of the speakers, I heard, "Private Richard Leslie, up front pronto."

Before I could check myself, I responded as I'd been conditioned, but my first name had been included in the command. To an officer, enlisted men had only a last name and a number. Still smelling of death, I stumbled to the foot of the stage, where Joey Brown reached down and helped me onto the platform. I was too astounded to salute Col. Jones separated from me by none other than Judy Garland.

The colonel faced the movie star. "Miss Garland, I've been informed that Private Leslie saved your life this afternoon as well as the lives of Mr. Brown and your crew. As you requested, you may reward this person with a kiss." Undistracted by the jeers and catcalls, he added, "You may proceed."

Judy Garland's lips pressed onto each of my cheeks felt delicious, but having Col. Jones refer to me as a *person* was the most astonishing. I shook Joey Brown's hand and saluted my commanding officer, waiting to be dismissed.

"Any soldier," he waved his hand to encompass the entire audience, "would have done the same thing, but Private Leslie happened to be in the right place at the right time." He glanced at me and said, "You may step down, Soldier."

I remained standing rigid, not overwhelmed at the situation but waiting to hear the magic word, "Dismissed." A stagehand cupped my shoulder and led me off stage. Returning down the aisle was like running the gauntlet, every soldier within reach cheering, slapping, and giving mock salutes. I returned to my tent and allowed my smile to continue until I fell asleep.

I didn't spend the entire six months isolated in the jungles of Negros. Our first R&R occurred in the city of Bacolod after 67 days and three camp moves farther out in the field. During that brief stay back in a somewhat civilized setting, I relearned the value of money, what pleasures it could buy. At the airport I took a practice jump to qualify for continued jump pay, and found a contact person who would fence the items Leining and I could pilfer from either governments, American or Japanese.

I had no interest in locally traded commodities such as fruits and vegetables that consumed the soldier's meager pay, but black market items the city folks craved. We only accepted American currency that accompanies our armies wherever they go. Transporting items from our various caches to the city was the fence's responsibility.

However, I made a few trips to the city whenever a Jeep became available, often at the cost of losing a stripe from my uniform. It would automatically come back to my shoulder any time I got involved in a firefight. Off and on, off and on. If only Velcro had been invented back then.

Patrols often began with a Jeep ride as far as roads were available followed by a hike through jungle or rugged terrain. With the luck of the draw, one or two of the squad would tend the Jeep while the others carried out the mission. A couple extra cans of fuel made a trip to town possible.

By midsummer our base camp had reached the mountains that separated West Occidental from East Oriental Negros. We had gained control of the high ground, and it was downhill for what was left of the Japanese army. The 34th Infantry pulled out, and the 503rd inherited the mop-up action for a second time. Some of our bloodiest action occurred those last few weeks as we attempted to clean up the aftermath, not realizing that six thousand Japs still hid out. Our companies were scattered throughout the island, each in desperate need of our four battery units. Our engineer units were busy repairing the damages the regiment continued to create.

Then rumors started about invading Japan's mainland. The marines had taken Okinawa, and B29's bombed Tokyo almost off the map, but the Japs refused to surrender. Their suicide strategy all but destroyed the American will to pursue the war, but our military was a machine full in control. Estimated American casualties from a mainland invasion would be in the hundreds of thousands.

Our particular mission, we learned later, would have been the Yokohama Airport with a total wipeout of the first three strings. As in Corregidor, battery units would have to accompany the infantry.

The tension increased when combat gear including parachutes got stockpiled, and we were put on ready alert for a mission at any moment. Companies were gathering around airports, and life in the camps became chaotic. In the midst of this turmoil, we were called to muster on the parade grounds for an announcement. The invasion had begun, we were sure.

Col. Jones stepped up to the stand, and the bulk of 503rd now bivouacked at this camp jumped to attention and saluted. We dreaded his message, but he was our esteemed leader, and to a man, we would follow him into hell.

He addressed us, "Men of the 503rd." He paused but didn't say, "As you were." Some men still saluting, others gaping, we heard, "Japan has surrendered. The war is over." The silence continued for a long minute, and then slowly developed into a cataclysmic roar. The 50-70% percent of us who would not have survived yelled the loudest. That would be each of us, we were sure.

We entered into a time span of no-man's-land when we were forbidden to shoot the enemy but they continued to shoot at us.

We were pulled back from our outer perimeters, but the enemy could have seen that as a buildup for a major assault. They weren't informed of their government's surrender until five days later, and many didn't trust the information. We saturated the jungle with leaflets dropped from the air to confirm what their officers had received from their government. Confusion reigned. Some higher-ranking officers committed ritual suicide, leaving a gap in their command structure.

Throughout the Negros campaign, we experienced individual Japs wandering toward us waving their arms, some even with white flags, only to pull the pin when they got within range. To us it seemed no different, unless an officer followed by his men made a surrender gesture.

We received the order to pull back, a vulnerable time for any squad in combat. One of my squad noticed him and yelled, "Jap!" On impulse I swung the 50 Caliber and let loose with a spray of bullets.

"Oops" or "Oh Shit," I can't recall which.

We packed up, pulled back and reported the incident. Apparently, mine wasn't the only one because existing squads were broken up; their automatic response would be to fire on Japs emerging from the woods.

Squabbles between the men over the spoils of war began after the officers had commandeered the most sought after souvenirs, Japanese officer's swords. I missed all the goodies, but reveled in the easy duty that followed. The enemy was no longer dangerous, and in many cases hardly recognizable as human beings. The first group I was assigned to guard had been isolated from their supply line and some were nearly starved to death.

I struck up an association with an officer who had been a student at Stanford on break visiting his family in Japan when the war broke out. The Japanese army immediately drafted him.

Another foot soldier had become my sort of valet. Although the prisoners were subdued, they still needed to be guarded. To me that meant leaning against a tree with my rifle in easy reach.

One lazy afternoon I called for my valet, handed him my rifle and said, "You guard your fellow prisoners. I'm going to take a nap." What the hell, the war was over, and he relished in the opportunity. Fortunately, he didn't get carried away and shoot any who refused to obey him. A short time ago, a dead Jap would have been a statistic, but after their surrender it would require an inquiry.

As we were slowly relieved of guard duty—I'm not sure what happened to the prisoners, either shot or, most likely, sent back to Japan, I supposed—we were transported to Dumaguete where our futures would be decided. I was short eleven points to earning a discharge, but I did not intend to return to civilian life. If my leaves home during and after training didn't work out, how much worse would civilian life be after a year and a half of combat. I realized I needed structure, often just to have something to rebel against, and I knew just how far I could go before I got into serious trouble. In civilian life, rules were vague and accidentally breaking them could create problems. I had accepted the military way of life, and without the threat of being shot every day, life would be pretty darn good. I would be safe!

My original squad of seven had survived without a loss or even any serious physical damage, emotional damage not yet apparent. We *borrowed* a Jeep and toured the countryside in search of war mementos to bring stateside, possible bragging rights or a good price on the black market. We approached a Jap bunker that looked ripe for the picking.

From this point I have two memory blackouts, one perhaps a daylong and the second at least a month long. The bunker had been booby trapped, and the rest of my squad took the full impact of the blast, me the only survivor. I recall a brief moment of shock and grief as I sat on my cot back in my squad's tent. I struggle to this day to recall what happened before or after that moment, but can only guess. Our bodies either dead or unconscious were discovered and brought back to camp. My injuries were not life threatening but my reactions threatened those around me after I learned of my friends' deaths. I must have gone berserk. My next conscious moment I was aboard a hospital ship in body restraints.

In my possession were the seven chips from that bar in California where we confirmed our friendship. I could only assume that they were handed to me before I went crazy. Maybe Geronimo had remained alive until he was satisfied that I was okay. He would have secured those chips for me to release his and Kilroy's and Jenkins and Heidt's and Reed's and Jennings's spirits.

The medics had sedated me and kept me in a coma for an extended period. When I came to, I had no fight left in me, not until years later when my war experiences returned.

Facts About the 503rd

Some facts to conclude the part of the Pacific Theater of WWII that I experienced. Of the 503rd seven airborne missions (Markham Valley,

Hollandia, Noemfoor, Leyte, Mindoro, Corregidor, and Negros), we never made a full regimental jump with all battalions, a total of 3,000 men. Our first jump was Markham valley in New Guinea before the artillery battery, of which I was a member, had been included. Hollandia, another New Guinea Providence off Soro Bay, was my first combat experience. In July 1945, Battalions A and C jumped at Noemfoor unopposed, the rest of us brought in by LCI's. Leyte was a partial jump to secure a runway that could not be saved because of the rainy season. (During this time, I and 33 other men were dropped into Leyte on an unsuccessful mission to secure a sugar mill.) Even on our most serious airdrop on Corregidor, the third string landed on the beach by-way-of LCI's. Then came Negros!

Except for five weeks in Australia, (I met up with the regiment at that point) the 503rd was continuously in an active combat zone from July of 1943 to the end of the war. I made three combat jumps including Corregidor and the limited jump that incurred 90% casualties, only three out of thirty four of us survived. My third jump was a routine practice jump during the Negros campaign. Between our beachheads and our jump on Corregidor, I spent eighteen continuous months in an active battle zone.

I bring up these statistics to help the reader understand my behavior during the Negros campaign, my final six months in the war, and all that happened since then. The 503rd again received orders to reinforce the 34th Infantry Division currently bogged down in Negros in the central part of the Philippines. We prepared to jump but for the third time it was canceled, and we made a beachhead landing, my fourth beachhead.

Five times we established a field camp as we worked our way from Bacolod on the Occidental sector of Negros to Dumaguete on the Oriental sector on the east side of the island across jungle and mountains. Our first move occurred in June when the Japanese strategy changed from offensive to defensive under cover of jungle and rough terrain.

The 34th Infantry left, and the 503rd continued to battle the Japanese alone. At the end of the war in August 1945, nearly 7500 Japanese surrendered to the 503rd Regimental Combat Team. Official War Department sources estimated that the 503rd killed over 10,000 Japanese, probably 4 or 5 for every soldier of the 503rd who was engaged in combat. As a machine gunner on each campaign, sniper with specified and general targets, and a participant on many patrols, I could not begin to estimate my contribution the 503rd estimated statistics.

However, I have documented in my mind my first and last kill, the young Japanese soldier in New Guinea and a Jap who maybe intended to surrender after the war officially ended, both incidents described above.

Official records place Japan's surrender on August 15, 1945, but we accepted our last platoon of prisoners September 14, five days before my twentieth birthday. Two months later, the 503rd ceased operations, and the regiment was finally deactivated at Camp Anza, California, on December 24, 1945. I survived to the very end, the last two months in and out of a coma. Ironically, my first clear memory occurred in a Catholic Church in Brigham City, Utah, during Midnight Mass on that same Christmas Eve. I can only estimate the date of my concussion and my squad's demise to be around mid October.

I made it through the war with my morphine needle intact, never having to use it on a fallen comrade or myself. A few of my comrades had been killed in my presence, mostly in Negros when patrols were sent to flush out the enemy, and some were injured, but none required or had need of morphine. Also, the cyanide capsule remained securely sewn in the hem of my field jacket.

As of 2013, less than 200 veterans from our regiment are still alive, 15-20 of us continue to perform role call at our annual convention. I am afraid 2012 will be my final reunion. In 2010, we voted a last man standing resolution to retire the colors at that time rather than incorporate them into the 11th Airborne. Other units have coveted our colors since the 503rd Parachute Regimental Combat Team ceased to exist in 1945.

Back at State Side

Needless to say, a part of me died in the Philippines, and the part that survived sustained damage.

Other than realizing I was restrained to a bed on a hospital ship, I have no memory of that journey or how and when we docked or how I arrived at Camp Hon, California. The two-week quarantine holds a shadowy spot in my brain. I understood they needed to see if I brought home any ugly microscopic creatures, and I was a bit curious myself. I had escaped malaria, typhus, jungle rot and the clap, but what might be floating throughout my blood system did concern me.

I agreed to remain isolated, but I did not accept it with any degree of patience. I wandered to the PX and gazed at all the items that would have been luxuries on the islands or totally unavailable.

When the girl behind the counter asked what I wanted—my stupid gaze must have exposed my confusion—I asked, "Do you have milk?"

"Yes. Would you like a glass?"

Of all the commodities I handled overseas, I don't recall ever having access to good old cow's milk. I must have ordered half a dozen glasses of it from that astounded server.

I recall being annoyed with nearly everyone who seemed to be in my way, but I don't think I got into any fights. That came later.

After quarantine, I requested a day pass to go to Riverside, curious if they trusted me to be on my own. I got the pass without reservation, and I didn't think anyone followed me.

If they realized how shaky I was, MP's would have escorted me, as they soon discovered were necessary.

I boarded the bus to Riverside directly to the bus stop near the bar where I had some business to complete.

"I need to see the manager." The bartender hesitated as if to say, *who the hell are you?* However, he called his boss from the back room. "Do you remember me?" I asked as the manager crinkled his face into a frown.

"Can't say that I do."

"About two years ago seven of us bought some Champaign."

"I remember. If you still have your chit, I will bring out a bottle?" He cast a curious but sympathetic glance and repeated. "Chits? Seven of them, if I recall."

"Yes. I have all seven of them."

He faced the bartender. "On the shelf behind my desk are seven bottles of Champaign. Bring them out here."

Silence until the bottles were lined up in front of me. The manager stammered, "All six of your buddies?"

"Yeah, every one of them." More silence. "Can I have your bar hammer?"

He handed me a wooden mallet used to break blocks of ice and stood back.

"Hey are you crazy?" The bartender stepped forward, but the manager held out his hand.

"Let him do what he has to do." Bang, one of the bottles exploded. "We'll clean up the mess when he's done."

Shattered glass and foamy liquid spread across the bar and splattered onto my uniform and the manager's shirt. The manager pulled one bottle from my final aim and said, "We have to drink this one." He popped the cork and filled two glasses.

I raised mine and said, "To all of us who tried."

We drank and he said, "You have honored their memories. Now you have to look out for yourself." I set my half-full glass on the bar. "You can keep this last bottle. I'm sorry about the mess." I left the bar and caught the bus back to Camp Hon.

The nurse on my ward took my damp jacket that smelled like booze and said, "I didn't expect you until tonight."

I muttered, "I can't take it," and flopped onto the bed. She respected my privacy.

A few days later I tried another day pass. I stopped at the bar to apologize for making the mess, but a different bartender told me the manager was out. I asked to use the phone to call a cab.

My sister had written me the address of my paternal grandmother in Whittier whom I had never met. Parked in front of her door, I told the cab driver to wait until I return or flag him off. A good thing I did.

A woman wearing a white tunic answered the door. "Yes."

"I'm here to see Mrs. Leslie. She's my grandmother."

Still blocking the door she turned and yelled, "Your son is here to see you."

"I don't have a son."

I interjected, "I'm her grandson."

"It's your grandson."

"I don't have a grandson."

Rejected, I returned to the cab and asked how much to take me directly to Camp Hon. I couldn't bear to ride that noisy bus back to camp. I lucked out by getting the same cab driver who took us to Coney Island in New York, or one just like him.

"Five dollars to get back to the bar where I picked you up. The additional miles on me."

How I wished that cabby were my grandparent rather than the one I just about met.

Bushnell Military Hospital in Brigham City, Utah

After numerous consultations with doctors, and I suppose with psychiatrists, I went to Bushnell Military Hospital in Brigham City, Utah, where wounded veterans from the Philippines were cared for, many of them amputees. I hadn't any missing body parts, but some of my mind had left me. I have no recollection of how I got there but most likely by rail with an MP escort. I can only guess at the interval between August 15, 1945 when Col. Jones announced the end of the war and Christmas Eve, 1945. Between those dates, I more or less estimate the sequence as follows:

Two months collecting prisoners and tending prisoners near Dumaguete while awaiting orders, a month aboard the hospital ship, and a month at Fort Hon, California. I must have been under close observation after arriving at Bushnell, but I can pin point my activity that Christmas Eve. I was staying at a hotel in Brigham City, probably experimenting with a two or three day pass. One snowy evening I met a girl a few years older than me as I wandered aimlessly around the town. Our conversation went something like this.

"Are you lost, Soldier?"

"I can find my way back to my hotel, if that's what you mean?"

"I was wondering where you were headed and if you'd like company."

"I'd kind of like to be left alone."

"Not on Christmas Eve. Come with me."

I obediently followed, or was towed by her arm down a snowy path to a church, its windows aglow with multi colored light. I wanted to run as the memory of a deadly church in Negros brought on a rush of guilt, but this girl clung to me.

"I'm taking you to Midnight Mass." She drew me inside the doorway, but I refused to advance beyond the back pew. Harmonic voices backed by an organ, candles flickering, and incense smoke rising put me into a sort of trance. The ritual performed by vested men and boys in front of the altar added to the effect. It was the most beautiful experience of my life.

When the performance ended and we stepped back into the snowy night, she said, "I want to go to your hotel with you."

As we walked a few blocks, I felt a wave of anxiety. At the lobby of the hotel I said, "I can't do this."

"If you want me to go, I will."

"I have to go home."

"Home?"

"The hospital."

She must have been frightened for me, because she helped me pack my duffel bag, check out at the front desk, and flag a cab. She gave the driver instructions and offered to pay the fare.

"I've got money." I stammered. "I'm sorry."

"So am I, Soldier." She held open the door to the cab. "So am I."

I mumbled, "Thank you," as she shut the door and the cab drove off. "For that wonderful experience."

Back at the hospital the nurse asked, "How come you're back so soon?"

"I just couldn't stay away." I curled into a fetal position on the bed and pulled the covers over my head. Like that night after my grandmother rejected me, I cried myself to sleep.

My doctors must have considered this episode a setback to my recovery, and I didn't offer much help by answering their questions with a "Yes, Sir," or "No, Sir," or the shortest possible answers. Their wearing uniforms did not encourage me to open up. I was locked inside myself, and I refused to show any feeling except anger, and even that was kept in check at the hospital.

Thirty Day Leave back Home

My doctor concluded that a 30-day leave back in Minnesota (in the dead of winter) with my family would break me out of my shell. They put me on a train with an M.P. escort who hung around me like *stink on shit* the entire trip. I have no idea what my mother knew of my condition or my situation; I doubt I wrote any letters and I don't remember receiving any. However, she was at the St. Paul Depot waiting with my younger sister, the older ones were married with families of their own. At least my arrival time had been communicated to her.

Much like Col. Jones presenting a battle ravaged Corregidor to Gen. McArthur, the M.P. said, "Mrs. Leslie, I am delivering your son to your care."

Our reunion was mostly silent, as if I had come home from a street fight expecting a scolding or even beating for my bad behavior. However, I suspect her anger wasn't directed at me.

Nothing felt right; my home, my bed, my old friends. In two years my childhood had been taken from me. I lasted two of the four-week furlough. I know my mother felt hurt, but she arranged for my trip back. She probably felt relieved of the pressure my hanging around the house caused. Even my sister seemed to walk on eggshells when we spent time together.

Return to Bushnell Hospital

A different M.P. but just as rigid and protective escorted me back to the hospital. I went directly to my bed, now occupied by some other sick soldier.

I yelled, "Get the hell off my bed!"

He just sat up and stared, too amazed to rise to the challenge. A good thing or one of us would have a need for the intensive care unit, and I don't think it would have been me.

Nurses and orderlies came running, but fortunately none of them tried to restrain me or even touch me.

"This guy is in my bed."

Just in time a familiar face showed up. "We weren't expecting you back. Your bed has been given to someone else."

"This is my bed!" I confronted the patient. "Get the hell off of it."

By then the doctor who had been assigned my case arrived and faced the staff members gathering out of curiosity more than any intent to help. "I'm sorry, there must be some mistake. This is Private Leslie's bed. Please move this patient to another bed."

I stood down; avoiding the fight that I didn't want yet felt I needed to relieve some of the pressure building inside me. I had my bed—my place in the world, for now.

I settled into a routine lounging around the hospital lobby and grounds. A group of German POW had provided maintenance inside and outside. Standing at a pool table, I glanced around for a partner, when a POW began mopping the floor.

"You want to play a game of pool?"

He shrugged and pointed to the mop.

"I'll check with the officer in charge."

When I returned with permission, we spent the rest of the afternoon playing pool. Some elements of my pre military life had begun to emerge. When he didn't show up one afternoon, I discovered he had been sent back to Germany.

Mustered Out

Just when I began to feel healthy and eager to return to duty, I was summoned to the paymaster's office where a sergeant who considered himself an officer sat behind a desk.

"Private Leslie." He glanced up at me and immediately broke eye contact. Shuffling some papers, he said, "When were you last paid?" More paper shuffling. "I see you took a cash advance back a Camp Hon."

"I can't remember. Some time back in Negros, I guess."

"Looks like you got three month's pay coming." He pinched his pencil tight and pressed it so hard to the note pad I was sure the lead would break. "Of course, none of that would be combat pay because the war had ended."

"Like hell, I'm still in combat."

"You aren't even in a combat zone, if one still existed."

"I was injured and brought to this hospital as a war casualty."

He looked up and peered at me from over his nose. "You appear to be recovered from your injuries." His attention back to his papers. "But that's beside the point. It's my duty to bring your pay status up to date." He mumbled as he scribbled some numbers on the pad, "Three month's regular Private's pay."

"Hey, I get jump pay. I'm a paratrooper."

"According to your record, you've done only one practice jump since Corregidor."

"Are you suggesting Corregidor was nothing more than a practice jump?"

"They're all the same to me. I have to exclude your jump pay any month a jump wasn't made."

"That rule is overlooked during combat when practice jumps aren't possible."

"I can grant you that, but combat ended three months ago. The Japanese surrendered if you recall."

Sarcastic remarks are tolerable from officers who need to assert their authority, but I was not about to allow a sergeant to get by with it.

"I want to see an officer."

"My rank is the best you're going to get, Private."

"I have a right to get higher authority, Sergeant."

"Watch that attitude, Soldier, or I will have to write you up. Then you'll get your officer at your court martial."

"In combat I've taken over squads where our sergeant in charge got shot."

"Are you threatening me?"

My mind flashed back to a drill sergeant during training that I threatened and he backed down. However, this was different and I had to walk a fine line. "I refuse to sign any pay voucher that doesn't include combat and jump pay."

"We'll see about that."

He got up and left the room with me still standing in front of a vacant desk. Soon he returned with a lieutenant. He returned my salute, and he told me to sit down while he did some calculating. Something did not smell right.

"I see you haven't jumped since the war ended."

"No, Sir, I haven't had the chance. But I am ready to jump right now if you will get me to an airport."

"I don't think you are in any condition to jump."

He was right but I began a protest. "With all due respect, Sir..."

"No need for that. We can overlook that little detail." He glanced at the sergeant and said, "I think $3000.00 would round off quite nicely."

The sergeant nodded his approval and even started to grin. Something was up.

"Three month's combat pay with jump pay added to mustering out pay. Three thousand dollars sounds pretty good, don't you think?"

"Sir, I'm not mustering out."

"Those are the orders. When we are finished with this transaction, you are a free citizen again."

"Sir, under military code, I am making a charge against you."

"Hold on soldier. You are not a civilian just yet. You will respect the uniform."

"I am respecting the uniform. The charge I am making under combat rules is against you as a person. I am still in combat as the pay voucher you just signed proves." I felt I had him at his own game.

"I cannot accept such a charge from a lowly private."

"Are you hiding behind your rank or just afraid to face a combat veteran in a fist fight?"

"That wouldn't be a fair fight. Wait right here. I will be right back." He glanced at the sergeant now forcing a grin off his face. "Be prepared to include all the details of this conversation in your report."

When a Lieutenant Colonel wearing an airborne uniform stepped into the room, I shot to my feet and saluted. All I could think of was Col. Jones.

He gestured for me and the sergeant to an *as-you-were*. "You just made a charge against an officer under combat code."

"No, Sir. Not the officer. Just the person wearing the uniform."

"Well, I can inform you that the officer has rejected your charge."

"Does that mean I won my point?"

"You have beaten him, and he now must answer to a reprimand, probably a loss of rank."

Such a swift decision in the military was unheard of, and I smelled a rat.

I stammered my confusion. "I, I..."

"You won your point, soldier, and with it comes an immediate but honorable discharge." He added, "According to the code of combat."

He beat me at my own game, I think, and I did not have the resources to research the code. Maybe none of it existed and this officer knew it. I tried reasoning with him. "I don't want to be discharged. I need to stay in. It's the only home I got."

"You'll do well as a civilian. You've shown great courage as a paratrooper, and now you deserve a bit of the quiet life."

"I demand you allow me to stay. My time isn't up, and I don't have enough points to be discharged."

"It's all part of the code of combat. You won, the officer you charged lost, and you are free to go."

"I won but I lost. It doesn't make sense."

"If the officer counter charged you, the case could go to a court martial with a possible dishonorable discharge and forget about the $3000."

He reached to shake my hand. "You've distinguished yourself in battle. Wear your medals with pride, you earned them." He left the room leaving me standing and the sergeant busy shuffling papers.

301

Home for Good?

I returned to Minnesota almost before the previous leave I cut short had ended. This time Rita met me at the station because my mother was busy doing laundry. When I walked into the house and saw her bent over a scrubbing board, all my anger vented at our poverty.

I said to my sister, "Come with me. We're going to get something."

Shortly after we returned, two deliverymen came to our door with a brand new Speed Queen washing machine.

My mother hugged me and cried.

Thus, I began life as Civilian Richard Leslie. Soon the $3000 disappeared and over the course of the next few years, my mother repaid that Speed Queen many times. Although the Army kicked me out, they never completely severed our relationship. I was required to report monthly to a certain lieutenant colonel at Ft. Snelling who asked me a lot of personal questions. I found this tiresome and unnecessary. I no longer held any rank that they could yo-yo; one stripe, two stripes, one stripe, two stripes. After about six months of this nonsense, I decided to skip a session.

My sister stood at the doorway to my bedroom and said, "There are a couple of soldiers at the door who want to see you."

"What do they want?" as if I didn't know.

"Get up and go see."

The intrusion didn't help the headache I'd been nursing from drinking the night before, and the two dozen White Castles me and my buddies consumed in the park after the bars closed put pressure on my stomach.

"Are they M.P.'s?"

"Just regular soldiers."

A sigh of relief. "Make them wait outside while I get dressed."

"They're in the kitchen talking to Ma."

This, I knew, would not be good. I dressed and confronted them. "What's up?" as I fought the impulse to stand at attention ready to be dressed down. For two years, they *owned* my body and my soul, and I might never be able to free myself of them.

A year or two later when I told the lieutenant colonel—asked permission—that I planned to marry, he asked to meet Norma, my fiancé. After a few pleasantries, he asked me to leave the two of them alone. Thus set together the two women in my life, my mother and my wife, who would ultimately free me from the military in exchange for a higher more effective authority. I owe my sanity to them.

Years later when I had my relapse back into combat, Norma stood by me and fought for my freedom. She wrote a second letter addressed to the president, the first one my mother helped me write back when I still fought being discharged.

That first letter requesting to be readmitted to the Army did make it all the way to the White House, the answer printed on White House stationary dated and signed by President Truman, or his automatic signing machine. Following a house fire, my family sorted through all my papers and the letter somehow disappeared. I hope the family member who pilfered it respects it for what it means to me.

Dear Mr. Leslie,

I had my staff review your war record and found it outstanding. You have done much for your country. It is time for your country to take care of you.

Regards,
Harry S. Truman
President of the United States

Years later, Norma's letter to the president lay on the kitchen table when I returned (escaped, I'd been told) from St. Peter's institution for the criminally insane. Even if the letter had been sent, Truman was no longer president nor would it have made it through the bureaucracy in Washington D.C.. However, it served as a testament to her devotion and perseverance to bring the father of her eight children back home after two years of incarceration. I reveled in her care until about a decade ago when she passed away.

I will rejoin her soon.

***

Nine months prior to September 19, 1925, God united two specks of Matter, and Richard Leslie sprung into life. To this embyro, God attached one elastic thread of Memory, its full length free to gyrate and stretch even beyond Richard's allotted eighty seven years on this planet. To Richard's wonderful gift I grasp and attempt to sing his life's song.

War made Richard crazy
His long life healed, Its melody lingers

Made in the USA
Lexington, KY
28 July 2017